Biographies

IN AMERICAN FOREIGN POLICY

Joseph A. Fry, University of Nevada, Las Vegas
Series Editor

The Biographies in American Foreign Policy Series employs the enduring medium of biography to examine the major episodes and themes in the history of U.S. foreign relations. By viewing policy formation and implementation from the perspective of influential participants, the series seeks to humanize and make more accessible those decisions and events that sometimes appear abstract or distant. Particular attention is devoted to those aspects of the subject's background, personality, and intellect that most influenced his or her approach to U.S. foreign policy, and each individual's role is placed in a context that takes into account domestic affairs, national interests and policies, and international and strategic considerations.

The series is directed primarily at undergraduate and graduate courses in U.S. foreign relations, but it is hoped that the genre and format may also prove attractive to the interested general reader. With these objectives in mind, the length of the volumes has been kept manageable, the documentation has been restricted to direct quotes and particularly controversial assertions, and the bibliographic essays have been tailored to provide historiographical assessment without tedium.

Producing books of high scholarly merit to appeal to a wide range of readers is an ambitious undertaking, and an excellent group of authors has agreed to participate. Some have compiled extensive scholarly records while others are just beginning promising careers, but all are distinguished by their comprehensive knowledge of U.S. foreign relations, their cooperative spirit, and their enthusiasm for the project. It has been a distinct pleasure to have been given the opportunity to work with these scholars as well as with Richard Hopper and his staff at Scholarly Resources.

Volumes Published

Lawrence S. Kaplan, *Thomas Jefferson: Westward the Course of Empire* (1999). Cloth ISBN 0-8420-2629-0   Paper ISBN 0-8420-2630-4

Richard H. Immerman, *John Foster Dulles: Piety, Pragmatism, and Power in U.S. Foreign Policy* (1999). Cloth ISBN 0-8420-2600-2 Paper ISBN 0-8420-2601-0

Thomas W. Zeiler, *Dean Rusk: Defending the American Mission Abroad* (2000). Cloth ISBN 0-8420-2685-1   Paper ISBN 0-8420-2686-X

Edward P. Crapol, *James G. Blaine: Architect of Empire* (2000). Cloth ISBN 0-8420-2604-5   Paper ISBN 0-8420-2605-3

DEAN
RUSK

DEAN
RUSK

Defending the
American Mission Abroad

Thomas W. Zeiler

IN AMERICAN FOREIGN POLICY

Number 3

**SR
BOOKS**

A Scholarly Resources Inc. Imprint
Wilmington, Delaware

Scholarly Resources Inc.
104 Greenhill Avenue
Wilmington, DE 19805-1897
www.scholarly.com

Library of Congress Cataloging-in-Publication Data

Zeiler, Thomas W.
    Dean Rusk : defending the American mission abroad /
Thomas W. Zeiler.
        p.   cm. — (Biographies in American foreign policy; no. 3)
    Includes bibliographical references and index.
        ISBN 0-8420-2685-1 (cloth : alk. paper). — ISBN 0-8420-2686-X
(pbk. : alk. paper)
        1. Rusk, Dean, 1909–1994. 2. Cabinet officers—United States
Biography. 3. Statesmen—United States Biography. 4. United
States—Foreign relations—1945–1989. I. Title. II. Series.
E748.R94Z45   1999
973.92'092—dc21
[B]   99-25315
                                                                                    CIP

⊗ The paper used in this publication meets the minimum requirements of the American National Standard for permanence of paper
for printed library materials, Z39.48, 1984.

To Jackson and Ella

About the Author

Thomas W. Zeiler, who earned his doctorate from the University of Massachusetts at Amherst, is the author of *American Trade and Power in the 1960s* (1992) and *Free Trade, Free World: America and the Advent of GATT* (1999). He is an associate professor of history at the University of Colorado at Boulder.

Contents

Introduction

The Lessons of History

"In 1969, the views that I held back in '61, '62, and '63 might be termed impossibly old fashioned," Secretary of State Dean Rusk explained after leaving office. "But I felt that the free world cannot afford to have the Communist world picking it to pieces by various forms of aggression and pressure at different points around the world and that if there was to be peace in the world, all nations large and small must have a right to live their own lives without being molested by force from outside their own borders. That was the basic concept of the United Nations Charter and seemed to be the conclusion that one would derive from the experiences of the 1930s that led us into World War II."*

"Look to the past as a means of weighing the present and the future," reads the inscription at the entrance to the Richard B. Russell Library at the University of Georgia in Athens, where the Dean Rusk papers are housed. Because history guided Secretary of State Rusk, these words and his own explanation, quoted above, capture the essence of his foreign policy in the turbulent 1960s. From his college days in the 1930s to the end of his tenure in government in 1969, Rusk's generation countered the totalitarian threats of fascism and communism. The experience taught him one lesson: aggressors must be confronted so that the dream of world peace and harmony can be achieved.

Rusk absorbed history and vowed not to be doomed to repeat it. Aggression, he believed, was the scourge of the twentieth century; international cooperation under the tenets of democratic liberalism was the force for good. When the timid European democracies responded to the outrageous demands of Adolf Hitler

*Dean Rusk Oral History II, John F. Kennedy Library, Boston, Massachusetts, 58.

during the 1930s by appeasement—granting territorial concessions in the mistaken hope of satisfying his insatiable thirst for domination—a vicious world war ensued. After the Second World War the Communist menace from the expansionist Soviet Union, from the People's Republic of China, and from lesser powers such as Cuba had to be deterred. In the Cold War struggle between the Communist Soviet-Chinese bloc of nations and the capitalist West, led by the United States, a nuclear conflict would have ended life on Earth. Rusk was determined to hold the line against Communist aggression.

That I have come to appreciate Rusk's part in seeing the Soviet empire fall is somewhat of a surprise, for at one time I shared the two basic reactions to this project that it has received from associates. Some have wondered why I would write about such a colorless figure, a boring bureaucrat seemingly lacking the pizzazz of the best and the brightest of the 1960s. Others remember Rusk as a myopic Cold Warrior, the so-called Chairman of the Establishment, whose blind anticommunism led him—dogmatically and unreflectively—to stand by the futile Vietnam War policy of President Lyndon Johnson to its disastrous end. Because Rusk was the quintessential representative of U.S. liberalism in foreign and domestic affairs, I believe that these criticisms are off the mark. I discovered in Rusk a quiet wit and sensitivity to other individuals and nations. To be sure, his computerized rhetoric of the Cold War could be grating, yet because Rusk was not merely a facilitator of policy or a yes-man to his superiors but a policymaker in a critical era in U.S. history, I found his story compelling.

There is much more to Rusk than his detractors suppose, not least because he lived through so much history. During his time, U.S. liberal values of protecting the weak and poor, of providing social justice and equality for all, reached their pinnacle of influence at home and abroad. It is this history that provides the context for his career and casts doubt on the claims of those who dislike his Cold War policies for supposedly being stymied by anti-Communist orthodoxy. This study, as a result, explores the ways that historical understanding, gained by experience and the application of analogies, marked Rusk's thinking. His was an exciting, dynamic, and controversial service as secretary of state. However much the Vietnam War battered his reputation as a liberal—for critics focused on the war in Southeast Asia rather than the staggering panoply of global issues that occupied Rusk—he held to principles learned over a lifetime.

Still, Vietnam cannot be ignored. That would be as out of place as asking Abraham Lincoln how much he enjoyed the theater. The war to prevent communism from conquering America's ally of South Vietnam is the central problem in any study of Rusk. I do not excuse him for Vietnam, but I sympathize with him. Why would such an intelligent, experienced, and, especially, well-meaning man be drawn into a tragedy that would ruin the Johnson presidency, tear the country apart, and deny Rusk his place in the pantheon of great American leaders? The answer is that Vietnam, like all Rusk's policies, was part of a plan to defeat aggressors, to put into practice his liberal internationalism—his idealistic vision of international law, order, economic development, and collective cooperation under United Nations rule. A special brand of liberal internationalism had been devised by President Woodrow Wilson near the end of the First World War, and Wilsonianism became the preferred course for those who lived through the hell of totalitarianism. Rusk's attempt to adapt Wilsonianism to the world explains the tragedy of the Vietnam War.

After sending the United States into war, President Wilson had enumerated his vision of a new international order in his Fourteen Points of 1918. Shunning the alliance-oriented power politics of realpolitik that idealists believed had led to a terrible conflict, Wilson promoted his fourteenth point, a community of nations bound under the auspices of a world organization. This League of Nations would resolve disputes and foster liberal internationalism. The League idea was Wilson's contribution to diplomatic idealism, or the overarching belief that nations could live in eternal harmony if given the means to cooperate.

Wilson's peace plan hinged on cooperation by the family of nations. Such "collective security" was institutionalized first in the League of Nations and later in the Charter of the United Nations after the Second World War. Both bodies were designed to provide the moral and legal guidelines for the settlement of international conflicts. Collective security would unite peaceful nations against aggressors. Countries would no longer enter individual alliances; they would join the League of Nations instead. The League would act as an arbiter and serve as a forum of public opinion to expose offenders to the democratic impulses of the world. If need be, the League would mobilize a concerted military force to stop aggression.

Wilsonianism, as the president's idealistic blueprint was called, proposed the conditions necessary for international compatibility.

The Fourteen Points also included calls for mutual economic expansion, disarmament, an end to territorial aggrandizement, and forthright, open diplomacy. National self-determination for people the world over, or the right of nations to decide for themselves their form of government, comprised eight of the points. Overseeing all of the objectives was the League. Wilsonianism aimed to render war obsolete and make the world "safe for democracy," but creating a Wilsonian system proved illusory. Because America's allies twisted Wilson's plan to suit their national interests, an effective League of Nations never materialized. The U.S. Senate rejected the Treaty of Versailles that ended the war and with it U.S. membership in the League, which undermined its power. Still, the president's call for a just peace and the need to confront aggression through collective security arrangements captivated liberals worldwide.

Rusk was one of the acolytes; idealistic Wilsonian ideology guided him at first. Then global events changed him. The rise of Japanese, Italian, and German fascism and militarism in the 1930s and appeasement of the dictators by the democracies convinced him that aggressors had to be confronted. Service in the Second World War then drew him into the practical world of policymaking. And the advent of the Cold War struggle against Communist aggression clinched Rusk's transformation, forcing him to adapt Wilsonianism to the power politics of the day. His shift toward realism, or the elevation of concerns for national security above moralism, did not erase his Wilsonian heritage in the postwar years, however. Instead, Rusk blended realism and idealism. He gave priority to considerations of power and security to combat Communist aggressors, hoping that once the United States successfully prosecuted the Cold War, international law and justice would rule the world. This idealist-realist fusion amounted to neo-Wilsonianism, the doctrine that defined Rusk's approach to the Cold War, including Vietnam.

Consider a grid with two axes, representing world politics. On one axis lies a large circle labeled idealism. Inside this is a concentric circle called liberal internationalism, within which is a Wilsonian circle, representing the idealistic adaptation of liberal internationalism under the League of Nations idea. The other axis, realism, intersects the idealism pole. Rusk's neo-Wilsonianism can be envisioned as a circle overlapping this intersection, part of it in the Wilsonian sphere and part in the realist orbit. For accuracy the axes would have to be viewed through a three-dimensional cone of time reflecting Rusk's embrace of realism during the Cold War as he reached, all the while, for his dream of a world run by Wilsonians.

Wilsonianism prompted Rusk to fight for the ideal of law, order, and justice, a world free from aggressors. Appeasement, the Second World War, and the Cold War taught him that aggressors had to be halted before that goal could be attained. In other words, realism—security against attackers—had to precede the structure of peace in the idealist framework. Rusk opposed aggression because he was a Wilsonian, but, significantly, idealist objectives required him to engage in the battle against communism that produced the Vietnam War. The tragedy of that conflict was thus an irony as well: realism in the service of idealism, or neo-Wilsonianism, actually undermined Rusk's ability to promote peace in Southeast Asia.

The tragedy lay in the fact that Rusk and other witnesses to the history of the midtwentieth century believed that aggression was aggression, whether it arose from big European powers or small Asian Communists. That was an understandable view for Rusk to take in light of his generation's experience with nazism. Hitler cast a long shadow, well past the Second World War. This legacy caused Rusk to fear other perceived aggressors, whoever they might be, and he was determined not to repeat the mistake of appeasing threats to peace. Nazism put Rusk on guard during the Cold War, and this defense against aggression led to Vietnam.

It should not be forgotten, however, that as secretary of state under President John F. Kennedy and President Johnson, Rusk remained an ardent believer in the U.S. mission to improve the world. An instinctive idealist, he cherished the democratic doctrines of the United Nations and injected morality and the rule of law into global affairs. His generation tried to apply internationalism before and after the Second World War. Even though Vietnam led him off that course, Rusk adhered to his principles, promoting—and largely carrying out—that mission. History showed him that resolute containment of communism would serve Wilsonianism's lofty goals of providing peace, security, democracy, and prosperity for all under the rule of law. Rusk would combat the Communists. In so doing, he came to epitomize the liberals' approach to the Soviet-U.S. confrontation. Neo-Wilsonianism undergirded the liberalism that prevailed in Washington during the long Cold War.

Rusk undertook the liberal mission at great sacrifice. In Vietnam this loss came in terms of lives, money, and prestige abroad. The war also stained his name and ruined a president. But Rusk honored the precepts of idealism while he engaged in power politics as a neo-Wilsonian. And he took full responsibility for his actions, bravely living with the results of his decisions. The key, he believed, was knowing what was right, a difficult task under any circumstances and certainly a monumental one considering the pressures of his very public job as secretary of state. Yet Rusk continued to make hard decisions and carry out unpopular policies in the cause of liberalism, the ideology he revered. Liberalism gave answers to the cruel lessons of history. The events he had lived through since the 1930s were heartless indeed.

Thus, Chapters 1 and 2, comprising the first part of this book, explore Rusk's evolution into a neo-Wilsonian, explaining his part in the great historic issues surrounding the two world wars and the onset of the Soviet-U.S. rivalry. These chapters set the stage for his tenure as secretary of state from 1961 to 1969, years in which the confrontation with the Soviet Union over the core, or the central area of European global power, developed into a struggle for control of the periphery, or the Third World—where most of the crises and all of the wars of the Cold War era occurred. The second part, Chapters 3 through 5, which examines U.S. policy toward the core of Europe and the regions of the periphery (Latin America, Africa, the Middle East, and Asia), is essential to understanding the motivating factors, circumstances, and thoughts that led Rusk into one of the more outlying areas of the periphery: Vietnam. The war in Southeast Asia constitutes the entire third part, Chapters 6 through 10.

In an attempt to fathom the development of a disaster, this study follows the sequence from boyhood to secretary of state, from core to periphery. The evolution of internationalist ideals into the neo-Wilsonian compromise with realism is the central issue in the Vietnam tragedy. History in the core and periphery loomed over the whole story and guided Rusk, the consummate Cold War liberal. The past was truly prologue for this man of impoverished beginnings, who ascended to the pinnacle of power at the very height of the American century only to exit the stage in a shroud of gloom. How Vietnam entrapped one of the most humane figures ever to serve in the government is the focus. But how Rusk made his way to the top; exercised power and judgment in the most benevolent way he could envision; faithfully followed to the letter the tenets of neo-Wilsonian doctrine as he constantly strived for a utopia of goodness in a dangerous world; and remained a most ardent, optimistic, if not ultimately successful, twentieth-century American liberal provides the heart of the story. Rusk's saga prompts reflection about the foundations on which the U.S. mission abroad rested in his century and may point us toward an understanding of how that charge should be undertaken in the years to come.

~

I received generous funding for this project from the John F. Kennedy Library, which awarded me the Arthur Schlesinger Fellowship and the usual good cheer from the archival staff, and from the Graduate School of the University of Colorado at Boulder. My appreciation goes in particular to Sheryl Vogt and her able staff at the Richard B. Russell Library at the University of Georgia, which possesses an archive rich in resources and professionalism.

Whipping this book into shape was largely the work of readers who cast a skeptical eye on my history, interpretation, and writing. Fred and Virginia Anderson helped me to fine-tune the argument and define concepts, Andy DeRoche assisted me with discussions of African affairs, Bob Schulzinger shared his expertise on Vietnam and Jess Strum and Michael Zeiler shared theirs on writing, and Tom Thomas corroborated my sympathetic view of Rusk as a figure who symbolizes the many ironies of U.S. history. I also benefited from discussions with Michael Schaller, Marc Gallicchio, and Don Oberdorfer. The editor of this series, Andy Fry, provided the closest commentary on anything I have written since my doctoral dissertation. I thank him for his care and insights. Rich Rusk kindly took the time to talk with me about his father and look over an early draft of the manuscript. All of these people greatly improved the book. Mary Rogat and Rick Rosen took care of business in Colorado during our absences; they were perfect neighbors.

My wife, Rocio, and two children, Jackson and Ella, pulled me away from the seriousness of writing, giving me—as they always do—a proper perspective on life. I hope that one day both kids will humble me even more than they do now by reading this book dedicated to them.

Chronology

1909

David Dean Rusk is born in Cherokee County, Georgia, on February 9

1917

General Pershing marches past Rusk's school; United States enters World War I

1918

Wilson campaigns for League of Nations; World War I ends

1920

Ho Chi Minh joins French Communist party

1921

Washington Naval Conference on disarmament (until 1922); Dean joins ROTC

1925

Rusk graduates from high school

1927

Rusk enters Davidson College

1929

Great Depression begins

1931

Japan invades Manchuria; Rusk embarks for Oxford as Rhodes scholar

1933

Roosevelt and Hitler take office; United States recognizes Soviet Union; Rusk resides in Germany

1934

Batista comes to power in Cuba; Hitler takes dictatorial powers; Rusk returns to England from Germany, finishes

studies at Oxford in spring, begins teaching at Mills
College

1935

German rearmament announced; Mussolini invades Ethiopia; First Neutrality Act

1936

Germany occupies Rhineland; Fascists sign Anti-Comintern
Pact; Congress renews Neutrality Act; Rusk begins part-time
law school at University of California at Berkeley

1937

Japan invades China; Neutrality Act revised as "cash and
carry"; Rusk weds Virginia Foisie

1938

Germany annexes Austria; Munich Pact signed

1939

Franco triumphs in Spain with German and Italian aid;
Nazi-Soviet Pact signed; World War II begins

1940

Japan, Germany, and Italy sign Tripartite Pact; German and
Soviet forces advance; U.S. gradual embargo against Japan;
Rusk enlists in army as captain

1941

Lend-Lease Act; Major Rusk reassigned to War Department
General Staff; Pearl Harbor attacked

1942

Rusk correctly predicts Japanese victories in Asia

1943

Rusk serves General Stilwell in China-Burma-India theater;
French paratroopers land in Indochina

1945

Yalta Conference; France as sole trustee in Indochina; Vice
President Truman becomes president at Roosevelt's death;
Charter of the United Nations Organization; Rusk appointed
to Operations Division of War Department; World War II
ends; Ho declares Indochina's independence; Korea divided

1946

Rusk appointed assistant chief of Division of International Security Affairs, State Department; Kennan's "Long Telegram" from Moscow; Ho begins war against France

1947

Rusk becomes director of State Department's Office of Political Affairs (UN desk); Truman Doctrine; Federal Loyalty Program; term "Cold War" coined

1948

Czechoslovakia falls into Soviet orbit; Marshall Plan (until 1952); Israel founded; Soviets blockade Berlin (June 1948–May 1949); Truman elected president

1949

Rusk appointed deputy undersecretary of state; Germanies formally divided; NATO founded; Mao Zedong takes China as Jiang Jieshi flees to Taiwan

1950

Senator McCarthy finds Communists in State Department; Rusk accepts demotion to assistant secretary of state; Rusk drafts NSC-68; Korean War (June 1950–July 1953)

1951

U.S.-Japan Peace Treaty; ANZUS Pact; Rusk calls China a "Slavic Manchukuo"; Red China aids Ho

1952

Rusk heads Rockefeller Foundation

1954

Dien Bien Phu falls; Ngo Dinh Diem becomes prime minister of South Vietnam; Geneva Conference divides Vietnam

1955

SEATO Pact; first Chinese offshore islands crisis

1956

Khrushchev comes to power; Suez and Hungarian crises

1957

Sputnik launched

1958

Khrushchev issues ultimatum on Berlin

1959

Castro comes to power; Nixon-Khrushchev "kitchen debate" in Moscow; NLF created; *Mid-Century Challenge to U.S. Foreign Policy* issued by Rusk's Rockefeller Foundation

1960

Soviets down U-2 spy plane; Castro signs economic agreements with Moscow; Kennedy elected president; Rusk appointed secretary of state; eighteen African nations gain independence; Congo civil war

1961

January	United States severs relations with Cuba
	Kennedy approves counterinsurgency plan for Vietnam
February	Congo's Lumumba assassinated
April	Bay of Pigs invasion
May	Dominican dictator Leonidas Trujillo assassinated
	Kennedy announces support for Multi-lateral Nuclear Force
June	Vienna Summit
August	Berlin Wall erected
	Alliance for Progress launched
September	Fighting between Katanga and central Congo government
	Congress approves Peace Corps bill
October	Soviets detonate largest bomb in history
	Mao walks out of Twenty-second Congress of Soviet Communist Party
November	Taylor-Rostow Report approved

1962

January	U.S. pilots bomb Binh Hoa
July	Geneva Accords on neutralization of Laos
September	Yemen crisis
	India-Pakistan clash
October	NLF stands its ground at My Tho
	Trade Expansion Act
	Cuban missile crisis (October 16–28)

Rusk's "eyeball to eyeball" comment on
Cuba blockade
China-India border war

1963

January   France's de Gaulle vetoes British membership in EEC
Battle of Ap Bac

April   *Jupiter* missiles in Turkey dismantled

May   South Vietnamese army fires on Buddhists

June   Immolation of elderly monk
Kennedy's American University speech
Kennedy visits West Berlin

July   Limited Nuclear Test-Ban Treaty

September   Dominican Juan Bosch ousted

November   Diem killed
John Kennedy assassinated

December   Kennedy Round of GATT (until May 1967)
Katanga rejoins Congo government

1964

January   Panama riots

April   Rusk visits South Vietnam

June   Rusk warns Turkey in Cyprus crisis
Civil Rights Act passes Congress
Seaborn mission (until August 1965)
Mandela and African National Congress
compatriots convicted

August   Gulf of Tonkin incidents and Gulf of
Tonkin Resolution

October   China detonates nuclear weapon

November   Congo rebels take hostages
Johnson elected president
North Vietnam increases troops in South

1965

January   Robert McNamara and McGeorge Bundy
advise larger U.S. commitment in Vietnam

February   Pleiku attacked
Operation Rolling Thunder (until 1973)

March   Marine battalions dispatched to Da Nang
Westmoreland requests U.S. troops
First teach-in at University of Michigan

April	Johnson's Johns Hopkins University speech
	Dominican crisis (until May)
May	Six-day bombing halt imposed in Vietnam
	Berkeley antiwar demonstration
	Johnson decides to send troops to Vietnam
September	Congress overhauls immigration law
November	Uruguayan youth tries to spit on Rusk
	Mobutu comes to power in Congo
	Ia Drang Valley engagements
December	Rusk's fourteen-point peace plan
	Christmas bombing halt in Vietnam (until January 1966)

1966

January	Fulbright Senate hearings (into February)
	Mao's Cultural Revolution (until 1976)
February	McGeorge Bundy resigns
March	France announces withdrawal from NATO
April	Johnson begins bridge building to Eastern Europe
June	Dominican Joaquín Balaguer elected
September	Attleboro operation (until November)
	George Ball resigns
November	Marigold Initiative (until February 1967)
December	Treaty bans nuclear tests in outer space

1967

January	Rusk meets student protesters
	China tests hydrogen bomb
	Cedar Falls operation
February	Phase A-Phase B plan, air war resumes
	South Vietnam forms constitutional government
	Junction City operation (until April)
April	Cornell students don death's-head masks at Rusk speech
June	Glassboro Summit
	Arab-Israeli Six-Day War
August	Punta del Este OAS Summit
September	San Antonio Formula
October	Rusk warns of nuclear-armed "billion Chinese"
	March on Washington

November   McNamara resigns
Wise Men tell Johnson to stay course in
Vietnam

1968

January   Tet Offensive (into February)
USS *Pueblo* incident

March   Rusk testifies at Fulbright hearings
My Lai massacre
New Hampshire Democratic primary
Johnson withdraws from presidential race

April   Martin Luther King, Jr., assassinated

May   Harriman-Vance mission to Paris

June   Robert Kennedy assassinated
Rusk stalls peace talks (into July)

July   Nuclear Non-Proliferation Treaty

August   Soviets invade Czechoslovakia
Riots at Democratic National Convention in
Chicago

September   Senator Humphrey endorses bombing halt

October   North Vietnam agrees to negotiate

November   Bombing halted in Vietnam
Nixon elected president

1969

Rusk steps down as secretary of state; Paris peace talks
begin; SALT I disarmament talks begin (and end in 1972);
Vietnamization of ground war

1970

Nixon announces incursion into Cambodia; Kent State
University erupts in antiwar protest; Rusk teaches at
University of Georgia (until 1984)

1971

Congress repeals Gulf of Tonkin Resolution; Calley court-
martialed for My Lai massacre; *Pentagon Papers* released;
Bretton Woods monetary system collapses; Quadrapartite
Agreement on access to Berlin

1972

North Vietnamese Spring Offensive; Watergate break-in;
Henry Kissinger and Le Duc Tho formulate peace terms;
Nixon reelected president; Christmas bombings

1973

U.S. cease-fire in Vietnam

1975

North Vietnam occupies all of South Vietnam

1985

Rusk testifies in Westmoreland libel suit against CBS

1991

Cold War ends

1994

Rusk dies at age eighty-five on December 20

1995

United States restores diplomatic relations with Vietnam

I

Emergence of a Neo-Wilsonian

1

International Idealist and Realist

Horatio Alger could not have written a better rags-to-riches tale. No Hollywood script could have more perfectly captured the essence of a poor boy making good and rising to the peak of power. Dean Rusk's background is the stuff of American legend. His was the quintessential success story of overcoming odds by diligence, devotion, irrepressible optimism, compatibility with his peers, impressive intellect, and, above all, loyalty to principles. When these traits joined with circumstances, the result was an active internationalism. As the United States ascended to global leadership, agonized through the Great Depression and an epoch of isolationism and appeasement, and triumphed in world war, Rusk was catapulted to prominence. Like his country, he embarked upon a crusade that meshed moralistic ideals with the diplomatic realism of power and security in a neo-Wilsonian framework. In essence, Rusk was situated squarely within the country's liberal tradition.

The Southern Scholar

Although he ended up at the top of the foreign policy establishment, Dean Rusk came from humble origins. Three Rusk brothers had emigrated from Ireland in the 1700s; Dean's father had settled in Georgia, in Indian country. One ancestor had become a prominent leader in Texas during the nineteenth century, but the Rusk family members were basically ordinary folks, hard-working small farmers who toiled on the land. Dean's father rented forty acres in northern Georgia's Cherokee County, on which he eked out a meager living by growing cotton and producing food for his large family. He could not make ends meet on the small farm, even though his children pitched in from sunrise to sunset. He had been trained for the ministry, but a throat ailment had forced him to abandon that ambition—a tragic turn of events for this learned man.

Born on February 9, 1909, the fourth of five children, Dean had a modest, sometimes impoverished, childhood. He was named for the horse that carried the doctor through a stormy night to attend his birth. Life was hard in Georgia. Pure drinking water was found only by chance, and with little milk in their diet, the children suffered tooth problems. They also lacked shoes. Their mother's health steadily deteriorated from a harsh regimen of housework, gardening, and child rearing. Only after procuring a job in the postal service in Atlanta when Dean was four was his desperate father able to move the family to a little house with an outdoor privy.

In Atlanta young Dean absorbed lessons from his school, his family, and the street. He was educated at home and then at a good experimental school. The teachers and their trainees stimulated the students through instruction on areas of the world, art, and drama. Dean added to his workload at age eight by taking a job in a grocery store. City life was exciting, especially after the family moved to the West End, where they had the conveniences of electricity and a telephone. Living near the railroad and factories, they met farmers who came into the outskirts of Atlanta for supplies. The railroad divided the Rusks' neighborhood from the area where black families lived, but Dean—raised by his parents to be as racially tolerant as the norms of the times allowed—had many friends within the African-American community. His later advocacy of civil rights reflected this experience, but what he most remembered were the divisions based on class. Although he could compete at school with the rich kids, he was not permitted to mix with them socially. Rusk's own poverty fueled his later focus on international aid and development.

Dean's minister-trained father and well-educated mother gave him a foundation in religion. The Bible was always present in the household, the commitment to Christian precepts followed in a quiet, private fashion. Dean absorbed southern Presbyterian doctrines, which taught a love of God, a self-effacing manner, a sense of duty and service, and a ceaseless work ethic. Ubiquitous sin had to be confronted. God had a plan for the world, in which devout Christians were expected to have faith. Rusk's loyalty, conviction in the validity of American values, grueling work schedule, and profound desire to fight communism were all the products of his religious upbringing.

In school, Dean embraced a southerner's love for the military. He joined the ROTC at age twelve, proud that his lineage included a grandfather who had fought for the Confederacy. (During the Cold War, he facetiously confessed on a security form that one of his relatives had tried to overthrow the U.S. government.) Rusk retained a reverence for the military; he idolized General George C. Marshall and often bowed to the Pentagon during the 1960s.

Southern, religious, and military influences instilled in Rusk a missionary's zeal to take part in a global crusade for peace and justice. Rusk did not hold a strict Calvinistic vision of good and evil, yet his view was fairly uncomplicated. The American mission was to spread democratic values the world over. The country must assume a global moral leadership. Dean had learned this tradition of Wilsonianism as a boy. Always curious about the world around him, he had brushed with greatness in 1918, at nine years of age, when the most influential thinker on foreign policy of the century— President Woodrow Wilson—visited Atlanta to campaign for his cherished League of Nations. As the president rode by, Dean waved a placard to show his support of internationalism and peace.

As a southerner, Dean also absorbed the Civil War tradition of militarism and honor that came from preparing to defend the country. When the United States entered World War I in April 1917, Dean was especially attuned to national politics. He never forgot a huge fire in Atlanta in May 1917 that was falsely rumored to have been started by German bombers. Dean also had the thrill of watching General John Pershing lead a parade past his school, yet it was liberal internationalism that struck a chord. Although the nine-year-old could not grasp the significance of Wilson's program, the president's visit left a permanent impression.

Wilsonian internationalism sparked Rusk's imagination, for he and the president shared important ideas. Rusk ultimately perceived that Wilson not only fought for the common man but also called for faith in Christian, and American, ethics. These values included a commitment to help the oppressed and to honor agreements. Morality must undergird foreign policy. War, an abhorrent means for solving disputes, served only as a last resort. Pacifism, however, was not the answer. Rusk, like Wilson, held an abiding faith in people's ability to govern and to better themselves if allowed to live in peace. Wilsonianism expressed principles related to Rusk's experiences and upbringing. In later life, genuinely hoping to extend its precepts to the entire world, he became a champion of internationalism, especially collective security.

This philosophy was not just heady idealism. International law would uphold these ideas; democracy would teach people that peace was not a utopian scheme to be obtained effortlessly but a goal requiring discipline. Vigilance was essential. It was the key to keeping the people on course, to grounding policy in legal doctrines, and to confronting those who would destroy the vision. Narrow patriotic nationalism, selfishness, and belligerence would be abandoned. Instead, nations would share universal values of peace and freedom to obtain their interests. They would join together in collective security arrangements to stop aggression and abide by the rules of international law, which would be established by a world organization. This was a most practical idealism, Rusk believed.

Meanwhile, Dean rose from poverty by means of his innate intelligence, schooling, and values. He compiled an impressive academic record, graduating from high school in 1925 at age sixteen after being named one of the best all-around students. The award was deserved: young Dean had added to his solid education in the classics, math, and science by becoming editor of the newspaper and yearbook, senior class president, and cadet commander of the ROTC battalion. He also earned forty dollars per month from the *Atlanta Journal* for writing a weekly column on school life.

Whether Dean would be able to further his ambitions was much in doubt, however: poverty prevented him from attending his father's alma mater, the private Davidson College in North Carolina. Buoyed by faith and ever mindful of his father's economic straits, Dean worked as a law clerk for two years to raise the tuition for Davidson. He considered a career as a missionary to China, but the Wilsonian bug had bitten him. He dreamed of working for the Foreign Service in the struggle for global peace. In 1927 he finally entered Davidson on financial aid, supplementing this funding by working odd jobs during his four years of study. Solid family ties, diligence, brains, and piety, along with an idealistic vision and patriotic faith in his country, combined to ensure his success at college. He graduated with honors in addition to various accomplishments in athletics and the ROTC. Dean majored in political science, focusing on foreign relations, international law, and the Wilsonian creed.

Dean's college years were a time of disarmament treaties and aversion toward war. Even so, Wilsonians were convinced that the League of Nations was the only hope for preserving peace. Dean grasped the legal aspects undergirding the League's covenant, but his service in the ROTC, as a reserve infantry officer, and his respect for the military convinced him that international law could not be upheld without a willingness to defend principles by armed force, if necessary. This shading of liberalism with realism was critical to the next giant step in his life.

Believing that study abroad would boost his internationalist aims, Dean won a prestigious Rhodes scholarship to Oxford University in England. During the application process he had answered an apparent paradox that reflected his liberal blending of security (realism) and peace (idealism). The Rhodes committee had been curious that although he exalted the military as an ROTC officer, once in England, he planned to study methods of achieving peace. The committee asked him if he could reconcile the fact that the eagle on the seal of the United States held an arrow of war in one claw and the olive branch of peace in the other. Surely, replied Dean, "the two must go together. Armed force and world peace are two sides of the same coin."[1] The committee was impressed with this neo-Wilsonian outline. In late 1931, at the age of twenty-two, the Phi Beta Kappa graduate from Davidson sailed from New York Harbor on his first overseas voyage. He would not live in the South again for forty years.

Age of Dictators

At Oxford, Rusk took to the life of a gentleman scholar, which included the discovery of Scotch whisky and the receipt of his blue, or varsity, letter in lacrosse. He thrived on the intellectual environment and the moral debates. Visits from such luminaries as Mahatma Gandhi of India made a strong impression. Gandhi, demanding Indian independence from Great Britain, looked meek but spoke harshly about the immorality of British rule. Rusk became fascinated by the "moral lapses" of Otto von Bismarck, the nineteenth-century German practitioner of realism, and he found in socialism the answers to living sensibly; any Protestant would agree that capitalism leaned too far toward embracing the immoral "calamity of private gain."[2]

Rusk (standing, second from left) at Oxford, as a member of the tennis team. *Courtesy Richard B. Russell Library, University of Georgia*

Most notable was the lesson that Oxford taught him about the constitutional system and international law. Engrossed in the lectures of John Brierly, the leading world-law scholar of the day, Rusk developed a lifelong interest in cooperation through global institutions and law. Influenced by Brierly, frustrated by U.S. isolationism (or the refusal to take a meaningful political role in international affairs), and appreciative of the transference to America of British beliefs in the individual and law, Rusk deepened his faith in internationalism.

The declining British Empire persuaded him that colonialism was dying. Well-bred Englishmen at Oxford wished to serve the empire, the huge conglomeration of dominions and colonies that stretched around the world. The subjects of these territories sought home rule and independence; the sun was setting on British power. Rusk exalted the British system of government, especially parliamentary democracy and constitutionalism, but he detested imperialism. The subjection of colonial peoples competed with every notion of liberalism that he held dear. A universal organization that would embrace the empire would be the answer to independence and would even save British power. In 1933 he won Oxford's Cecil Peace Prize for his essay on this issue.

Meanwhile, more acute threats had emerged. After seizing the north Chinese province of Manchuria in 1931, Japan received a mere slap on the wrist from the League of Nations. Rusk also watched Adolf Hitler come to power. He determined that legal restraints on nations were imperative, but, like other liberals who feared the aggressors, he advocated force as a deterrent. Pacifism, the popular nostrum of the day that called for people in the European democracies and the United States to refuse to participate in military service, provided only the illusion of peace. Rusk believed that some realism was needed.

Rusk's disgust with the appeasement of dictators by the flaccid democracies heightened his devotion to activism, even by arms. Many years later he remained "personally convinced that this combination of pacifism, isolationism, and public indifference—attitudes prevalent not only at Oxford but also in the Western democracies generally—contributed immeasurably to the events that led to World War II."[3] Security and war were, therefore, integrated into his Wilsonian agenda. Rusk's later allegiance to the containment doctrine, designed to limit Soviet expansion during the Cold War, reflected this neo-Wilsonian view.

Fascism, militarism, and the appeasement of dictators shocked Rusk and the world. As peace marchers campaigned for paper disarmament treaties, and cynical politicians bowed to the aggressors, the pace quickened toward war. The League's weak response to the Japanese invasion of Manchuria disappointed Rusk, as did its feeble reaction to Italian dictator Benito Mussolini's attack on Ethiopia and the vicious Spanish civil war that began in 1936. Like other observers, Rusk underestimated the Fascists. But he learned that collective security was a hollow promise when placed under the flawed doctrine of appeasement. "We must be prepared to go to war in order to prevent war," he declared in a striking statement of the realist belief that raw power, not Wilsonian appeals for morality and negotiation, was the key determinant in global affairs.[4] This view, however, also signified his desire for a foreign policy designed to preserve the rule of law. The failure of mediation required collective security. For that reason he applauded the diplomatic recognition of Russia in 1933; the Soviets and the Americans could jointly confront Japan. Such collective security was an essential response to the dictators' aggressive acts prior to the Second World War.

In 1938 the crushing blow came with the infamous Munich Pact, whereby the European democracies handed over part of Czechoslovakia to a war-mongering Hitler. Munich came to symbolize the sin of appeasing aggressors. U.S. isolationists had tried to distance their country from the European mess. They passed legislation preventing the United States from trading with or aiding nations at war; unlike in World War I, this time the country would remain a true neutral. Both before and after Munich, neutrality legislation hamstrung President Franklin Roosevelt, keeping him from supporting the democracies against fascism.

Roosevelt prodded Americans toward involvement, seeking to quarantine lawlessness by bringing U.S. diplomacy to bear in the court of global opinion. The president was an internationalist who urged a concerted effort by the democracies to oppose violators of international treaties. With his country outside the League of Nations, however, Roosevelt could do little but signal displeasure; he also sought to avoid exciting isolationist fury, which he feared would embolden Germany, Italy, and Japan. Rusk agreed with the president that the triumph of law and moral principles on which peace and freedom rested—the very essence of liberal internationalism—could be upheld only by an active engagement in world affairs. He recoiled from the Munich Pact that appeased Hitler. A decade later he would draw an analogy between the imperialism of the Nazis and the expansion of communism under the Soviet Union. Appeasement at Munich made an indelible impression on Rusk. "In the Thirties, they said Manchuria was too far away to matter and I found myself at war in Burma," he would tell Vietnam War protesters. "Now they say you cannot believe all the rhetoric out of Peking, which is what they said about Hitler—and six million people were exterminated before anyone believed it. These aren't new ideas. We heard them before and we didn't get peace."[5]

The pre-World War II years were a disquieting period for Rusk as well as for a world immersed in economic depression and living at the point of a gun. He recognized the appeal of Hitler for Germans; in fact, he was deceived, at first, by the dictator's professed peaceful agenda. But Nazi ideology soon confronted Rusk in the universities and churches, and Brownshirts met him in the streets. Rusk was even arrested at rallies where he argued with German authorities about their racial policies. The German experience taught him a lesson about confronting bullies, but Rusk remained, at heart, a Wilsonian who placed his faith in the conference table rather than in brute force. His Cecil Peace Prize essay at Oxford verified this posture; he advocated a British Commonwealth subsumed under the League of Nations. As the democracies continued to tempt thieves by appeasement, however, Rusk distanced himself even further from pacifism.

In Service to the Nation

Rusk earned his degree at Oxford in 1934, and, after being snubbed by the State Department, accepted a position as a professor at Mills College in Oakland, California. He would not gain entry into the government until after the Second World War, when the Rhodes scholarship, wartime service, and contacts would lend him credence with the Ivy League elite of the State Department. For now he taught government and international relations, and he married one of his students, Virginia Foisie. She had recently returned from Japan, and both she and Rusk were known as Mills College's experts on foreign affairs. Both were certain that international law was the only brake on the spiral of world conflict.

The Germans, the Italians, and the Japanese were on the march. Rusk urged students and faculty toward interventionism, denouncing the restraints on President Roosevelt's ability to aid friends abroad. Rusk shunned pacifism, demonstrated in Oakland to protest the sale of scrap iron to Japan, and wept before his international relations classes in frustration over the passivity of the democracies. This crisis period in history forever marked Rusk and his generation, who became advocates of collective security to make the world safe from totalitarian aggression.

America's turn from isolationism came too late to stop Hitler from going to war in 1939. At the end of the following year, Rusk did his part by taking command of an infantry company at the rank of captain. If the appeasement era had caused him to question Wilsonian idealism, the Second World War pushed Rusk even further toward realism. Because of his study overseas, the U.S. Army regarded him as an expert on the British Empire. In 1941, assigned to a military intelligence division in Washington, DC, Rusk went to war as a major and became a specialist on Asia, a region that would captivate him for decades to come.

Major Rusk focused on South Asia, Southeast Asia, and the Western Pacific, and he came into contact with such leaders as General Marshall and General Joseph Stilwell, who oversaw the U.S. aid program for China. Early in the war, Rusk briefed Marshall and others on events in Malaya from intelligence data he had gathered. He then turned to Burma and China; working closely with Stilwell, he accompanied the general, along with Roosevelt, to major conferences such as the Cairo meeting in 1943. The reserved and diplomatic Rusk proved a perfect counter to the fiery Stilwell, whom Roosevelt recalled at the end of 1943. In December 1944, Rusk was

Major Dean Rusk in the China-Burma-India theater, 1943. *Courtesy Richard B. Russell Library, University of Georgia*

appointed deputy chief of staff of the entire China-Burma-India theater.

Rusk watched Japan advance throughout Asia, all the while learning more and more about the geography, politics, and economy of this large, disparate region. He learned firsthand of the rifts between Chinese Nationalist leader Jiang Jieshi (Chiang Kai-shek) and Stilwell. He also gained a fuller understanding of the evils of colonialism, an awareness of communism's appeal, and some recognition of the difficulties facing military campaigns on the Asian land mass. Flying dangerous missions in the Burma theater and witnessing the viciousness of the war (and emerging civil war) in China solidified Rusk's belief in Wilsonian ideals as the foundation of a peace that could only become reality through constant vigilance against aggressors.

The Second World War, like the Munich Pact, was a transformative event for Rusk, as it was for so many of his generation and for the United States as a whole. The war convinced Rusk and others that America was the sole bastion standing in the way of dictatorship, abject poverty, and global chaos; it was the U.S. mission to save the world *for* democracy and *from* totalitarian evil. The era also shaped his career. His schooling, his native intelligence, and, not least of all, his timing—as he reached maturity during the age of appeasement and served his nation in the world war—propelled Rusk to prominence.

Rusk's beliefs, his status as a protégé of the highly esteemed Stilwell and Marshall, and his lucid reporting and problem solving won him the Legion of Merit with the Oak Leaf Cluster. Stilwell had even included Rusk on a list for promotion to brigadier general. Rusk's talents would not be tested in the military, however. Instead, they landed him a position in the War Department's Operations Division, the postwar planning staff. This appointment came thanks to the personal instructions of General Marshall, who had been impressed by Rusk's work with Stilwell. The timing was crucial, for Rusk took his post in July 1945 as briefing papers were being prepared for the Potsdam Conference on arrangements in postwar Europe, the United Nations, and policy in Asia, including the defeat of Japan. He focused on the military aspects of the United Nations Security Council (a priceless position for a Wilsonian) and would become responsible for a decision of great magnitude.

Because of his Asian expertise, Rusk was asked to choose a dividing line between U.S. and Soviet liberation zones on the peninsula of Korea, a decision predicated on the assumption that Seoul, the capital of Korea, should be in the U.S. sector. Rusk's recommendation was accepted, making him instrumental in the division of the two Koreas. This bisection led to armed conflict five years later, a heightened Cold War, and Rusk's belief that communism in Asia must be stopped. Korea forever loomed large in his policy calculations. Rusk had become indispensable as a postwar foreign affairs expert.

Work on the United Nations earned him a brief posting in the State Department's Division of International Security Affairs in early 1946. Another stint in the War Department preceded his return to the State Department—under Marshall's command—as the director of the Office of Political Affairs in early 1947. Rusk replaced Alger Hiss, who would soon become a victim of the anti-Communist Red Scare, and Marshall elevated the job to the level of assistant secretary. Rusk oversaw a cherished area: policy regarding the United Nations. With his wartime experience and acceptance into the privileged club of the State Department and Marshall's sponsorship, Rusk began his ascendancy through the echelons of the department. He emerged as a major foreign policy figure as his mission of putting liberal, legal, and moral internationalism into practice materialized. Only one obstacle blocked this vision: the Soviet Union's resistance to Rusk's brand of universal values.

The Cold War

Faced with growing tensions with the Russians, Rusk adjusted his Wilsonian ideals. The Cold War struggle between capitalism and communism was emerging. Conflicts over Greece, Iran, Eastern Europe, atomic weapons, and the United Nations bolstered Rusk's pursuit of liberal internationalism, but the lessons of appeasement and now the renewed threat of aggression diverted him from Wilsonian practices. Nonetheless, Rusk was closer to the idealists in his division than to such tough-minded believers in power politics as Soviet expert George Kennan and Assistant Secretary of State Dean Acheson, who doubted the efficacy of the United Nations and championed realism in dealing with the Russians.

Rusk was willing to be pragmatic. He recognized the need for President Harry Truman to back the creation of a Jewish state in 1948, for instance, in order to woo votes at home. But Rusk also remained a steadfast anti-imperialist and a thorn in the side of State Department Europeanists, who supported colonialism. And to their further irritation, he constantly advocated the intervention of the United Nations for legal solutions to conflict. Unlike both Kennan, a Sovietologist and the father of the containment doctrine of confronting Soviet expansion, and Acheson, the pivotal secretary of state who molded early Cold War policies, Rusk was a legalist—a believer that a strict reliance on law must undergird U.S. diplomacy. Peace and security would be jeopardized unless policy was placed squarely behind the legal structure of the United Nations. Although he understood that the Russians would confound the United Nations, he was determined to make the organization work. To realists, Rusk appeared as an internationalist ideologue.

Although the analogy of Russian expansion to Nazi tyranny was important in Rusk's thinking, it was the carnage of the Second World War that really made the United Nations imperative in his mind: "The human race had paid fifty million lives to draft that Charter. Our minds and hearts had been purged in the fires of a great war, and the UN Charter represented the best that was in us at the time." Nations had been given a second chance, and Rusk refused to let the world lose the peace again. The security organization "seemed mankind's last great hope."[6] Rusk took the moral high ground. The United States must act in concert with other nations and honor its creed. Freedom took precedence over colonialism, even if the latter was in U.S. interests. This position frustrated Kennan and Acheson. The latter once responded to Rusk's moralizing by exclaiming, "Damn it, Dean, the survival of nations is not a matter of international law." Rusk disagreed: "In a nuclear age, the survival of nations may depend upon international law."[7]

Law—the setting of international standards of conduct and morality—was the key for Rusk. The United Nations was the tool to protect human rights, mediate disputes, and ensure that nuclear weapons—including the U.S. monopoly of the atomic bomb—were eradicated. Rusk vigorously pursued this liberal vision. He understood, however, that liberalism had to be rooted in international cooperation and in achieving national interests. Such pragmatism was particularly important after the Second World War, when communism menaced vulnerable nations. Thus, he looked to the UN Charter as the umpire and enforcer of peace. Rusk blended internationalist morality with both traditional realist values that focused on national interests and the use of power to achieve them. In his eyes the fusion of peaceful idealism and national security was seamless.

The logic was simple. Inheriting the Wilsonian belief that the world could be remade, Rusk became an activist in the cause of liberal internationalism. The United States would crusade on behalf of universal interests to combat communism. Liberal internationalism, then, was the ultimate objective; upholding the charter of the United Nations was the goal. National security policy was the means to that end. That was Rusk's neo-Wilsonian mission: defeat the enemies of liberal internationalism through collective security and usher in an era of global relations based on international law. In short, Kennan and Acheson were too gloomy about the prospects for cooperation. Rusk devoted himself to furthering U.S. interests, which he equated with the dream of fairness and freedom for all nations. Rusk helped formulate policies to confront Soviet expansion by relying as much as possible on the United Nations. He adhered to articles in the charter that compelled nations to refrain from using force. He urged them to resolve conflicts by collective action. Like the U.S. Constitution, the UN Charter was sacred. Because the United States dominated the United Nations— thanks to the large majority of countries in the General Assembly and the Security Council that supported U.S. policy—Rusk hoped to use the organization to secure Wilsonian ideals.

This legalistic view of the world actually led Rusk toward hardline anticommunism. Although opportunities to avoid the Cold War had been lost in the rush of events and in the quite substantial American paranoia, he never accepted that the United States shared equal blame with the Soviet Union for the conflict. For Rusk the "origins of the Cold War arose from this doctrine of world revolution and actions by various Communist countries to try to move that revolution ahead by force."[8] Surely, Rusk realized that Americans had met their match; communism—the idea that economic and social classes must be abolished to create a system of complete equality among people—also had a crusading element, much in the style of Wilsonianism. Rusk's problem was not so much with communism as it was with the Soviet Union, whose goal, he believed, was to use the ideology as a disguise to mask traditional, territorial expansionist objectives.

Kennan believed that although Soviet leader Joseph Stalin was a threat, he would be cautious in extending Soviet power. Therefore, he advocated that the United States contain Russian expansion but seek order and stability in global affairs, choosing the areas and nations of importance to take a stand against communism and letting the others go. This was realist doctrine. Rusk, on the other hand, who saw Stalin as a ruthless dictator who pursued totalitarian ends that clashed with international law, thought that Kennan was too soft on the Russians. Rusk backed the containment policy, but he did not shy away from upholding Wilsonian values. Stability was impossible without justice, and Soviet rule was not just. For Rusk, containment promoted not only a balance of power but also a moral global system.

This broad worldview had positive and negative consequences. On the positive side, Rusk was one of a handful of officials who cared about underdeveloped areas. Acheson and Kennan were Eurocentrics who had only peripheral interest in the Third World. Rusk brought attention to these regions. On the negative side, he promoted the globalization of the containment doctrine. That is, the Cold War was extended to all parts of the world in a mission to assert Wilsonianism. Rusk wanted allies to recognize the threat of communism. In Korea the threat was real; elsewhere communism was hardly distinguishable from nationalism, or the desire for independence from great powers. Wilsonian moralizing brought UN doctrine into the developing world, but it also injected the Cold War into these regions. The results were often detrimental to the target countries, and, as in Vietnam, sometimes to the United States as well.

Thus, the Cold War impinged on Rusk's universal vision of global peace. It simply had to, for the first step toward creating a Wilsonian order of liberal internationalism was to halt aggression.

Rusk sounded the alarm each time the Russians, in his eyes, tried to create a stronghold outside their borders. His brand of realpolitik —a pragmatic use of the United Nations as a tool of U.S. diplomacy—showed that Cold War realism often overshadowed his goal of liberal internationalism.

The Truman Doctrine exemplified the evolving neo-Wilsonian compromise. On March 12, 1947, the president disappointed Rusk and decided to bypass the United Nations and obtain congressional approval for economic aid to Greece and Turkey, both menaced by communism. This pledge to confront Communist subversion in the Near East was then expanded to the entire world, and it became known as the Truman Doctrine of containment. When he read the president's intended speech to Congress, Rusk demanded that the United Nations be given a role in mediating the dispute. Acheson and Kennan refused, even though Truman alluded to the United Nations without granting it a function. And Rusk, who was only the assistant chief of the Division of International Security Affairs, was forced to acquiesce. In reaction to the Truman Doctrine, however, some congressmen and journalists denounced the country's unilateral action against communism. Like Rusk, they wanted the United Nations and international law to be intimately involved.

Although he was uncomfortable that the United Nations had been sidestepped, Rusk—preferring a tough expression of resolve against the Soviet bloc—accepted his defeat. For Rusk the choice in the eastern Mediterranean was simple: the United States could either defend Greece and Turkey "or watch the USSR become the dominant power throughout the region."[9] This was the thinking of Cold Warriors; this was the type of realism that blended with Rusk's dogged faith in internationalism.

This approach was consistent with his views on the use of force. He advocated a large military body under the United Nations to give the organization more credibility as a peacekeeper. As the Second World War had come to an end, Truman had bowed to pressure and withdrawn U.S. forces from overseas. No single air group remained in Europe; no army division was ready for combat. The defense budget had been significantly reduced. Rusk considered these cutbacks a mistake. Without troops to resist him, Stalin expanded Soviet influence and territory, initiating the Cold War. Thus, military force protected liberalism, in the guise of protecting Western interests against the Russians. Article 43 of the UN Charter allowed for the arming of member states and the Security Council. To Rusk's chagrin, the U.S. military and Secretary of State George

Marshall rejected the proposal because they feared that it might be viewed as a cynical ploy to build up America's own power through the United Nations and because they considered the force too small to confront Stalin.

Rusk also wanted the United Nations to oversee the Marshall Plan, an ambitious program for European economic recovery involving $17 billion in U.S. aid. The plan was designed to jump-start Western European economies in order to erode the appeal of communism so prevalent among destitute Cold War allies. Marshall Planners, however, scorned the idea that the United Nations could guide the enormous assistance package. In 1948, as these issues evolved in ways contrary to his wishes, Rusk further conceded his legalistic principles to the pressing demands of the Cold War.

Universal Idealism under Stress

Such acquiescence allowed Rusk to survive bureaucratic turf wars. He was famous for his loyalty to higher-ranking officials, even when he disagreed with them. His allegiance to Truman's unilateral power politics, and later to Lyndon Johnson's expansion of the war in Vietnam, exemplified this fealty. This trait gave him a more extensive Cold Warrior image than he deserved. But loyalty, and his ability to get along within the State Department, earned him the respect necessary for advancement.

Rusk's circle of acquaintances included the key figures of the day: Marshall; Dean Acheson, Marshall's successor as secretary of state; and Undersecretary Robert Lovett. Other associates were powerful Republicans such as Senator Arthur Vandenberg, who shepherded the North Atlantic Treaty Organization (NATO) through Congress, and foreign policy adviser John Foster Dulles. Rusk shared much in common with Dulles, who became President Dwight D. Eisenhower's secretary of state. His Dulles-like view of the world as a struggle between the immoral Communists and the moral West led Rusk to endorse the militarization of the containment doctrine by supporting defense pacts and assistance programs.

That his principles were subsumed under national security prerogatives by the late 1940s did not turn Rusk from the fight for international law. He still vigorously opposed colonialism. Faced with imperial powers determined to retain their colonies and with a secretary of state (Acheson) who cared little about stopping them, Rusk campaigned for the independence of colonies under the guidance of the United Nations. European allies, and Acheson, argued that these colonies (the Dutch East Indies; French Indochina; British India, Burma, and Malaya; and Italian Libya) were key components of the Western alliance. If given their independence, they would fall into the hands of the Communist bloc. But Rusk viewed colonialism as an immoral anachronism. How could the United States and the United Nations promote principles of freedom and democracy while denying self-government to a majority of the world's people?

Maneuvering within the United Nations, Rusk supported the creation of Indonesia from the Dutch East Indies, an independent India, freedom from Britain for Palestinian Jews and Arabs, and a trusteeship for Libya. These accomplishments were not without conflict—the partition of India and Pakistan brought disorder and war. The same was true for Indonesia. And France refused to give up Indochina, prompting Vietnamese revolutionary leader Ho Chi Minh to continue his struggle against imperialism.

Rusk was not able to deter the White House from recognizing the state of Israel when the British mandate ended in May 1948. Like other officials in the Departments of State and Defense, he protested that protecting the strategic Middle East through a United Nations trusteeship to attract the oil-rich Arabs was more important than providing a homeland for Holocaust victims and winning Jewish-American votes in the presidential campaign, but he obeyed the stricture that the president had the final say over policy. Rusk was ultimately content that anticolonialism had prevailed on most fronts, even if, as in the case of Libya, the Soviets could take credit for the independence. His worldview fit with the neo-Wilsonian Cold War consensus of idealism restrained by realpolitik.

Having proved his loyalty to Truman and to his superiors in the State Department and having exhibited expertise in many foreign affairs crises, Rusk was promoted to the position of deputy undersecretary of state in the spring of 1949. He became a key liaison in Congress for Acheson, who depended on Rusk's knowledge of the world, his ability to solve problems caused by bureaucratic rivalries, and the respect he had garnered on Capitol Hill. By all reports, Rusk was popular as he reached the top of the State Department. A patient, unpretentious man, he earned a reputation as an intelligent, resourceful, and calm decision maker. His mild and often witty temperament facilitated his rise to the highest ranks of leadership; his patrons included a range of top officials, from Marshall and Acheson to Republican leaders. Hard work, skill, and contacts served him well. Above all, faith in the containment doctrine, which required his support for top policymakers through loyal service, paid off. Neo-Wilsonianism provided the ideological and strategic guide with which to chart the rough waters of the Cold War.

With a diligence unparalleled in the State Department, Rusk worked long hours under self-imposed pressure. Although he was well liked, he had few friends and sacrificed his family life for his seven-day-per-week job. By 1949 he and Virginia had had their third child, but Rusk rarely took time off to socialize. His family lived in a small apartment outside of Washington, and he occasionally played bridge or a round of golf. But this workaholic—now a balding, stocky man of forty with a soft Georgian drawl—was devoted to making and explaining foreign policy and to running interference for Acheson in Congress.

To ease the strain, he smoked several packs of cigarettes each day and imbibed Scotch at night. Neither impaired his abilities, at least not until the end of his tenure as secretary of state, when he came under enormous pressure to negotiate peace in Vietnam. Both habits alleviated his great sense of responsibility. Rusk profoundly believed that his role was to defend democracy. Sincerely holding that the constitutional system bestowed obligations on every citizen, he felt compelled—actually driven—to serve his country.

Rusk was an excellent midlevel bureaucrat. He delegated authority but gave guidance to subordinates. His mind was supple and quick, able to grasp complex issues and make succinct, convincing observations. In the dog-eat-dog world of politics, he also became a good tactician. Rusk flourished behind the scenes, getting along with most officials, soothing egos, intervening in squabbles, and pursuing bipartisanship in Congress. Above all, he was known for not tipping his hand; he remained publicly noncommittal and firmly opposed to expressing his personal view on an issue. Testimony to Congress, for instance, hardly ever deviated from the administration's line, even if he did not agree with it. He liked the limelight but not prying reporters. He steadfastly refused to comment on matters that he considered confidential, and he cautioned others to do likewise.

The value of such a company man was not lost on Acheson and Truman, or later on Kennedy and Johnson. In an era of divisive party politics, when the former pair found that they were targets of Republican party disdain, the president—who had been trained in the world of boss politics in Kansas City—appreciated Rusk's loyalty. And Acheson took Rusk into his very small circle of confidants. By the early 1950s, Rusk was a man of influence.

It is clear that for Rusk there were career advantages to adapting strict Wilsonian principles of universal collective security to the more narrow ideological doctrine of containment, but there was also a price to pay. It was not that Rusk believed that he was sacrificing his soul to join the foreign policy elite; the Cold War compelled liberals to make hard choices. They could hold to their beliefs in the hope of achieving harmony around the globe; Truman's secretary of commerce, Henry Wallace, pursued this course by demanding reconciliation with the Russians, and he was banished from power in 1946.

At the same time, liberals had qualms about such hard-line realists as Acheson and Kennan, who approved of heightened U.S. security policies abroad and opened the way to rigid anticommunism at home. Some liberals took the road that Rusk traveled, connecting realism to universalism. By the late 1940s, Soviet-U.S. conflict had made a mockery of the UN ideal. There was no cooperation, except within the discrete Western and Soviet camps. That realization did not deter liberals like Rusk from hoping for a better day, but it imposed a framework that left little room for pure Wilsonianism.

Rusk's observations about the world—the tragedy of the 1930s when the democracies had not confronted aggressors, the horrors of world war—had pushed him toward a more unilateral foreign policy and the advancement of security concerns above global consonance. His assessment of the Communist threat led him away from youthful ideals and toward realism. Yet by remaining loyal, as he said, "to our basic principles and to joint action with others who share them," Rusk managed to keep the overall goal of world peace in view.[10]

Notes

1. Dean Rusk, with Richard Rusk, *As I Saw It*, ed. Daniel S. Papp (New York: W. W. Norton, 1990), 62.

2. Dean Rusk to his father, December 18, 1932, Box 1, Series I, Dean Rusk Collection, Richard B. Russell Library, University of Georgia, Athens (hereafter cited as UGA).

3. Rusk, *As I Saw It*, 66.

4. Thomas Schoenbaum, *Waging Peace and War: Dean Rusk in the Truman, Kennedy, and Johnson Years* (New York: Simon and Schuster, 1988), 50.

5. Milton Viorst, "Incidentally, Who Is Dean Rusk?" *Esquire* (April 1968): 181.

6. Rusk, *As I Saw It*, 136.

7. Ibid., 98. See also Warren I. Cohen, *Dean Rusk* (Totowa, NJ: Cooper Square Publishers, 1980), 8.

8. Rusk, *As I Saw It*, 129.

9. Ibid., 140.

10. Dean Rusk, "Universal, Regional and Bilateral Patterns of International Organization," U.S. Department of State *Bulletin* (hereafter cited as *DSB*) 22 (April 3, 1950): 530.

2

Among the Best and the Brightest

The Cold War changed Dean Rusk's approach to foreign policy. He had hoped that the United Nations would become the forum for conflict resolution, but neither superpower wanted it to take that role. When the United Nations failed to meet Rusk's expectation, he became a liberal interventionist. This Cold Warrior engaged the Soviets, for they had, in his view, "an insatiable appetite for their objectives. There is no limit to their goals."[1] Without abandoning his Wilsonian roots, Rusk became an architect of the tough stance against communism, particularly in Asia. Although few of the vestiges of idealism were apparent in his outlook, the very prosecution of the Cold War defended this ideology. His neo-Wilsonian views corresponded with those held by most of the foreign policy elite; as a member of this club, Rusk had reached its top ranks by 1961.

Perils of Communism

The Cold War entered a perilous period in 1949. Russia had already swept democratic Czechoslovakia into its orbit; then, in 1948, it shut off Western access to Berlin, the German city divided between wartime allies. The Soviet blockade precipitated what was the gravest crisis to date in the Cold War. The United States airlifted supplies to the stranded West Berliners and bluffed the Russians by sending bombers equipped to carry nuclear weapons to bases in England. During the emergency, Rusk sought a role for the United Nations by maintaining pressure on the Soviets within the Security Council. The Soviets abandoned the blockade in May 1949, but the superpower conflict had intensified.

Signs now pointed toward a protracted conflict between the United States and the Soviet Union. Germany was divided in two, Moscow tested its own nuclear bomb, and Western nations created NATO. Rusk approved of this defensive alliance against Soviet expansion in Europe that linked the United States, Canada, and ten Western European nations. It was a step toward fulfilling principles of Wilsonian collective security. Support of NATO as a legal entity, however, distanced him somewhat from the universal ideals of Wilsonianism, for the alliance grouped one set of nations against another. The victory of Chinese Communist Mao Zedong (Mao Tsetung) over U.S. ally Jiang Jieshi (Chiang Kai-shek) in 1949 further emphasized his Cold War liberalism.

The rout of Jiang and the Nationalist Chinese, who fled to Taiwan, reverberated in the United States. The world's most populous nation, Red China might now serve as an inspiration to others seeking to change the status quo in Asia. The United States had long tried to protect China from imperialism, but now communism ruled. Right-wing, Red-baiting anti-Communists, led by Senator Joseph McCarthy, accused the State Department of employing traitorous subversives who had let Jiang "fall" to the Communists.

Rusk was disappointed by Jiang's defeat. It was "a great tragedy—that the Chinese people, with their tremendous energy and potential, were now wedded to Communist ideology and allied with the Soviet Union," he lamented.[2] His wartime experience in the China-Burma-India theater made him agonize particularly over this tragedy. The McCarthy-era Red Scare raised the stakes for containment in Asia, which meant that all areas of the region, including French Indochina (Vietnam, Cambodia, and Laos), must be denied to the Communists. This crusade became Rusk's signal contribution to the Cold War.

Rusk took this position to answer McCarthy's outrageous charges as well. Anti-Communist hard-liners in Congress attacked the administration for being soft on communism. Republicans seized the "loss" of China as a means to discredit Truman and the Democrats. In this political maelstrom, Rusk exhibited the loyalty that would exemplify his tenure as secretary of state a decade later. He volunteered to be the lightning rod for the State Department by requesting a demotion to assistant secretary of state for Far Eastern Affairs. In this way he might deflect criticism from such vulnerable officials as Acheson to himself. This sacrifice meant a fall from the lofty perch as the State Department's third-ranking member to the third tier of the bureaucracy.

A stunned Acheson was so moved that he later lobbied President Kennedy to consider Rusk as secretary of state. (He also claimed to have kissed Rusk on both cheeks out of gratitude, although Rusk denied it.) Rusk took the heat. He called in his chips, drawing on such contacts as John Foster Dulles and Republican friends in Congress to halt the attacks from Capitol Hill. He then clearly stated that McCarthy's charges endangered U.S. security. They "not only create disunity and bitter feelings inside the country at a time when national unity is needed most but they cause our friends abroad to wonder what kind of people we are."[3] Lacking evidence of a conspiracy, McCarthy had better shut up.

Rusk had revealed another one of his strengths—a knack for handling Congress in sensitive circumstances. Like the Foreign Service diplomats on China, Rusk was vulnerable to the Red Scare because he argued that Jiang's corruption had brought about his own downfall. Rusk helped to formulate the China White Paper of 1949 that showed the truth to this allegation. Yet he also built the bipartisan consensus in favor of containing China. Seeing Mao as a puppet of Moscow, Rusk joined other administration members in persuading Congress to deny the People's Republic of China a seat in the United Nations and to sever diplomatic relations for over two decades.

By 1950, Rusk had blanketed Asia under the threat of communism. His contempt for colonialism came second to his conviction, for instance, that France's presence in Indochina was necessary to combat the Russians. Rusk worried that the Indonesian government was being infiltrated by Communists; aid in building a police force would shore up that nation. Rusk decided that the Communist threat in the region was equal to that in Europe. Containment would be difficult in Asia, however, for the Communists had an easier task, as he put it, of "trying to tear down" what "we are trying to build."[4]

Rusk had toughened in a tough year. He epitomized the liberal, Cold War consensus that a stand against communism was in order. As such, and appropriately enough, he helped draft NSC-68, a national security agenda that recommended massive defense spending to contain Soviet imperialism the world over. Accepted by President Truman in the summer of 1950, NSC-68 signaled a change from containment in certain regions to a worldwide, globalized extension of national security programs. In private, Rusk doubted the supposed ubiquitous intentions of Stalin and rued the day that the Cold War had spread into Asia. But for public

consumption, he became a leading voice of the crusade for globalized containment. And he had a hand in almost every major policy
issue in the Cold War.

The Cold War tied together Rusk's principles. The United States
must shun isolationism, for it had a stake in a peace that could be
obtained only by carrying out the elementary task of providing for
national security. The UN Charter must be upheld "as the minimum standard of conduct required of all," regardless of political
philosophy or national character. But the Russians were not play-
ing by the rules of acceptable conduct, and they had now yoked
the Chinese to their policies. They were aggressors, a threat to peace.
To stop them, he said, "American strength must be joined with the
strength of others" in collective security.[5] In the Rusk equation, security against communism was part and parcel of liberal internationalism—Cold War-style.

Korea and the Chinese Threat

The onset of the Korean War in 1950 validated Rusk's desire for a
forceful presence in Asia to stop Communist penetration. The Korean peninsula, divided in accord with Rusk's recommendation,
placed Americans in the South and Russians in the North. Both
nations had aided their zones, but—to Rusk's chagrin—the U.S.
contribution had been reduced during the Truman years. Although
he agreed with the accepted view at the time that the possibility of
war was remote, Rusk wanted to display resolve in Korea.

That Korea was a lower priority for defense than Japan and the
Philippines seemingly gave the North Koreans a green light to
launch an invasion of South Korea on June 25, 1950, designed to
unify the peninsula under communism. As the first senior official
to learn the news of the attack, Rusk was shocked as North Korea
rolled through the South with ease. Hearing of the assault while
dining with Secretary of the Army Frank Pace, Rusk urged Acheson
to let him lobby UN Secretary General Trygve Lie to call a meeting
of the Security Council.

Characteristically, Rusk involved the United Nations, for the
attack challenged "the entire concept of collective security won at
such cost during World War II."[6] South Korea and the United States
had no security treaty, but Washington had responsibilities there.
Yet instead of a unilateral response, the United Nations would send
troops after a vote in the Security Council. That approach appealed
to world opinion and had worked in confronting the Soviets in the

Near East just after the Second World War. Involving the United Nations also placed Rusk's cherished imprimaturs of international law and morality over military action. With Moscow boycotting the United Nations in protest of the U.S. refusal to seat the Chinese delegation, the Security Council passed resolutions for UN troops to repulse the invasion.

The United States carried the burden of the fighting. As an adviser in Truman's war cabinet, Rusk applauded as two divisions of U.S. troops and various UN units halted the North Korean advance within a month. By September 1950 the daring tactics of General Douglas MacArthur had driven the Communists out of South Korea, back across the 38th parallel. MacArthur continued his assault into North Korea, right to the Chinese border. But Mao countered with a force of over two hundred thousand troops in late November that sent the Americans reeling southward in retreat.

Rusk advised Truman not to expand the war by attacking China, for winning would be impossible. But he also won a battle against the Joint Chiefs of Staff, who advocated a complete withdrawal of troops from the peninsula. Rusk prevailed on the president to hold the line until there was a cease-fire; American prestige was at stake. Winston Churchill had held out against Hitler in the darkest days of the Second World War, Rusk argued, and Truman must do so now. Truman agreed. Unfortunately, hanging on in Korea set a historical precedent for staying the course in Vietnam fifteen years later.

Rusk was optimistic about the situation in Korea. If China had legitimate reasons to intervene, then the whole matter could be turned over to the United Nations for resolution. But, he said, if Chinese "intervention is part of a pattern of wider Communist aggression, I think the free world is going to put up a solid front."[7] The United States could not give an inch to Chinese- or Soviet-sponsored communism, which encouraged outlaw behavior from rogue nations like North Korea. International law must be upheld.

Mao and Stalin were not behind every conflict in Asia, Rusk knew, but he had few doubts that the Communist bloc eyed the region. At best the Chinese were a destabilizing force in the area; at worst they were an expansionist menace serving Russian whims. Issuing one of the sharpest attacks by any U.S. official against North Korea, Rusk accused the Chinese Communists of preparing for the treacherous assault on South Korea long before it was actually launched. The People's Republic of China was no free agent; the "puppet master is Soviet," he declared in 1950.[8] Policy in Asia became predicated on the threat of Chinese-Russian expansion. To

Rusk his country faced "great peril," for the chances of a "general war" waged by Moscow and its satellites had increased substantially. The United States had entered a period of "attempted intimidation" in which its national unity would be tested. "We must keep steady nerves, remain calm, and understand that we *have* to prepare to face the main threat,"[9] said Rusk. The Cold Warrior would battle to the end.

The Korean War ultimately ended in 1953 in a stalemate that reestablished the division of the peninsula at the 38th parallel. China had eventually sent over one million troops and had lost one-half of that number. That sacrifice impressed Rusk. For him the lesson was obvious: the United States had to be firm in containing communism in Asia. Korea was the historical benchmark of the Cold War that verified the anti-appeasement approach. Rusk approved of most hard-line containment policies. Truman integrated Japan into the alliance against communism by signing a peace treaty in 1951, ending the postwar U.S. occupation but retaining troops and bases. The United States signed a defense treaty with the Philippines that same year, as well as the ANZUS pact—proposed by Rusk—between Australia, New Zealand, and the United States. In a change of policy painful for Rusk because he despised the unscrupulous Jiang, the United States would also defend Taiwan from the People's Republic of China.

Significantly, Rusk was lukewarm to calls for a "Pacific NATO," a Southeast Asian Treaty Organization (SEATO) of regional nations. He noted that many of these countries were too politically and economically unstable for the alliance to work. And he did not want the United States to organize security for Asians; regional security would be more successful if they devised their own arrangement, he believed. (Yet Secretary of State Dulles would create SEATO in 1955.) If Rusk questioned SEATO's form, however, he certainly agreed with the intent. The people of Asia deserved to live under the principles of Wilsonian democracy and prosperity. He envisioned a grouping of anti-Communist Asian nations linked to the West, a collective-security arrangement that would undercut the appeal of aggressive communism. This was not imperialism; rather, the question was whether all Asians would "be subjected to a Communist reign of terror and be absorbed by force into the new colonialism of a Soviet Communist empire."[10] That defense of SEATO's aims drove Rusk to endorse war in Vietnam years later.

Rusk accepted SEATO because of his perception that China threatened U.S. interests and peace. In a hyperbolic speech in May

1951 delivered to the China Institute in New York City, Rusk drew a stark picture. Mao's regime was, he said, "a colonial Russian government—a Slavic Manchukuo on a larger scale. It is not the Government of China. It will not pass the first step. It is not Chinese." He later disclaimed the remarks as merely a taunt to Beijing, but they appeared to express the desire for conflict, not negotiation, in Asia.[11] His words created a furor. The press considered them a radical reversal in State Department policy toward China. Secretary Acheson had earlier indicated that the United States would live, unhappily, with Mao. Now the diplomats, particularly Rusk, seemed more inflexible. To liberals, Rusk seemed to signal a shift in U.S. policy toward a belligerent stance that served the whims of the mercurial Jiang. They took Rusk to task for being too zealously anti-Communist, for issuing a near ultimatum designed to quiet Red-baiters and President Truman's GOP critics. The assistant secretary clearly lacked the reflective nature of a mature statesman, left liberals concluded.

Rusk could not have befriended Mao in the charged atmosphere of the 1950s, but his rhetoric did not soothe fears. Instead, it exacerbated hatred toward China and created the scary image of monolithic communism in Asia. Turmoil in the region was blamed on the Soviet-Chinese axis. Such thinking set the stage for the burden of Vietnam. It must be said, however, that when Rusk made the statement, Washington was fraught with tension. Truman and Acheson were under the gun from McCarthy. The Korean War was going badly; containment seemed to be unraveling, like Truman's presidency. Rusk spoke in haste, but he also loyally deflected criticism from the White House. Moreover, mainstream Cold War liberals agreed with both his assessment of China and the need to assist such nations as the Philippines, Malaysia, and French Indochina in their fight against Asian communism.

Preparing to leave the State Department in late 1951, Rusk voiced the principles of the United Nations under the guise of realism. He likened the United States to a benign tomcat, guarding the mice from the evil Communist predator: "We feel that there will be no pouncing if the free world thoroughly demonstrates it will not accept that sort of thing." Wilsonianism was but a memory at the height of the Cold War, yet Rusk's neo-Wilsonian purpose of peace through vigilance remained. War was easy to make; avoiding conflict was much more difficult. The best way to achieve peace was to prove to enemies that war would "mean disaster for them. If that is a prayer," said Rusk, "I think it's a very good one."[12]

The Rockefeller Foundation

Having completed the Japanese peace treaty, obtained aid for France's effort in Indochina, and seen the Korean War stabilized, Rusk looked around for new work in the foreign policy field. As a Truman appointee, he was not optimistic about his chances for government service. The Republicans were likely to gain the White House in 1952. Rusk knew that he was not long for the State Department. His friend Dulles, a Republican, recommended him for the presidency of the Rockefeller Foundation. Rusk would remain a consultant to the State Department but would have at his disposal sizable financial resources to maintain his internationalist mission. He would also, of course, finally earn a decent salary while enjoying life removed from the pressures of policymaking. Exiting Washington amid glowing press reviews, Rusk took over the Rockefeller Foundation in June 1952.

Headquartered in Manhattan, the Rockefeller Foundation had long focused on domestic issues. Rusk continued this tradition by starting new programs that funded education, libraries, and the arts. Along with aid to minority and antipoverty programs—of interest to Rusk because of his own background—the Foundation promoted radical studies such as those on human sexuality by zoologist Alfred Kinsey. From inquiries into food supply, population, and public health to esoteric research on plant behavior, hookworm disease in the South, and behavioral science, Rusk's institution reflected a liberal's concern for development. It also reflected a liberal's approach to the Cold War in the 1950s. Rusk hoped to eradicate the excesses of McCarthyism (and ably defended the Foundation against charges of subversion) and to maintain a strong but adaptable national security policy that did not shun negotiation with the Soviet bloc. Regarding Asia, his field of expertise, Rusk took an active interest.

On China, remarkably, Rusk showed a desire to negotiate. If the People's Republic were to be admitted into the United Nations, Mao must assure that Taiwan would be left unmolested and that Ho would no longer receive Chinese aid. Rusk advocated a Two-Chinas policy, of seating Taiwan and the People's Republic in the United Nations while seeking to isolate Mao from Russia. One way to drive a wedge between the Communist powers was to encourage trade between Beijing and the West. A start would be to normalize U.S.-China relations, which meant a shift from hard-line containment. The plan collapsed in 1956, however, when Congress unanimously resolved against admitting Beijing into the United Nations. Dulles would not budge; the resolution similarly scared President Kennedy half a decade later.

Rusk was willing to look for ways to ease tensions and even end the Cold War. He was not soft on communism but clung to the lessons of appeasement and North Korean aggression. The Rockefeller Foundation urged an increase in defense spending. But nonmilitary responses to communism were also feasible. When Soviet leader Nikita Khrushchev announced that the Russians had greater development appeal in the Third World than the United States, Rusk took heart. Economic competition could change the nature of the Cold War, easing the superpowers away from deadly nuclear solutions to their problems. This position was consistent with President Eisenhower's attempts to tone down the Cold War as well as the liberals' pursuit of peaceful coexistence with the Soviet Union. Under Rusk's guidance, the Rockefeller Foundation funded courses at American University to promote the nonmilitary contest by teaching a better understanding of the new Russia.

Khrushchev drew U.S. attention to the underdeveloped areas of the globe. Rusk's memories of his childhood poverty and the later transformation of the rural South into a productive region inspired him to seek development in the Third World. Concentrating on health, education, and agricultural output, Rusk sought to "get involved with the great mass of humanity in the Third World."[13] He shifted the Rockefeller Foundation's focus from domestic to international poverty. Studies within the Foundation led to the creation of a program of technical aid, funded by $5 million per year, to train Third World leaders to exploit their national resources. Efforts to increase food supplies yielded the hardy miracle rice of the Green Revolution that staved off starvation in India, Mexico, the Philippines, and elsewhere. Population studies led to birth-control programs, the eradication of viruses forestalled epidemics, and investigations into unconventional fields like cloud chemistry and marine biology advanced knowledge about sustainable life. Rusk's Rockefeller Foundation forged the liberal vision of distributing global wealth more equitably.

In the late 1950s, as colonies prepared for independence and as the Cold War stabilized in Europe and moved into the periphery, Rusk's programs took on greater significance for U.S. foreign policy. But, as a latent Wilsonian, Rusk was also deeply committed to the humanitarian service of the Foundation. As a result, he gave a grant to a Colorado college that began planning for a "peace corps" of

American volunteers who would travel abroad to assist in basic projects of development.

Rusk also remained wedded to the United Nations, giving dozens of speeches throughout the 1950s that built a case for the importance of using the organization to promote democratic solutions to conflict. Still, Rusk was not such an idealist that he would subject all U.S. diplomacy to UN deliberations. Events like the Suez crisis of 1956 and confrontations over the Chinese offshore islands of Quemoy and Matsu in 1955 and 1958, when the United States sought to protect Jiang by signing a defense pact with Taiwan, convinced him that the superpowers would act independently of the United Nations if it suited their interests. The international body could not be expected to bring peace by itself. Yet because open debate, in the court of world opinion, might prompt searches for alternatives to violent action, Rusk continued to defend the United Nations in front of the realist skeptics.

The Rockefeller years also had an impact on his career. He was a behind-the-scenes adviser to the political establishment. Most notably in this regard, he directed a national study of foreign policy. The report, *The Mid-Century Challenge to U.S. Foreign Policy*, was drafted by the prestigious Council on Foreign Relations and issued by the Rockefeller Foundation in December 1959. Largely Rusk's document, it surveyed both the great transformations that lay ahead as the colonial era came to a close as well as the dangers of nuclear arms. Above all, the study eschewed passivity for creativity in foreign policy. A willingness to pursue interests must coincide with a search for cooperation. The Soviets sought domination, as proved by a second crisis over Berlin in 1958. Rusk concluded, however, that the United States could shape the world's future.

In the document, and in later articles, Rusk explained his typically optimistic conviction that a strong president, working with a loyal secretary of state, could inject foreign policy with dynamism, idealism, and realism. In his eyes, the relationship of Acheson and Marshall to Truman—not the presumed passive role of Dulles to Eisenhower—served as a model for an activist approach to a changing world. The foreign policy elite, based in the Council on Foreign Relations, endorsed this idea. Hardened Cold Warriors and leftist liberals alike thought along the same lines. The former, represented by Acheson, knew Rusk to be a foe of Communist expansion; the latter, such as Chester Bowles and Adlai Stevenson, appreciated Rusk's reliance on the United Nations. They agreed, essentially, with his neo-Wilsonian stance. Most important, the recognition that the

United States must seize the opportunity of leadership in a rapidly changing world appealed to Senator John Kennedy.

A Consensus Secretary of State

Kennedy epitomized dynamism; the older Rusk did not. But after his very narrow electoral victory in November 1960, the new president needed a cabinet that would not threaten conservatives in Congress or the business community and that would convince the people of the United States and the world that his youth enhanced, rather than diminished, his potential for leadership. Kennedy searched for a secretary of state who would fulfill these requirements.

In fact, Kennedy discussed possible choices with Rusk. The first was former Secretary of Defense Lovett, who begged off because of health problems and advanced age. Stevenson was next, but he had angered Kennedy by angling for the Democratic nomination for president in 1960. Bowles, the opinionated and dovish Democratic spokesman on foreign policy, was too liberal. Kennedy looked to Senator J. William Fulbright, a Democrat from Arkansas, but his support for racial segregation made him vulnerable in Congress. Rusk suggested that Fulbright would revert to his liberal values once removed from Congress, but Kennedy would not have him. Averell Harriman, erstwhile emissary to presidents from Franklin Roosevelt to Jimmy Carter, was considered too old at age sixty-nine. David Bruce withdrew himself from candidacy and was subsequently appointed ambassador to Great Britain.

That left Rusk. The respected Lovett recommended him for the position. Although a Democrat, Rusk was an intimate of top Republicans and could help Kennedy in Congress. Rusk also had the credentials in education, government service, crisis diplomacy, ideology, and intellect. He actually had much more experience in foreign affairs than the presidents he served. To be sure, he enjoyed running the Rockefeller Foundation, but, as he told his brother Parks after being offered the post, "If I don't take it, all that experience will be wasted."[14] Rusk was also a humble man; he had long worked behind the scenes, having attained his status without politicking inside the Washington Beltway. Although he was generally confident in his convictions and in his abilities, Rusk exhibited a disarming lack of assurance when offered the post of secretary of state. When Lovett approached him at the annual meeting of the Rockefeller Foundation, Rusk was visibly shocked. He promptly listed his liabilities. He had had contacts with Kennedy during the

1950s, when both had focused on foreign aid programs, but he certainly was not in Kennedy's circle. He later told Kennedy that his financial situation was so bad that he could afford only one term at the moderate pay the position offered. And did Kennedy not know that Rusk had backed Stevenson during the Democratic primaries? The president-elect just laughed.

Rusk wanted the post, even if it meant leaving behind a comfortable life. For eight years he had worked normal hours; returned home to Scarsdale, New York, most nights for dinner; and spent weekends enjoying his family and weeding dandelions in his front yard. He accepted Kennedy's offer out of a sense of duty, because his ambition had been piqued, and because Lovett (who sat on the board of the Rockefeller Foundation) made it possible for Rusk to make the financial sacrifice by arranging a generous termination allowance from the Foundation. Kennedy accepted Rusk because of his competence, experience, and bipartisan appeal and because he recognized that Rusk would be a loyal and unassuming subordinate in the making of foreign policy, which suited Kennedy's image-making needs. Thus, returning to the spotlight, Rusk moved his family from New York to Washington. But he had traveled much farther than that. Appointed secretary of state on December 12, 1960, Rusk had risen from obscure poverty to the highest foreign policy position in the world's most powerful nation.

Integrity to a Fault

In his official capacity, Rusk never got particularly good press. Not an insider in the president's circle and obsessed with confidentiality, he seemed too serious about his job. He was famous for his closemouthed, deferential style. One story tells of Kennedy asking Rusk about a classified matter as the two sat alone in the Oval Office. Rusk replied, "There are still too many people here, Mr. President."[15]

In an administration of bright and talented whiz kids, Rusk was both more ponderous in thought and much older than most. He was known as "square" by the Washington jet set. With the temperament of a bureaucrat and intellectual, Rusk had none of the shoot-from-the-hip bold glamour of the best and the brightest who surrounded the dashing president. In the Oval Office one day, Kennedy sent his three-year-old daughter, Caroline, to Rusk's side to inquire about the situation in Yemen. Rusk was taken by surprise, but when he heard the president chuckling in glee behind a curtain, the seemingly tedious secretary of state played along. Throughout the 1960s, Rusk remained an enigma to Americans. This bland bureaucrat with a Buddha-like public image became a symbol of the elite class of Washington, a target for the liberal press and Vietnam War protesters. He sought to cover his tracks, to sit quietly and advise presidents in private. He was proud of his style, of providing his bosses a chance to sound off without fear of publicity. He was not verbose, not interested in grandstanding; he was not like other administration members.

Rusk became the bedrock of both Kennedy's and Lyndon Johnson's foreign policy teams, a steadying influence in times of crisis, of which there were many. Certainly, he was not given to creativity; he hewed close to his experiences and history. As he explained, "Ideas are not policies. Besides, ideas have a high infant-mortality rate."[16] Rusk kept his presidents on course. Lacking the shine of Camelot, he proved indispensable in guiding two administrations along the tortured neo-Wilsonian course of idealism and resolute anticommunism. At age fifty-one, Rusk heard doubts about his suitability in the administration while he drew praise as a veteran Cold Warrior. Kennedy's own men, and those enamored by the Camelot myth, brushed him aside as unimaginative, predictable, and wooden. Yet he was certainly appreciated for his service to the nation. Those who knew him from the Rockefeller Foundation found him "approachable, a real liberal" who was down to earth, warm, and practical.[17]

The new secretary of state could not have been more unlike the president. Kennedy had grown up Catholic and wealthy and was driven politically. His wit, youthful restlessness, and pragmatism contrasted with Rusk's dry humor, reticence, rigid adherence to principles, Protestant convictions, and modest background. Kennedy loved the limelight; Rusk operated behind the scenes. Kennedy also relied on his impulsive brother Robert, the attorney general, who often clashed with the seemingly staid Rusk. But the president and Rusk got along.

Rusk was especially valued as a veteran policymaker with close associates on Capitol Hill, a man who could soothe fat egos in Congress. Kennedy understood politics and the need to treat legislators with care. More than that, Kennedy and Rusk shared views about the world. Both understood the stakes in the Cold War and the need to be tough but flexible toward communism. Both World War II veterans also voiced the rhetoric of American-style altruism: progress, positivism, freedom. In his first State of the Union

President Kennedy came to appreciate the wise and mature Rusk as time went on.
Courtesy Richard B. Russell Library, University of Georgia

address, Kennedy alluded to the eagle on the Great Seal of the
United States, with an olive branch of peace in one claw and a
bundle of arrows in the other. Just as he had years before on his
Rhodes scholarship exam, Rusk welcomed the symbolization of
peace and strength. Kennedy and Rusk had much in common.

Rusk settled into bureaucratic life in 1961, pressing onward with
the beliefs that had shaped his career. He recognized the imperative of a strong defense, for he saw aggression as the world's most
serious problem. But even as the two superpowers confronted each
other, it was imperative that they negotiate. Rusk believed in talking; he was a diplomat who stressed the rule of law and shied away
from dramatic brinkmanship. Principles of justice and law could
resolve disputes and thus undergird a lasting peace. Above all—
and more so than the presidents he served—Rusk continued the
liberal crusade for human rights and legalism. The Soviet Union
was both a security threat and menace to global civil rights, just as
the segregation of black Americans in the United States undermined
freedom at home. Rusk carried his Wilsonian ideals into the
Kennedy administration.[18]

As secretary of state, Rusk held over seventy press conferences,
met over five hundred foreign dignitaries, and logged one million
miles of travel. Nearly sixty years old when he stepped down in

1969, he was called by one journalist the "Lou Gehrig of government."[19] Rusk served eight years, longer than all of the more than sixty secretaries of state in American history except one, Franklin Roosevelt's Cordell Hull. As a policymaker, Rusk saw his job as that of presidential adviser and spokesman for foreign policy. His schedule included fifteen-hour workdays, seven days per week, with very few nights alone with his family. Only on weekends did he forgo his tie. His wife endured as their social life declined dramatically. Both Kennedy and Johnson had to insist that he take vacations. During Rusk's eight years in office, he took only seven weeks off; in 1967 he worked on Vietnam issues during the Christmas and New Year's holiday weekends. Not surprisingly, Rusk suffered occasional physical and emotional strain, including headaches, stomach problems, and nightmares.

Rusk's decision-making style did not ease the burden. He focused on presidential advising, Congress, foreign officials, and traveling. He delegated power to subordinates, seeking advice from assistant secretaries and undersecretaries on all important issues, a pattern that earned him respect from the lower ranks. Bureaucrats were doubly thankful when Rusk employed many victims of McCarthy's anti-Communist witch-hunts. But freedom for subordinates led to disorganization and to the ascendance of advisers from outside the State Department, prompting the president to question Rusk's reliability. Early in his administration, Kennedy expressed his uneasiness by often bypassing Rusk on key matters.

Nevertheless, Rusk's unobtrusive leadership served his boss. Mindful of others' opinions, the secretary of state encouraged the kind of give-and-take sought by Kennedy. He preferred to discuss matters with the president after noisy meetings. He disagreed with Kennedy only in private and downplayed any friction between them. He was also the only member of the cabinet whom Kennedy did not call by his first name, a practice that Rusk approved of as appropriate to the relationship between a president and his secretary of state. As a result of his style, Rusk remained a shadowy figure who was undeservedly described by such liberal detractors as the voluble Kennedy court historian, Arthur Schlesinger, as being made of "ice water."[20]

Although stoic in public, Rusk was anything but a sphinx in private. He kept family matters out of the limelight and was closemouthed with relatives—even his wife—when issues upset him. Even during the worst days of Vietnam, however, he was known to laugh easily; he was a good-natured, soft-spoken colleague who

The Rusk family. Standing is son David. Seated, left to right: son Richard, wife Virginia, Dean, David's wife Delia, and daughter Peggy. *Courtesy Richard B. Russell Library, University of Georgia*

bowled and played bridge, poker, and tennis. His obvious self-effacement was refreshing. When asked whether being secretary of state made him famous, the burly, bald, and round-faced Rusk replied in jest that beautiful young women now smiled at him in the streets.

He disdained flashiness. Once he was photographed leading an entourage of State Department officials on a bowling outing. When he visited his alma mater, Davidson College, where he had played center on the basketball team, he sank long shots at the gym. One day, while teaching his son Rich how to drive in the streets of Washington, the car stalled. After Rusk got under the hood and cleaned the air filter, he was oblivious to a policeman's puzzling over the secretary of state's greasy hands. This everyday man described himself as looking like a bartender; others compared him to a big koala bear with a Mona Lisa smile.

Rusk had his faults, to be sure. His inability to stem the infighting in his department forced Kennedy to step in and reorganize it in late 1961. Never successful at managing the State Department with total efficiency, he quipped during a museum visit that an exhibition of abstract art reminded him of a day at the office. As he shied away from public diplomacy, he earned the undeserved reputation of being stiff and unapproachable. Yet during the crises of the Kennedy years, Rusk grew closer to the president. A faltering Kennedy came to rely increasingly on the secretary of state's calm determination and on his profound foreign policy convictions.

From a poor boy in Georgia to secretary of state was a storybook achievement drawn straight from the American dream. The appointment capped a dazzling five decades of life. Rusk had lived through the formative years of twentieth-century U.S. foreign affairs, including debate over liberal internationalism, the rise of fascism, the eras of appeasement and isolationism, the Second World War, the onset of the Cold War, the conflict in Korea, and the rise of the Third World in the global agenda. Throughout these times, he had retained his faith in Wilsonian ideals and the principle that international law and morality should guide the world.

Rusk had experienced firsthand the terror of aggression, militarism, intimidation, and outlaw behavior. Like almost all U.S. leaders, he tried to square a legalistic vision with the harsh realities of national interests. For practical purposes, this was an impossible task, he reasoned, because "the Communist world has dedicated itself to the indefinite expansion of what it calls its historically inevitable world revolution. The cold war is simply the effort of communism to extend its power beyond the confines of the Communist bloc and the effort of free men to defend themselves against this systematic aggression."[21]

Forcing U.S. officials toward realism, the Cold War was a magnet that tore Rusk from the idealism he so hoped to bequeath to the world. Soviet-American conflict was an ordeal inflicted on the world and on Rusk. He kept his faith that one day the principles of international law and morality, guided by the UN Charter, would become a reality. Until then, as a good liberal, he would meet head-on the severe test of Communist confrontation in the 1960s. "The conflict between the Communists and the free world is as fundamental as any conflict can be," observed Rusk. "Their proclaimed objectives and our conception of a decent world just do not and cannot fit together."[22] The Russians might have changed tactics, by focusing on competition rather than expansion, but they were wedded to their goals. As a result, the Kennedy years would see the gravest crises of the Cold War era, especially in the central, contested core area of the world: Europe.

Notes

1. Viorst, "Incidentally, Who Is Dean Rusk?" 181.

2. Rusk, *As I Saw It*, 157.

3. "Rusk Cites Damage in McCarthy's Charges," *Atlanta Constitution*, April 8, 1950, 5.

4. Dean Rusk, "Underlying Principles of Far Eastern Policy," *DSB* 25 (November 19, 1951): 825.

5. Dean Rusk, "The Stake of Business in American Foreign Policy," *DSB* 21 (October 24, 1949): 631–32.

6. Rusk, *As I Saw It*, 162.

7. Quoted in *Atlanta Journal and Constitution*, November 19, 1950, 9.

8. Cohen, *Dean Rusk*, 60.

9. John T. Carlton, "Dean Rusk Says Soviet Is Ready to Risk War," *Atlanta Journal and Constitution*, February 25, 1951, in State Department folder, Box 17, I.A., Thomas Schoenbaum File, Dean Rusk Collection, UGA.

10. Cohen, *Dean Rusk*, 75.

11. Rusk, *As I Saw It*, 173.

12. Dean Rusk to Robert Allen, April 24, 1951, State Department folder, Box 17, I.A., Thomas Schoenbaum File, Dean Rusk Collection, UGA.

13. Rusk, *As I Saw It*, 182.

14. Ibid., 195.

15. Ibid., 197.

16. "Quiet Man," *Time* (December 6, 1963): 25.

17. *New York Times*, December 13, 1960, 1.

18. Schoenbaum, *Waging Peace*, 265–67.

19. Joseph Kraft, "The Dean Rusk Show," *New York Times Magazine*, March 24, 1968, 34.

20. Benjamin Read Oral History, JFKL, 35.

21. Ernest K. Lindley, ed., *The Winds of Freedom: Selections from the Speeches and Statements of Secretary of State Dean Rusk, January 1961–August 1962* (Boston: Beacon Press, 1963), 140.

22. Viorst, "Incidentally, Who Is Dean Rusk?" 180.

II

From Core to Periphery

3

Bearing the Burden in Europe

In 1960, in a famous scene from the Cold War, Soviet Premier Nikita Khrushchev erupted in anger over U.S. spying, banging his shoe on a podium in the United Nations. The incident was symbolic of his desire to strut on the world stage. He had every reason to do so. The new Kennedy administration would bear the brunt of Khrushchev's mighty ambitions. In the late 1950s, Soviet technology seemed to outpace U.S. advances. The Russians developed a nuclear arsenal replete with missiles capable of hitting targets continents away. Khrushchev boasted that these weapons came off assembly lines methodically, like sausages. In 1957 the Americans, who had long believed that they had an edge in the arms and space race, were stunned when the Soviets launched *Sputnik*, the first space satellite. When Vice President Richard Nixon proudly displayed his nation's color television sets at the 1959 American National Exhibition in Moscow, the Russian premier countered that his country would soon surpass the United States in consumer-goods production just as it had in missiles. In April 1961, just a few days before the disastrous Bay of Pigs invasion in Cuba, Soviet technology triumphed again: Yury Gagarin became the first human to orbit Earth.

Americans were excited, surprised, and worried. Democrats charged that a so-called missile gap existed—the Soviets, it seemed, enjoyed superiority over the United States. The claim was shown to be false, as testing of the Atlas, Thor, Minuteman, and Polaris missiles retained the U.S. advantage. But fear of Russian technology persisted, enough so that the Central Intelligence Agency (CIA) continued high-altitude spying with its new U-2 plane that overflew Soviet facilities. In 1960, Russian antiaircraft shot down a U-2, capturing its pilot, Gary Francis Powers. This was the incident that led to Khrushchev's demand for an apology as he banged his shoe at the United Nations. Soviet prestige had never been higher.

The arms and space race represented one of the battle sites between communism and capitalism in the 1960s. Proclaiming the ultimate triumph of communism through wars of national liberation in the Third World just days before John Kennedy took office, the Soviet premier threw down the gauntlet to the United States on the global political front. Boldly, he embraced Fidel Castro in Cuba when the Americans cut ties with the island that lay just ninety miles from their shore. He also sought to oust the Western powers from Berlin, a city occupied by the former World War II allies since 1945, which was a showcase of both Cold War camps. It was clear that Khrushchev intended to upstage the novice Kennedy.

Secretary of State Rusk took a moderate approach to Moscow. He understood that the superpowers had few bilateral problems. Tension arose instead "over the nature of the world to come"; that is, the two sides waged an ideological battle.[1] As the opposing forces maneuvered for advantage, they clashed in dangerous ways. Khrushchev, Rusk determined, intended to bolster Russian prestige in the world and answer the internecine challenge from China with his bluster. The Soviets sought "détente through intimidation" in the early 1960s.[2]

American conservatives suspected that Kennedy was soft on communism and too inexperienced to contest the crafty Khrushchev. Kennedy defused the criticism with lofty rhetoric, bold responses, and expert crisis management. In his inaugural address, he asked Americans to "pay any price, bear any burden, meet any hardship, support any friend, oppose any foes to assure the survivial and the success of liberty." The undemonstrative, neo-Wilsonian Rusk played a central role in the effort to contain the Communists and achieve the end goal of liberal internationalism. No contradiction existed between the search for security and peace; defense and ideals went hand in hand. Invariably the historian, Rusk explained that the Cold War was "a struggle in the long story of freedom between those who would destroy it and those who are determined to preserve it."[3] Peace through strength, negotiation and military power, law and order—all were a balancing act in the Kennedy-Rusk policy of taking a fresh look at relations with the Soviet Union.

The Berlin Crisis

The central battleground of the Cold War since 1945 had been the core of Europe. A second crisis over the city of Berlin, initiated by Khrushchev in late 1958, culminated in the erection of the Berlin Wall in August 1961. Yet enemies were not the only problem. NATO allies and trade partners were demanding a new relationship with the United States. The crisis in Berlin gave way to a lower-intensity debate over the course of the alliance.

The stakes were high in Berlin. Territory, prestige, and the possibility of a nuclear conflict were all involved. In the crisis of 1948–49 a Russian blockade had failed to drive the three Western powers from their occupation sectors. Ten years later, Moscow demanded that the United States, France, and Great Britain leave West Berlin, a glittering capitalist bastion sixty miles from the West German border that lured emigrants from East Germany. Hoping to solidify the alliance of Communist nations, weaken NATO, and stem the flood of highly trained refugees into West Berlin, Khrushchev wanted to put the city under East German control.

Berlin

Airports

Occupation Zones

U.S.   British   French   Soviet

Divided Germany

The Russians issued an ultimatum: if the West refused to leave Berlin, the Soviets would deem it a free city and turn it over to their ally, the German Democratic Republic (East Germany). The NATO nations would be compelled to acknowledge the city's new status and to negotiate access routes with East Germany, which took orders from the Russians. The Communists would put an end to free access between East and West Berlin, and the East German refugee problem would be resolved. Moscow insisted on a settlement over Berlin on Soviet terms.

Advisers counseled Kennedy to hang tough while they prepared to negotiate. In early June 1961, Kennedy met Khrushchev in

Vienna to discuss Berlin. When Rusk joined the talks, he worked to keep them general and to avoid nit-picking over details. He hoped that by drawing on his service at the Rockefeller Foundation and by impressing Khrushchev with his knowledge of farm productivity—a topic of deep interest to the Soviet premier—he would be able to establish good relations. Rusk also made Berlin's importance clear. Aggression would not push the United States out. The 2.25 million people living in free West Berlin constituted a population larger than that of one-third of the countries in the United Nations and were responsible for the production of more wealth than well over one-half of these nations. The city was a vital security interest, a hard-won prize from the Second World War, and a symbol of American resolve in the Cold War. All four occupying powers deserved the right to be there. The United States owed West Berliners a secure future. It was imperative, warned Secretary of State Rusk, that the two superpowers refrain from engaging in "a dangerous game on top of the roof of a house in which millions of people were going about their daily work."[4]

Khrushchev was just as unyielding. Viewing the president (just two months after the Bay of Pigs disaster) as a vacillating amateur in world affairs, the Russian premier reissued his demand that the West vacate the city or deal with East Germany on occupation rights. Then he turned up the heat, threatening war if the United States interfered with his plans. "Then there will be war, Mr. Chairman," answered Kennedy. "It will be a cold winter," he said, if Moscow is bent on conflict. Kennedy did not cringe in the face of such bullying, but he was stunned by the "full weight of Soviet pressure and the full weight of the ideological commitments of the Soviet Union," Rusk recalled.[5] Rusk also knew that diplomats never talked of war unless they really meant it. Fearful of Khrushchev's ultimatum, for a war involving nuclear weapons would bring an end to civilization, he labored to find a way to end the crisis.

Berlin dominated administration attention for the rest of the summer. Former Secretary of State Acheson pushed for a military buildup, including nuclear weapons, to force the Russians to back down from their ultimatum. Others found this idea appalling: a military move would escalate the crisis; negotiations might bring a compromise. True to form, Rusk remained circumspect. It took a long six weeks for his department to present Kennedy with a reply that echoed Acheson's. Berlin was no place for compromise. It was Moscow that had changed the game. The United States should sit tight, talking the issue to death and holding the line. Take "the peels

Rusk tries to lighten the mood at the Vienna Summit in June 1961. At the table to his left are Kennedy, Khrushchev, and Foreign Minister Andrei Gromyko. *Courtesy of the John F. Kennedy Library*

off the banana and look at the heart of the matter," he told Foreign Minister Andrei Gromyko. It was up to Russia to decide whether policy would be conducted by agreement or would "resort to the law of the jungle." The United States welcomed discussions but would not leave Berlin unless forced out.[6]

Rusk's mid-July 1961 memorandum to Kennedy emphasized U.S. contractual rights and obligations in Berlin and NATO. Neither West Germany nor France wanted to negotiate; every nation feared war. The crisis was yet another violation of international law propagated by the Soviet Union since the Second World War. Rusk advised a tough stance, including a military buildup, but he hoped to defuse the tension through exploratory talks. Speaking to the nation on July 25, 1961, as the Berlin crisis intensified, Kennedy adopted Rusk's approach. America would stay in Berlin and maintain access to the city, bolstered by an increase in military personnel and spending. He proposed a civil defense program to build nuclear fallout shelters at home in case of war. But he also considered means to satisfy both sides. Kennedy made it clear, Rusk noted, that "we and the free world must prepare ourselves to be firm and to defend our rights, if necessary, in that city" while leaving "room for discussion."[7]

The Communists forced an endgame. Under pressure from East Germany and from hard-liners in Moscow, Khrushchev sought to resolve the crisis. Thirty thousand East German refugees had fled to West Berlin in July alone. On August 13 the Russians began building the Berlin Wall to keep East Germans from "voting with their feet," Rusk noted with disgust.[8] It is unclear how surprised the administration was by the construction of the barbed-wire fence, which was soon replaced with concrete blocks. But neither Rusk nor Kennedy saw any need to take action to knock it down. As Rusk explained, "The wall was not an issue of war and peace between East and West; there was no way we would destroy the human race over it."[9] And, after all, the barrier was in the Soviet, not Western, zone of the city and thus removed from U.S. authority. To boost morale in West Berlin, which had sagged to the desperation point, Kennedy sent a contingent of fifteen hundred soldiers across East Germany to Berlin to reaffirm access rights, and Vice President Lyndon Johnson announced to Berliners that the American commitment to their freedom remained firm. But privately, Kennedy admitted that the Berlin Wall, however inhumane, had attained the goal of ending the crisis.

Rusk, too, held the view that the outcome served U.S. interests. The wall showed the bankruptcy of Communist ideals. Within a few weeks, the Russians again damaged their prestige by announcing resumption of the nuclear testing that they had agreed to halt in 1958 as they engaged in test-ban talks. His image tarnished, Khrushchev withdrew the ultimatum on Berlin. The firm stand taken by the United States had paid off. This was realist calculation at its best. Rusk knew that neither West Germany, nor France, nor Britain would have gone to war over Berlin. There was no reason to think that Moscow would have backed down either. During the Soviet invasion of Hungary in 1956, the United States had made it clear that it would not use military means to prevent Russian control over Eastern Europe. There was no cause for Kennedy to have altered this policy and use force to protect West Berlin; the wall was, as Rusk later explained, a "gate in the Iron Curtain," not a cause for war.[10] The key, therefore, was to deescalate the crisis and leave intact the status quo, a negotiated, neo-Wilsonian approach endorsed by the NATO allies.

The tactic of awaiting Russian moves had allowed the United States to remain in Berlin. Rusk began access negotiations with Foreign Minister Gromyko a few months after the wall went up. Keeping an eye on the status quo, Rusk was as purposefully repetitious as the long-winded Gromyko as the two sparred over Berlin. In one instance in mid-1962, when Khrushchev followed a statement about peace with a threat to close the air corridor, Rusk jested pointedly with Gromyko: "From now on, I am going to listen with two ears to establish which is the real Mr. Khrushchev."[11] Periodic harassment along the U.S. access route to Berlin renewed tension now and then, but a frustrated Khrushchev turned to other arenas, notably Cuba, in an attempt to pry the Americans out of Berlin.

In 1963 the Soviet leader pulled Rusk aside during a treaty-signing ceremony: the NATO allies would not risk a nuclear war over Berlin, he contended, so why should he think that the United States would? "Mr Chairman," replied Rusk, "you will just have to take into account the possibility that we Americans are God damn fools."[12] The war of words turned down the flame on the Berlin hotspot for the rest of the Cold War. The Berlin Wall, though regrettable to the United States, was the harsh reality of preventing World War III. President Kennedy clearly appreciated the contribution of his calm and resolute secretary of state.

The German Question

The deescalation of the crisis did not mean the end of preoccupation with German issues, however. When it came to Europe, Germany was a major concern, especially when considered in historical context. The so-called German Question was still a topic high on every nation's agenda.

The Soviets were, of course, a consideration. Foiled by the Berlin situation, in 1962 Khrushchev had warned West German Chancellor Konrad Adenauer, who was on the verge of retirement, that West Germany would "burn like a candle in the very first hours" of a war if Bonn made unreasonable demands.[13] That statement had prompted Rusk to announce that Berlin and West Germany were vital U.S. interests, and in June 1963, Kennedy traveled to the Berlin Wall and proclaimed his famous words of unity before 60 percent of the West Berlin populace: "Ich bin ein Berliner" (I am a Berliner).

But West German ambitions for unification with East Germany were also a worry. Ever since the expansionist dreams of Bismarck and Kaiser Wilhelm II, German ambitions—the German Question —had been the subject of scholarly and public debate. Hitler had brought the German Question to the fore again, and during the Cold War the West had to stand guard against the menace of

Kennedy gazes back at the Berlin Wall from a platform in June 1963. *Courtesy of the John F. Kennedy Library*

totalitarianism. History had made Germany suspect. Rusk related an experience to elucidate this point. During his Oxford days, he had canoed in the lakes around Neue Babelsburg in Germany. Returning to the bank where he had left his canoe while lunching one day, he found that it had been stolen. The police eventually retrieved the boat and punished the culprit, but they also fined Rusk five marks for "tempting thieves."[14] The lesson was clear: the democracies should always take care. Germany and other potential threats required constant monitoring.

West Germans demanded attention during the 1960s, but history had shown that they should be neither isolated nor strengthened too much. Rusk believed that the German issue of reunification was the sole European problem that could trigger a nuclear war between the superpowers. In a neo-Wilsonian bargain, therefore, containment of the Federal Republic's ambitions far preceded its dream of unity with East Germany. This approach was difficult when applied to the independent-minded Europe. West Germans welcomed the U.S. nuclear umbrella, but they wanted a voice in decisions concerning the atomic arsenal and, possibly, a chance to develop their own stockpile. That alarming prospect led to an American idea in 1963 to give alliance members some say over nuclear weapons without diminishing any of Washington's authority over NATO. West German Chancellor Ludwig Erhard went along with this rather condescending policy in the hope of enhancing the American defense of his nation and giving Bonn some say of its own.

The Federal Republic had become a formidable power in its own right. It was a key to NATO security as well as the economic engine of the new Europe, led by the six-nation customs union, the European Common Market. Although fears of Soviet attack waned during the decade, the superpower conflict was still in effect. West Germany, which occupied the front line in Europe as a base for three hundred thousand U.S. troops, had be treated with care. Bonn's political role was even more crucial. The West Germans could help offset the disengagement efforts of General Charles de Gaulle, who had led the French resistance to the Nazis during the Second World War. To be sure, this grand hero wanted German power contained, but on French, not American, terms. As his rivalry with the United States over Europe created tension within the Atlantic alliance, the German Question lingered.

America's or Europe's Europe

Before he went to Vienna, Kennedy made a celebrated stop in Paris to discuss Berlin and other issues with General de Gaulle. If anyone gave the administration a harder time in Europe than Khrushchev, it was de Gaulle, with whom communicating was, according to Rusk, "a little bit like climbing on your knees up a mountainside to talk to the oracle."[15] De Gaulle questioned Washington's ability to defend Western Europe from Soviet nuclear attack or from France's historic German enemy. He also resisted U.S. economic penetration that was harmful to French farmers and threatened to change the cultural tastes of the populace. He hoped that the European Common Market would redress his perceived power imbalance in the alliance. And he opted to tread independently on security policies and global politics by weakening U.S. leverage in NATO and building up French military strength.

In short the general assailed U.S. dominance in the core of Europe. He distrusted America's willingness to defend Europe and despised U.S. meddling in European political affairs. His vision posited a Germany unified and reintegrated into a Western Europe free from superpower troops and led by France. Washington would balance out Russian nuclear strength but would play only a minor role in regional politics. To his chagrin, however, the Americans would not let French nationalism undermine the alliance against communism.

Obligated to defend its allies, the United States maintained about one million troops and related personnel, as well as a stockpile of nuclear and conventional weapons, in Western Europe. In addition, the Kennedy defense budget expanded from $43 billion to $56 billion by 1962 to bolster European security. But these expenditures strained America's international balance-of-payments account, or the difference between earnings and spending abroad. Economically, U.S. leadership was in trouble. De Gaulle took advantage of the fact that the United States had run a worsening deficit of a few billion dollars for several years. He converted the dollars spent in France into gold, draining the precious metal—the basis of U.S. currency—from Fort Knox and spooking financial markets. The infant Common Market, moreover, was already an able U.S. trade competitor.

The dilemmas were clear. The United States was paying the price of postwar success: the rebuilding of Europe. Now, noted Rusk, Europeans were more assertive and nationalistic. Yet these "comfortable and fat" allies were not pulling their weight by sharing the burden of security expenses with the United States.[16] During the Kennedy and Johnson years, therefore, the recommendation circulated that a resurgent West Germany should offset costs by buying more U.S. military goods and adjusting fiscal and monetary policies. The idea was that the Europeans should help solve the payments imbalance, because the United States could no longer afford to subsidize unilaterally the NATO defense network. But de Gaulle fired back that such talk showed that the United States could not be counted on to defend its allies, even as he badgered fellow Europeans to reduce U.S. influence in the region.

Rusk helped develop a strategy to overcome the predicament. Under the "Grand Design," the United States and Europe would join an "Atlantic partnership" to share the benefits and burdens of their alliance. An economic, military, and political bloc, the partnership would accommodate the independence-minded Europe but would face down the Soviet Union. By integrating West Germany more intimately into NATO, Kennedy hoped to unify Western Europe and prevent the joining of the two Germanies. This was one reason that he had abandoned the Skybolt missile program, under which Eisenhower had promised to sell nuclear weapons to the British, advocating a NATO-wide missile system instead. In economic relations, Kennedy sought to bring Great Britain into the Common Market—for Rusk "one of the great constructive undertakings of our time"—in order to prevent the customs union from turning to trade protectionism.[17]

For the secretary of state it was imperative that the United States react wisely to economic renascence in the core represented by the Common Market. In so doing, the Kennedy administration would promote cooperation, maintain the postwar liberal trade order under which so many nations had prospered, and show the Russians that they could not compete with the West. "We must be able to work together in harnessing the free world's economic strength for our common purpose," Rusk announced in early 1962.[18] Thus, the U.S.-Common Market relationship had to look outward, embracing the notion of nondiscriminatory commerce for the mutual benefit of all. The benefits would also be political. Rusk envisioned the partnership in neo-Wilsonian terms, as a means to promote interdependence within the Atlantic community, encourage cooperation through international institutions, and meet Khrushchev's challenge of economic competition with a united bloc of Western countries.

Free trade had long had a political element. Protectionism in Europe might split the West; protectionism at home signaled the return of U.S. isolationism. Free trade safeguarded liberties enjoyed under capitalism. It maintained the two-decade-old tradition of economic liberalism between the Western nations. By boosting productivity through the free exchange of goods and services, prosperity would increase. Growth and economic gain would then enhance political stability, one of the best ways to resist the insidious intrusion of dictatorship. This was the free-trade dogma most ably voiced by such southern Wilsonians as Roosevelt's secretary of state, Cordell Hull, its great champion, and Rusk. The real and propaganda value of free trade was priceless. In a jab at both Soviet policy in Berlin and at U.S. protectionists, Rusk lauded the political benefits of trade liberalization. Free trade proved that "successful societies don't have to imprison their own people behind barbed wire and walls."[19] Britain's entry into the Common Market under the Grand Design would add another floor to the sturdy edifice of the Atlantic community.

A major trading power, Britain had applied for membership into the Common Market in August 1961. Kennedy inserted in his Trade Expansion Act, his key legislative endeavor in 1962, a provision to eliminate all tariffs from goods traded mainly among the Atlantic powers. Without British entry into the Common Market, the provision would be nullified. Because Britain accounted for a significant amount of U.S.-European commerce, its absense might encourage the Europeans to focus on regional trade at the expense of such outsiders as the United States. In January 1963, de Gaulle vetoed Britain's application on the grounds that London would act as Washington's agent, a sort of Trojan Horse that would undermine the Common Market. Other Europeans counseled Rusk not to cause a stir; the general would not back off in any case. Hoping that more amenable leadership, under which the Common Market could be expanded, would soon come to power in France, Rusk and Kennedy took the advice. Later, Rusk advised President Johnson to ignore de Gaulle's obstructionism, but the Frenchman had rendered the Atlantic partnership a lost cause.

Kennedy had not been able to overcome French suspicions about the Grand Design. De Gaulle's desire to be the centerpiece rankled Rusk, who criticized the general for "living in an anachronistic dream world of the France of Joan of Arc and Louis XIV."[20] Yet Rusk hoped to find a way to unify the alliance and bypass Gaullist obstructionism. A week after the January 1963 veto, the implications for military aspects of the alliance became clear when France signed a treaty of friendship with West Germany that shunned the Grand Design. The Berlin crisis had raised West German doubts about Kennedy's willingness to end the division of Germany. De Gaulle fueled the flames. He sought a nuclear deterrent of his own, removed from American (NATO) control. The French leader was convinced that the United States would sacrifice Western Europe in a nuclear war; Europeans would be better off controlling their own destiny, counseled de Gaulle.

Rusk, Kennedy, and Johnson had an answer. In order to assert the primacy of the Atlantic alliance over Franco-German leadership, the administration suggested the creation of a fleet of ships carrying nuclear weapons and manned by all NATO nations. Rusk assured Congress that this Multilateral Nuclear Force of two hundred nuclear missiles was consistent with NATO's goals of containing the Soviet Union and unifying the alliance. The plan wooed the West Germans but not President de Gaulle. The Multilateral Nuclear Force gave the West Germans their first chance to participate in nuclear decisions, and it weakened de Gaulle's appeal. The general saw through this ploy; the United States would not give up its veto power over the firing of nuclear missiles. The idea faded away when West Germany pledged anew its allegiance to the Atlantic alliance but also extended a hand to France. When de Gaulle vetoed the Grand Design and Congress expressed its concerns about relinquishing command of nuclear missiles, the Multilateral Nuclear Force plan died.

Rusk shrugged off the rejection. If the allies did not want the Multilateral Nuclear Force, so be it. There was no need to push it on them; their lukewarm response would only sour Congress. On Capitol Hill, when conservatives criticized Rusk for having no backup plan, he countered that Dulles had had no such contingency when France had rejected the European Defense Community idea in 1954. Rusk pledged, however, that the United States would keep its six divisions in Western Europe and would reduce only non-combat personnel. There was no alternative to a U.S. presence in Europe, he would explain from 1963 onward by repeating the history of the early Cold War. Even de Gaulle acknowledged that. And Rusk vowed to come up with some kind of partnership regarding nuclear arms; the general would not have it.

The blows to U.S. prestige kept coming. To assert their independence, the French refused to sign the Limited Nuclear Test-Ban Treaty of July 1963 (thus permitting them to test nuclear weapons wherever they wanted), recognized the People's Republic of China (disdained by the United States), and in 1966 booted NATO troops and bases out of France. Johnson ordered an angry Rusk to let the general run his course; a vendetta was not in U.S. interests. Still, the secretary of state tweaked an embarrassed de Gaulle by asking if U.S. cemeteries, full of American soldiers who had liberated France, should be removed from French soil along with NATO. More moderately, Rusk reflected on the soundness of the alliance. He credited NATO with diminishing the Soviet threat in Europe and therefore warned against dismantling it. In any case, NATO would succeed without France if need be. Indeed, the alliance members moved the military headquarters to Brussels and took NATO's political body, the Council, out of Paris too. De Gaulle would not be allowed to undermine the Western bloc on Rusk's watch.

U.S. interests did not suffer unduly from Gaullism, yet the threat to collective security was clear. Nevertheless, the alliance remained intact and prosperous. The Federal Republic, prevented from unification with East Germany, remained a close ally. Chancellor Erhard fell from power in late 1966, replaced by a government more open to French designs but willing to unite only economically with its Communist counterpart. Fissures were only natural in the U.S. relationship with Western Europe. But by the end of the decade, the United States and its allies had helped clear the way to détente with the Soviet Union. The Cold War actually abated in the core.

Having recovered from World War II, the allies wanted an equal status with, and independence from, the United States. Like other officials, Rusk sometimes failed

"COME—LET US REASON TOGETHER!"

To the Americans, Charles de Gaulle often took on an air of grandeur. *Courtesy of* The Minneapolis Star Tribune

to fully recognize this elemental fact. He was upset when the United States was asked to take the lead only to have no other ally follow. After all, he declared, the Europeans were not innocent bystanders in the Cold War. They were the issue. The United States was not going to fight the Soviet Union about polar bears in the Arctic; it would go to war over Europe.

The real problem in allied relations, however, resulted from the fact that Europe now stood on its own feet. The Grand Design lay in tatters because the United States no longer had the same leverage over its allies that it had had during the immediate postwar period. The Europeans could orchestrate their own self-defense. History understandably overburdened Rusk, who worried about a recurrence of appeasement or early Cold War dangers. When it came to matters of European security, however, he can be forgiven for erring on the side of caution.

Regarding Europe, the United States often had less trouble with the Soviets than with its allies. Spain is a case in point. Madrid demanded either admission into NATO (which many Europeans refused because they despised dictator Francisco Franco) or a security treaty with the United States in return for renewed base agreements for the American military. Eventually, Spain secured both a pledge of protection and increased aid. Then, in 1964, Turkey and Greece stood at the brink of war after Archbishop Makarios III of Greece sought independence for the contested island of Cyprus. Both nations were members of NATO. Rusk prevented a Turkish invasion, and an opening for Moscow, by sending Undersecretary of State George Ball with a firm message to Turkey that the United States would not defend its NATO ally. A UN peacekeeping mission restored calm. Meanwhile, the crisis showed that problems within the Western camp could be as dangerous as those between the superpowers.

Still another example of inter-allied tensions occurred in the economic field. The Kennedy Round of the General Agreement on Tariffs and Trade (GATT) ended in 1967 after four years of American and Common Market bickering over agricultural protectionism. Furthermore, the United States began to take a closer look at Japan, which came out a winner at the Kennedy Round of international trade negotiations. The Japanese boasted growing trade surpluses with the United States, adding to the international payments burden that so taxed the U.S. Treasury.

Because of the financial burdens of maintaining security and the inroads on its former commercial dominance, the United States suffered larger and larger payment deficits, which put even more dollars in the hands of its allies. Like de Gaulle, they cashed in dollars for gold, using convertibility as leverage against U.S. policies. The dollar, the principal medium of exchange after the Second World War, was in jeopardy as the Europeans, and then Japan, drained the U.S. Treasury throughout the 1960s. Negotiations to resolve the problem ensued in the International Monetary Fund and on a bilateral basis. Talks eventually led to the 1971 collapse of the postwar Bretton Woods system of fixed exchange rates, which the United States had fathered. The monetary reforms weakened the standing of the dollar and raised doubts, once again, about U.S. hegemony in the core.

Added to the economic woes, which included growing trade deficits with allies, were other conflicts that troubled the West and Rusk. The 1960s witnessed dissent against U.S. cultural imperialism—the so-called Americanization of Europe—through protests against the infusion of blue jeans, movies, Cokes, and other products. And some Europeans—the Swedes, the French, the Labour party in Britain—harshly criticized U.S. policy in Vietnam. Other Europeans complained that Johnson neglected their interests. The charge had merit; even Rusk seemed so preoccupied with Vietnam that by mid-1962, he had turned over European affairs to Undersecretary Ball.

Disarmament

Rusk slighted European concerns not only because of Vietnam but also because the primary issue of nuclear disarmament with the Soviet Union drew his attention. After months of stalled disarmament negotiations with the Russians in Geneva, during which time both superpowers engaged in atmospheric testing, the United States and the Soviet Union agreed in 1963 to prohibit nuclear tests in the atmosphere and underwater. The harrowing Cuban missile crisis had terrified both sides; they had come to the brink of nuclear war. In a speech at American University in Washington, DC, in June 1963, Kennedy held out an olive branch of peace to the Soviets. Rusk was instrumental in putting the president's rhetoric into action.

That nuclear arms were the ultimate danger was understood by Rusk. Placed in the hands of rogues, they could be used to blackmail peaceful nations. Also weighing heavily on his mind were the possibility of a mistake, "the awesome destructive power of modern weapons and the speed with which they could be delivered," and the fears generated by the uncontrolled momentum of the arms race itself. The Titan missile's single warhead alone could destroy Moscow, and the United States had thousands of these and other missiles. Soviet atmospheric testing in August 1961 had unleashed a massive fallout of atomic debris that had degraded land, water, air, and outer space. "We can only be safe to the extent that our total environment is safe," Rusk warned.[21]

Rusk also recognized the irrelevance of nuclear weapons to decision making. After the carnage at Hiroshima and Nagasaki, the United States would never again use such atomic weapons, even against the Communist bloc. Consequently, enemies could call the U.S. bluff; a new approach was needed. Driven by his fear of nuclear war, Rusk developed a relationship with Soviet Ambassador Anatoly Dobrynin, with whom he negotiated a framework for disarmament throughout the 1960s. On October 30, 1961, when the Soviets tested the largest bomb the world had ever seen, with more power than all of the explosives used in the Second World War, Rusk intensified his disarmament efforts.

The ban might prompt the Russians to open up a bit and ease the arms race. Rusk's Wilsonian roots were amply evident. He parried Soviet efforts to obtain an edge in testing because of, as he put it, "our joint and primordial responsibility for slowing an arms race that threatened the survival of the human race."[22] The Limited Nuclear Test-Ban Treaty, prohibiting explosions everywhere but underground, would lead to a safer world by building trust between two enemies. In his first visit to the Soviet Union, to sign the treaty in August 1963, Rusk called the document "a turning point in the affairs of mankind" as he acknowledged Khrushchev's toast to "peace and friendship."[23] Rusk's disarmament talks added to this significant accomplishment. He helped Kennedy and Khrushchev create the foundation of détente, which would arrive half a decade later under President Nixon. Critical was momentum toward arms control. Rusk was appalled, he told Russian Foreign Minister Gromyko in October 1963, that the superpowers were building nuclear arms faster than the rate of obsolescence. No innocent in this deadly game, the United States would try to ease the danger.

Rusk met with Krushchev, who was still reeling from the Berlin and Cuban crises, in Moscow and at the Russian leader's country vacation spot. The secretary of state held out the possibility that the United States might be forced to use nuclear weapons to defend Berlin. He also told the press that the test-ban treaty was only a first step—it neither ended the Cold War nor guaranteed against nuclear war. He expected no miraculous change in the Soviet Union. The aim was merely to keep the Cold War within tolerable bounds, to build freedom without resort to weapons of mass destruction. Rusk was adept at blending firmness with diplomacy, even politely losing a game of badminton to the aging Khrushchev. Pulling out all stops to push the Russians toward peace, Secretary Rusk moved closer toward ending the terrifying history of the early Cold War and getting on with his internationalist mission.

Urging Senate ratification of the test-ban treaty, Rusk recalled the past eighteen years of Cold War struggle. In 1946, lobbying for his UN plan to limit atomic weaponry, Bernard Baruch had explained that nations had "to make a choice between the quick and the dead." It was now clear that massive arms would not win the conflict. For too long, people had lived in the shadow of fear. The treaty allowed the Soviets and the Americans to replace terror with hope, despair with confidence. "Peace would cease to be only a dream and will begin to acquire solid reality," Rusk exclaimed, if the superpowers used the test ban as a springboard toward détente.[24]

The Limited Nuclear Test-Ban Treaty was one of Rusk's unheralded successes; his reputation for toughness won Senate passage.

He contended that the treaty was a step toward peace, but he did not mean to imply that the Cold War was winding down. He rejected a total ban on testing as impossible to verify. A partial moratorium allowed the military to conduct necessary underground testing and maintain scientific facilities. He would be ready to restart atmospheric explosions if the Soviets did so. Realist thinking won congressional conservatives' support for the treaty; Rusk's idealist vision of disarmament and peace convinced the liberals. Cold War liberalism triumphed.

The superpowers worked on many fronts in this early epoch of détente. Each opened additional consulates in the other's country. They established a telephone hotline between the two capitals to defuse crises. In late 1963, Kennedy agreed to sell wheat to the Russians to prevent a famine. And by 1971, Rusk's efforts to ease tensions over Berlin had led to an access agreement for the Western powers into the city. Johnson and Rusk also launched a bridge-building campaign for Eastern Europe, which would encourage détente by ensuring a peaceful settlement of the division of Europe but would steer West German ambitions away from unification with East Germany. Bridge-building contacts between West and East Germany, also known as Ostpolitik, would be limited. The effort included extending most-favored-nation trade privileges to the Communists, but the plan ran aground. Congress refused to act on an East-West trade bill until the mid-1970s, and the Soviets eyed the policy as a means to drive a wedge between Russia and its allies.

Still, momentum for negotiations on nuclear arms continued. A December 1966 treaty banned testing in outer space, which Rusk saw as having the potential to become a new battlefield in the Cold War. Alarmed by China's explosion of an atomic bomb in 1964 and by the fact that five nations had joined the nuclear club, Rusk persuaded the NATO nations to accept a treaty to stem the spread of nuclear weapons. The advent of nuclear proliferation required an agreement to ensure that fissionable material would not be diverted into weapons. And the Soviets favored any means of preventing West Germany from becoming a nuclear power. As a result, in July 1968 the superpowers and dozens of other nations signed the Nuclear Non-Proliferation Treaty at the United Nations.

Rusk lamented the many nonsignatories, including rogues like China and such volatile neighbors as Israel and Egypt, India and Pakistan, and Brazil and Argentina. But the treaty was another landmark in U.S.-Russian relations. The superpowers soon embarked on arms-limitation talks, although these discussions were scuttled when the Russians invaded Czechoslovakia in August 1968. Despite this setback, progress in superpower relations was commonplace by the time Rusk stepped down as secretary of state. By examining antiballistic missile (ABM) defense systems, he had laid the groundwork for the 1969–1972 Strategic Arms Limitation Talks (SALT I). Because he feared that deployment of ABMs would allow each side to build more effective offensive weapons, he worked hard to prohibit all but a few token systems. SALT I put his approach in place and ushered in the era of détente for which Rusk had greatly helped set the stage.

Despite the improved relations, Rusk did not lower his guard against Moscow. Nuclear arsenals attested to mutual superpower distrust. Beijing's militancy only detracted further from the idealists' hope for ideological coexistence. As Rusk told journalists in 1966, the Soviets were still a threat. When Khrushchev had turned 70, he bantered, the world had celebrated him as an affable grandfather, but when he was 68 1/2, he had put missiles in Cuba, and at 67 he had threatened Kennedy with war over Berlin. The Cold War continued.

Nevertheless, after the crises in Berlin and Cuba, discussions with the Russians encouraged a sense that a new era of peaceful coexistence had begun. Rusk even had the bold idea for a joint reduction in U.S. and Soviet defense budgets. Neither side was keen on the plan, however, least of all the United States with its burgeoning expenditures on Vietnam and high employment in the defense industry. Alarmingly, because nuclear disarmament was unachievable and war was unthinkable, both superpowers kept building their arsenals to prevent the other side from attacking. That was the grim logic of mutually assured destruction, aptly named MAD. But the war in Southeast Asia also had a salutary effect on relations with the Soviet Union. Secretary Rusk and President Johnson persevered in arms control and détente even as they grew more deeply mired in the Vietnam War. They regarded peace as a better option than nuclear war.

The Soviet invasion of Czechoslovakia in August 1968 and fear of a similar attack on Romania put Russian-U.S. negotiations on a back burner during the last months of Rusk's tenure. The Cold War was not over, lamented Johnson, as he watched the Russians end the brief Prague Spring of political openness and greater contact with the West by rolling tanks into Czechoslovakia. Yet Rusk still sought to apply Wilsonian ideals within the context of the Cold

War. He understood that Europe remained contested ground. The Czech crisis reminded observers that bridge building touched deep fears in Moscow. It also showed that NATO and a strong defense were necessary in Europe. The Johnson administration was disturbed by the comparisons of Czech repression to its actions in Vietnam. When violence shook the Democratic National Convention in Chicago just a few days after the Russian invasion, youth protesters raised signs reading "Welcome to Czechago."[25]

Still, détente endured. Addressing the United Nations in October 1968, Rusk took the Russians to task for their actions in Prague. The intrusion reminded him that the world was just four to five years removed from two great crises—Berlin and Cuba. He warned against exaggerating the prospects of détente, for the Czech incident undermined movement toward this end. Yet he also held out hope: "Let us say very plainly to the Soviet Union: The road to détente is the road of the [UN] Charter."[26]

Rusk hoped that the superpowers could continue to settle their differences, as they had over Berlin and nuclear arms. He also labored to keep the Western alliance intact, a task that often proved more difficult than managing tensions with Moscow. For this reason, Rusk insisted that the United States must remain in Europe to provide security but that the allies must contribute more to the partnership. Meanwhile, West German power was contained by preventing reunification while making enough concessions to Bonn (nuclear weapons sharing, bridge building to Eastern Europe) to satisfy this crucial ally. It was imperative for the United States to build a more peaceful world and prevail in the struggle against communism. By the end of Rusk's tenure the dark days of nuclear crises in Berlin and Cuba were far behind, replaced by détente—a stability and balance of power in the volatile superpower relationship. Rusk had managed the considerable accomplishments of easing superpower tensions and containing German aggression, thus relegating the German Question to mere historical debate.

Allegations that Rusk cared only about Vietnam by the mid-1960s are false. Indeed, he minimized the effects of Vietnam on U.S.-Soviet relations. Rusk personally managed the 1967 Glassboro Summit in New Jersey between President Johnson and Soviet Premier Aleksey Kosygin toward that end, and he held up the bombing of Haiphong Harbor in North Vietnam so as not to antagonize the Russians. Above all, the issue of disarmament continued to draw his attention; because nuclear war remained his one great fear, he stayed involved in matters relating to the core.

Détente between the superpowers brought many benefits as well as at least one major drawback: the Cold War became less dangerous in Europe, and the Soviet Union, the United States, and the People's Republic of China turned to confrontation in the periphery, or Third World. This was where the rest of the world lived and where, as Rusk lamented, millions of people suffered from Cold War tensions.

Notes

1. Dean Rusk, interview on "The Today Show," *DSB* 44 (February 27, 1961): 307.

2. John Lewis Gaddis, *Russia, the Soviet Union, and the United States: An Interpretive History*, 2d ed. (New York: McGraw-Hill, 1990), 242.

3. Lindley, *Winds of Freedom*, 140.

4. Memcon, March 20, 1962, National Security Files (hereafter cited as NSF), Box 186, USSR: Subjects—Gromyko Talks-Rusk, 3/11–27/62, JFKL.

5. Dean Rusk Oral History III (hereafter cited as DROH with interview number), John F. Kennedy Library, Boston, Massachusetts (JFKL), 165.

6. Memorandum of Conversation, Dean Rusk and Andrey Gromyko, October 18, 1962, NSF, Box 186, USSR: Subjects—Gromyko Talks-Rusk, 7/21–10/18/62, JFKL.

7. Lindley, *Winds of Freedom*, 164.

8. James N. Giglio, *The Presidency of John F. Kennedy* (Lawrence: University of Kansas Press, 1991), 83.

9. Rusk, *As I Saw It*, 223.

10. Dean Rusk to Eleanor Lansing Dulles, October 1, 1971, Folder 9, Box 2, Series IV:D, Dean Rusk Collection, UGA.

11. *Time*, March 23, 1962, Box 110, V.D.3, Thomas Schoenbaum File, Dean Rusk Collection, UGA.

12. Dean Rusk anecdotes, September 16, 1981, Box 4:1, Series V:A, Dean Rusk Collection, UGA.

13. "Secretary Discusses Berlin in Filmed Interview," *DSB* 48 (January 28, 1963): 136.

14. Dean Rusk, interview on "The Today Show," *DSB* 44 (February 27, 1961): 309.

15. DROH IV, JFKL, 178.

16. Rusk, *As I Saw It*, 261–62.

17. Lindley, *Winds of Freedom*, 86.

18. Dean Rusk, "U.S. Trade Policy—Challenge and Opportunity," *DSB* 46 (February 5, 1962): 197.

19. Dean Rusk, "Trade, Investment, and United States Foreign Policy," *DSB* 47 (November 5, 1962): 689.

20. Schoenbaum, *Waging Peace*, 358.

21. Lindley, *Winds of Freedom*, 288.

22. Rusk, *As I Saw It*, 252.

23. Schoenbaum, *Waging Peace*, 363–65.

24. Dean Rusk, "Nuclear Test Ban Treaty Signed at Moscow," *DSB* 49 (August 26, 1963): 314.

25. Frank Costigliola, "Lyndon B. Johnson, Germany, and 'the End of the Cold War,' " in *Lyndon Johnson Confronts the World: American Foreign Policy, 1963–1968*, ed. Warren Cohen and Nancy Tucker (New York: Cambridge University Press, 1994), 209.

26. Cohen, *Dean Rusk*, 300–303.

4

Watchful Neighbor
over Latin America

One major success of post-World War II U.S. foreign policy had been the insulation of the Western Hemisphere from communism. Despite leftist threats, notably in Mexico and Guatemala, the Soviets had not gained a foothold. Yet liberalism had not prevailed either. In order to uphold the Monroe Doctrine, which prohibited outside intervention in the Americas, the United States had interfered in Latin America on numerous occasions.

Frequently heavy-handed and imperious, sometimes beneficent, and often neglectful, the American Colossus of the North had tried to be a good neighbor by eschewing intervention as long as political stability and prosperity reigned. When Cold War battlefields moved to the periphery, however, U.S.-Latin America policy added the containment of communism to the traditional goals of maintaining order and safeguarding U.S. economic interests. Fidel Castro's Cuban government provided the challenge. "We regard this regime as temporary," sneered Secretary Rusk, who could not disguise his disdain for communism in the Western Hemisphere.[1]

Aid and Development

Rusk mixed economic aid and military assistance to bolster progressive leaders in the region and dampen the appeal of the left. This was idealism overlaid by realism—the neo-Wilsonian pursuit of peace by subverting enemies. Reliance on trade, aid, and investments would be the rule, except when communism reared its ugly head. Then military responses would take precedence.

True to the promise in his inaugural address to stimulate growth and social progress in Latin America, President Kennedy launched the Alliance for Progress in August 1961. Enlisting U.S. businessmen in the effort to end poverty, illiteracy, and disease, the United States pledged $20 billion in assistance for ten years and proposed economic and social stabilization plans, to which the administration added its own assistance schemes. Billions of dollars flowed to Latin America.

Rusk was a devotee of development, as he had shown during his Rockefeller Foundation days. He urged reforms on a broad front, including education, health, productivity, and capital investment, just as his native South had experienced in years past. But while the wealthy were an obstacle to Latin American reform, he saw the left as the ultimate danger. The Communist state deprived people of a livelihood. "Wherever communism goes, hunger follows," he said. Recently, Communists had added Latin America to their hit list, trying to subvert the "orderly social progress" of nations in the hard transitional period leading to modernization. Pledged to a "mammoth ten-year effort" under the Alliance for Progress, the United States would cultivate "human and material resources," dedication to "national spirit," and the "fair expectation of social justice." However, at stake in this internationalist program, declared Rusk, the Cold War liberal, early in 1962, was the "security of the free world today."[2]

The Alliance for Progress and foreign assistance policies did not end poverty or social distress. During the 1960s, Latin America sustained progress in land reform but the drive for literacy floundered, unemployment rose, and per capita agricultural output declined. Economies grew by a paltry 1.5 percent. Infant mortality rates in this Decade of Development showed only slight improvement over rates in the 1950s. And in the first five years of the Alliance for Progress, nine coups against elected governments took place.

By the time Lyndon Johnson took office in late 1963, the Alliance for Progress had stalled. Rusk blamed an overdependence on the United States. He pushed for a Latin American common market that would institute the rule of self-help out of poverty. As he asked Congress for a huge increase in funding for the Alliance in 1967, he warned Latin Americans that Washington would be only a junior partner. Upon his retirement he reasoned that decreased reliance on the United States had prompted a period of progress in taxing, investment, education, public health, and productivity in the region.

President Johnson in particular was committed to bettering relations with leaders in the Western Hemisphere. The United States grew very close to Mexico, for instance, during his tenure. He also exercised personal diplomacy at the 1967 Punta del Este Conference, a hemispheric summit where he lavished affection on his fellow heads of state. However, both he and Rusk were locked into a Cold War mentality in which aid was predicated on the notion that regionalism would build stable governments that adhered to market capitalism and anticommunism.

As a result, the Alliance for Progress lost its way and eventually ran out of gas. Although experts debated the causes (an unanticipated population boom, the inability of Latinos to reform, modifications by the administration that vitiated the program, ponderous bureaucratic planning), placing aid in a Cold War context hurt the Alliance's chances. It forced nations to adapt their economies to private enterprise rather than to socialism, to the benefit of the wealthy and multinational corporations. Meanwhile, military spending rose and internal security forces were strengthened under Kennedy and Johnson. The Alliance might have represented "enlightened anticommunism" to Rusk, but the stress on national security in this supposed "Marshall Plan for Latin America" thwarted social progress.[3] In the end an unhappy state of affairs emerged from Rusk's grand strategy: anticommunism overruled Wilsonianism.

If internationalist ideals did not prevail, military realism did. Arms flowed to friends to ward off leftist rebels and socialist threats to entrenched governments. Police forces in Latin America received $56 million from the United States between 1961 and 1973. Honduras, Nicaragua, Venezuela, Colombia, Guatemala, Peru, and Bolivia—many of these nations run by dictators—numbered among the beneficiaries. This subversion of development stemmed in large part from the perceived threat of Castro, who provided a powerful example of liberation to the oppressed. This Cuban totalitarian, warned Rusk, hoped to infuse the region with communism. The great "tragedy," he stated, was that "an alien ideology which is seeking to extend its dictatorial system to all of Latin America" had gotten a jump on the neglectful United States.[4] For Rusk, order took priority over justice in Latin America. He mourned the detour away from social issues, for he saw the Alliance for Progress as "an effort to energize and mobilize the free peoples of this hemisphere to get on with the great historic task of economic and social development."[5] But Communist Cuba blocked the way.

The Bay of Pigs

In 1959, Fidel Castro, a thirty-three-year-old lawyer turned revolutionary, overthrew Cuba's corrupt dictator, Fulgencio Batista. Americans initially welcomed his social reforms, but Castro soon alienated Washington. He cracked down on his opponents, executing over five hundred Batista supporters and exiling thousands of others, and transformed his revolution into a Communist movement bent on giving the Soviet Union a beachhead at America's back door. When Castro signed a loan and trade agreement with the eager Khrushchev in 1960, after nationalizing major American holdings in Cuba, the Eisenhower administration imposed an economic boycott; ordered the CIA to train Cuban exiles to overthrow Castro; and, just before John Kennedy's inauguration, severed relations with Havana.

Rusk's approach was informed by the Cold War. He despised Batista, yet Castro had betrayed Cubans, dictatorially violating civil rights by censure, jail, and execution. Worse, Castro's links to Moscow menaced U.S. security. Consequently, Rusk would not tolerate Cuban self-determination, even though this principle was a hallmark of liberal internationalism. Castro had subjected his nation to "Marxist-Leninist doctrines," claimed the secretary of state, "at the very time when this answer to economic and social problems has proved itself to be brutal, reactionary and sterile" in Sino-Soviet satellites.[6]

Nevertheless, Rusk worried when he discovered the proposed Bay of Pigs operation. An invasion of Cuba by exiles trained by the CIA at a remote site, the action would raise questions about U.S. adherence to law and the doctrine of nonintervention, policies that had been followed at least in theory since the 1930s. Because Castro had enough support to thwart the invaders, Rusk also doubted the chance for success. He favored continuing the boycott, yet he remained silent. He later confessed that his failure to voice his skepticism clearly at meetings did not serve Kennedy well. Arthur Schlesinger and Undersecretary of State Chester Bowles, both liberals, also scored Rusk on this count.

Not until days before the invasion did Rusk approach Kennedy with his misgivings. He worried about pitfalls noted by the Joint

Chiefs of Staff and was convinced that Kennedy's inexperience and love of James Bond-like scenarios were leading the president down a catastrophic path. It was not just that the landing could go awry; foreign policy and principles were at stake as well. If the U.S. hand were exposed, the Russians might retaliate in Berlin, or the Organization of American States and the United Nations could censure Kennedy for acting unilaterally and for violating international law. Anxious for the chance to unseat Castro, Kennedy was undaunted. The ever-loyal Rusk went along.

The calamity began on April 15, 1961. The brigade of exiles sailed from their secret training base in Guatemala. Squandering the element of surprise, they failed to knock out the Cuban air force. Reporters soon sniffed out the CIA's complicity in the attack. Two days later 1,453 men hit the beaches of the Bay of Pigs. Spooked that, as the operation became public, it would bring down a hail of censure around the globe, Kennedy decided to cancel another air strike that would have provided cover for the brigade. He was advised on this course by Rusk and McGeorge Bundy of the National Security Council. Rusk had also managed to prevent the deployment of U.S. military forces. Castro's alert units mopped up the invaders: aircraft crippled landing vessels, and militia gunned down the men as they came ashore. Many were captured later in the surrounding swamps. As Castro boasted in triumph—114 members of the brigade lay dead and 1,189 were imprisoned—Kennedy kicked himself for approving the mission.

The Bay of Pigs operation was an unqualified debacle. It was "one hell of a way to close out my first hundred days as secretary of state," Rusk lamented.[7] It was the darkest hour for Kennedy and amateur hour for the intelligence apparatus. Feeling fortunate that, even with clear justification, the United Nations had not turned on the United States, Rusk toiled to save Kennedy from the international and domestic fallout. The disaster had resulted from arrogance, bad planning, and shoddy coordination. Kennedy respected CIA advice; after all, the agency had ousted a leftist government in Guatemala in 1954 and had come close to assassinating Castro. He also marginalized the State Department by running policy out of the White House. Rusk sought to minimize the American presence in the invasion by reducing U.S. aircover for the exiles. Even this modest input led CIA advisers to suspect Rusk of attempting to abort the operation. Rusk did, in fact, have misgivings about the plan, but he had been too silent on the issue and Kennedy had been too determined.

The Soviets were equally determined to protect Cuba. This was the most ominous outcome of the Bay of Pigs operation. Premier Khrushchev sent an angry message to the White House promising to defend Castro from further attacks. Rusk persuaded the frantic Kennedy not to be baited, and he blamed himself for not having insisted on a thorough review that would have revealed the futility of the operation. The failure had even broader ramifications, however: Cuba became an obsession for Kennedy.

Castro emerged as a Cold War symbol, a target of U.S. wrath. Chastened but emboldened by the Bay of Pigs, Kennedy determined to get rid of the Cuban leader. The CIA intensified its covert efforts and assassination plots. Meanwhile, the administration used a combination of diplomacy, propaganda, economic sanctions, and a covert sabotage plan (called Operation Mongoose) to isolate, destabilize, and eliminate Castro. In a display of resolve, forty thousand U.S. military forces undertook exercises in the Caribbean area in the spring of 1962. Kennedy pledged to uphold the Monroe Doctrine and fight communism; Castro panicked, fearing another invasion. Cuba was now a battleground of the Cold War.

At a meeting of the Organization of American States in 1962, Rusk found most nations in agreement with the U.S. view on Cuba. The OAS ousted Castro because his Communist ideology threatened to destabilize the hemisphere. But one other concern weighed heavily on America's friends: outside intervention. Rusk feared that the Soviet Union might use Cuba as a base to intimidate the United States. Castro was merely a "smirking sycophant for the Communist bloc." But the use of Cuba "as the means through which extracontinental powers seek to break up the inter-American system" would not be tolerated.[8] Kennedy made good on that pledge.

The Cuban Missile Crisis

When a journalist prodded him early in his second year as secretary of state for his forecast of world events, Rusk responded that if "1962 should prove to be a year without crisis, it would be a most reasonable and most welcome year."[9] His wish did not come true. While dining with the West German foreign minister on the evening of October 15, Rusk received an emergency call. Soviet missile sites had been detected in Cuba. The president required his advice. Intelligence reports confirming the sites awaited Rusk at the White House early the next morning.

Khrushchev believed that Castro needed extensive Soviet protection from the United States. Bolstering Cuba with nuclear missiles would not only solve that problem but also provide such strategic advantages to the Russians as new leverage over Berlin or parity in weaponry. Fearing another invasion, Castro had pleaded for Russian aid. He understood that the Soviets welcomed him as an ally as a means to prosecute the Cold War. These were the seeds of the Cuban missile crisis of October 1962.

Pressure from Republicans, who made Castro an issue in the mid-term elections, had prompted surveillance missions in late August 1962 to investigate their claim that Moscow was building a missile base in Cuba. Spy planes photographed Russian surface-to-air nuclear missiles (SAM), defensive weapons used to shoot down aircraft. Rusk was impressed. Propped in their launchers, the SAMs looked like "one hell of a missile."[10]

Based on these findings, Kennedy warned Khrushchev against taking any menacing steps in the Western Hemisphere. The Russians responded to this and other stern messages by repeating that any attack on Cuba would mean war. President Kennedy stood his ground. When construction of a Soviet medium-range ballistic missile base was detected in Cuba on October 15, alarm bells went off in Washington. These weapons could knock out all U.S. military bases and missile sites and every U.S. city short of Seattle. The task was clear: the missiles and bases must be removed. The thirteen-day crisis, the most dangerous event of the Cold War, had begun.

Employing the Executive Committee (Ex-Com) of foreign policy and military advisers, the Kennedy administration scrambled for answers. Why were the Soviets building the bases, and what could be done about them? Determining Khrushchev's motivations was guesswork, but considering the fact that the Russian premier knew the bases would be easily detected, Rusk discerned a number of reasons behind the rash move. Moscow had to have larger goals than mere defense of Cuba. Rusk was certain that the Russians wanted the ability to knock out U.S. defenses; after all, the number of missiles in the sites doubled the known Soviet capacity to strike at the United States. Politically, Khrushchev might have acted to impress the Chinese, who were skeptical of Soviet fortitude in prosecuting the Cold War. The missiles would also alter the balance of power in Latin America, provide the Soviets nuclear parity with the United States, and possibly offer a means to force Kennedy out of Berlin. It was a trading ploy, reminiscent of the Russians' clever

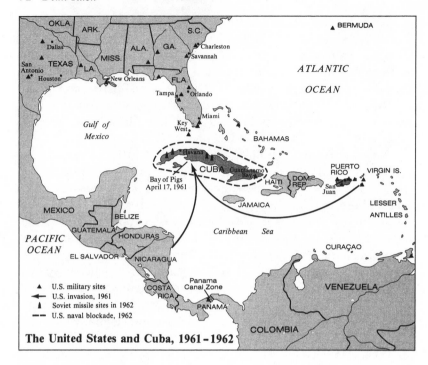

The United States and Cuba, 1961–1962

Legend:
- ▲ U.S. military sites
- ← U.S. invasion, 1961
- ⚑ Soviet missile sites in 1962
- – – U.S. naval blockade, 1962

move against Hungary in 1956, when the Suez crisis preoccupied the United States.

Recent research into the Soviet archives and revelations from the taped transcripts of Kennedy administration meetings have shown that determinations by Kennedy, Rusk, and the rest of the Ex-Com about Russian intentions were remarkably accurate. Ex-Com basically viewed the Cuban missiles in global terms. As the president told the Joint Chiefs, "The problem is not really so much war against Cuba. But the problem is part of this worldwide struggle with the Soviet Communists, particularly, as I say, over Berlin. And with the loss of Berlin, the effect of that and the responsibility we would bear."[11] Like Rusk, Kennedy had in mind the Suez-Hungary parallel but also, at bottom, the notion that beyond their immediate danger, the missiles posed a political challenge to American resolve against aggressors.

The missile crisis was a nightmare come true. Communism posed not just an ideological threat to the United States but now, for the first time, a direct military one as well. This was the first time that the Soviet Union had moved missiles outside of Eastern Europe. For Rusk, it was a completely "reckless and hazardous approach" with "both military and, of course, political ramifica-

One reason that Castro and Khrushchev placed missiles in Cuba was to undermine the United States' time-honored Monroe Doctrine. By Jim Berry. Reprinted by permission of Newspaper Enterprise Association, Inc.

tions." It was truly astounding, and distressing, that Khrushchev had gone to the nuclear extreme.[12]

The administration decided to parry the Russian thrust. At an Ex-Com meeting on October 16, Rusk noted that although the United States should not be "moved to general war" and should avoid unilateral measures, Kennedy must act decisively. "I do think we have to set in motion a chain of events that will eliminate this base. I don't think we can sit still," he told the president.[13] The Soviets could not be allowed to blackmail the United States, destroy U.S. credibility by deploying such weapons ninety miles off the Florida coast, or psychologically devastate the Free World. If the United States did not respond to aggression, then the nation's allies would question its pledge to defend them.

Resolving the crisis without sparking a nuclear exchange was a monumental problem. Rusk saw two options: a quick but risky strike to eliminate the base, or, if there was time, a diplomatic effort to formulate sanctions. This was also an opportunity to persuade the Cubans to break with Moscow. Word had to get to Castro that he was "being victimized here"; the Soviets were setting him up for "destruction or betrayal."[14] Rusk preferred a firm yet unprovocative stance. Highly trained soldiers, perhaps 150,000, must be called up immediately. The U.S. naval base at Guantanamo Bay, at the eastern end of Cuba, must be reinforced, along with bases in the southeastern United States. The American people must also be informed, as they had been during the Korean conflict.

In addition, covert activity must create confusion in Cuba while allies were alerted. Regarding the allies, Rusk expected a Soviet counterreaction somewhere in the world. Latin American friends had to be given time to meet such retaliation. Meanwhile, if NATO allies were not told in advance about "the very great danger" awaiting them once the United States struck at Cuba, they would be furious and the alliance might crumble. More than anyone else, Rusk pushed for political preparations together with military actions. And, of course, Khrushchev must be informed that Kennedy was on to him, which would give him the "chance to pull away" before war broke out. There would be no question of bargaining Berlin for Cuba. The premier might be "just a little crazy," but he should have no misconceptions about the "importance of Cuba in this country," asserted the secretary of state.[15]

The reticent Rusk occupied a key advisory position for Kennedy, particularly because he counseled both patience and limited military action. He sought to eliminate the missile sites and to do so quickly, before they were operational, without igniting a larger conflict. By encouraging Ex-Com to explore every alternative before taking any drastic steps, Rusk played the devil's advocate, opposing Vice President Johnson, Defense Secretary Robert McNamara, National Security Adviser McGeorge Bundy, Dean Acheson, and General Maxwell Taylor, chairman of the Joint Chiefs of Staff, all of whom pushed for an air strike against the sites and against military facilities in Cuba without prior negotiation.

At first, Kennedy leaned toward this option. Rusk concluded that a surprise attack would prompt a Russian strike at Berlin, South Korea, or U.S. missiles in Turkey. It might be worth the risk to appear firm, yet it was a perilous gambit. Khrushchev, Rusk feared, had inadvertently opened a Pandora's box of American outrage and retaliation. Rusk recognized the possibility for escape from this dilemma in McNamara's suggestion that a naval blockade be placed around Cuba to prevent Soviet ships from delivering more missiles. That action would buy time in a far less bellicose manner than an air strike, which might kill thousands of Russians and Cubans without succeeding in destroying all the missiles. The influential Robert Kennedy was pivotal in promoting this option. In his view a surprise air strike, similar to the Japanese attack in 1941 on Pearl Harbor, would make his brother "the Tojo [Japan's wartime premier] of the 1960s."[16]

Rusk helped gain the consensus for the blockade alternative by convincing hawkish Ex-Com members that it was a strong measure. Air Force General Curtis LeMay, for instance, hated the idea. "This is almost as bad as the appeasement at Munich," he told the president.[17] Rusk pondered that assertion, but because the blockade was limited, it was less inflammatory than an air strike. The logic for the blockade was simply more compelling than military action. World opinion would denounce an assault, Rusk warned.

State Department legal counsel confirmed that an attack would be a violation of international law. Because the United States had already been burned by the Bay of Pigs, Rusk admonished in seeking a neo-Wilsonian balance, the "legal case was very important." A blockade approved by the Organization of American States on the grounds of maintaining regional security, on the other hand, was legal. An air strike could follow the blockade if President Kennedy was not satisfied that the missiles in Cuba already were being withdrawn.[18]

On October 19, even as Rusk made his case, intelligence analysts confirmed that two missile sites were operational, each having eight medium-range SS-4 missiles already on launchers and eight more ready for a second attack. Another set east of Havana would be primed in a week, and two sites for SS-5s (intercontinental missiles with a 2,200-mile range) could be completed in six

U.S. reconnaissance aerial photograph of Cuban missile site. *Courtesy of the John F. Kennedy Library*

weeks. Caution had to be the rule, especially in view of the fact that the Joint Chiefs of Staff were recommending an unannounced strike that might shock the Russians into nuclear war. On October 20, Ex-Com decided on a defensive "quarantine" (since, in legal parlance, warned Rusk, a "blockade" was an act of war). This was not a perfect solution, since missiles already in Cuba might still remain, but it was the safest. Khrushchev would have time to ponder his options under pressure but without being backed into a corner. President Kennedy sided with Rusk.

The missile crisis now reached its most dangerous point. As the president prepared a televised speech for Monday, October 22, to explain the blockade to the American people, the State Department planned to warn NATO allies of a possible Soviet attack and to call emergency sessions of the United Nations and the Organization of American States. The tension mounted. Rusk informed Soviet Ambassador Dobrynin, who was not privy to Khrushchev's decisions, that the United States knew about Russia's offensive missiles. On Monday afternoon astounded congressional leaders also learned about the circumstances in Cuba.

Kennedy made his speech at 7:00 P.M. explaining the threat of the missiles, announcing the blockade to prevent the landing of more weapons, and demanding that the existing sites be dismantled and the missiles removed. He incorporated Rusk's point that the initial aim was to stop Soviet activity and then work through the United Nations to inspect the sites. Kennedy urged the "captive people of Cuba" to rid themselves of "foreign domination." Rusk endorsed the president's reference to the appeasement era, which, Kennedy observed, "taught us a clear lesson: Aggressive conduct, if allowed to grow unchecked and unchallenged, ultimately leads to war."[19]

The ball was in Khrushchev's court. He could respond with a nuclear strike, and he proceeded toward this end by ordering Soviet forces to combat readiness. The Warsaw Pact, the Communist equivalent of the NATO alliance, did the same. Cuba also went on alert, preparing for a U.S. invasion. Americans went to bed that night with the knowledge that they might not wake up. But they did awake on Tuesday, October 23, to face a full-blown crisis. Analysts had been up around the clock monitoring Soviet movement. At least the worst had not yet happened, Rusk gleefully told Undersecretary of State Ball: "We've won a great victory: you and I are still alive!"[20]

Denouncing the blockade as a belligerent act and as a violation of international law, the Russians erected new border checks between West Germany and Berlin. More ominously, twenty-five Soviet ships edged toward the U.S. blockade line that comprised sixteen destroyers, three cruisers, an antisubmarine aircraft carrier, and over 150 other vessels. Russian captains were under orders to stay on course, and, on Wednesday, submarines joined the cargo fleet sailing toward Cuba. Soviet forces in Cuba—an estimated 35,000—armed themselves with tactical nuclear weapons. War was imminent.

Meanwhile, Rusk made headway on the diplomatic front. The NATO allies, even the difficult Charles de Gaulle, supported Kennedy's firm line. Discussions begun in the Security Council of the United Nations injected some calm into the crisis. The Organization of American States unanimously endorsed the quarantine, giving it an imprimatur of legality. It meant even more for Rusk: "My God," he exclaimed at an Ex-Com meeting on October 23, this vote would, in all probability, prevent the Russians from launching "an immediate, sudden, irrational strike."[21]

What would happen when the Russian ships reached the U.S. Navy vessels, which had moved farther out in defiance of civilian orders, nobody knew. The answer came on Wednesday night, October 24. The president and his advisers sat nervously, some pale, others near hysteria, as they awaited word from the navy. Soviet vessels edged closer toward the waiting American ships. Robert Kennedy described his brother's movements: the president's "hand went up to his face and covered his mouth. He opened and closed his fist. His face seemed drawn, his eyes pained, almost gray."[22] And then news came. The Russian ships had stopped short of the blockade line; some had changed course. Seated next to the president in the Cabinet Room, Rusk whispered to McGeorge Bundy what would become one of the most famous quotes of the crisis: "We were eyeball to eyeball, and the other fellow just blinked."[23] The next day the ships turned back toward the Soviet Union, and the worst had passed.

The crisis was not over, however, for Khrushchev determined to ready for operation the missiles already in Cuba. The CIA reported that the Russians had put building in Cuba into high gear. Missiles might be operational within a few days. Rusk understood that if the missiles were up and running, it would be extremely difficult to persuade the Soviets to remove them voluntarily. Ex-Com was back to square one—considering an air strike before it was too late.

The administration began preparations to invade Cuba the following Tuesday. Numbering 100,000 men, five combat divisions of the Army Strategic Reserves were readied for action. Tanks rolled from Texas into Georgia, and troops were sent to southern Florida, the staging area for the invasion. Troopships also steamed from the Panama Canal while 7,000 marines reinforced the Guantanamo Bay base. The Strategic Air Command shifted to war alert for the first time ever, sending 550 B-52 bombers into the air loaded with nuclear weapons. The order to the B-52s was purposely sent uncoded to ensure the Soviets' full comprehension of the seriousness of the situation. The Russians were informed that their missile bases would be destroyed.

Latin American allies urged caution, aware that a large number of Cuban casualties would create long-term resentment in the region. The superpowers once again stood eyeball to eyeball, but the way out was clear: "We don't believe that there should be insuperable difficulties in reaching a solution," Rusk explained on Thursday morning, October 25, "if those responsible for the threat are prepared to remove it."[24] Diplomacy now took over, with Rusk as a central figure. On Friday he learned that the Soviets were willing to remove the missiles under the supervision of the United Nations in return for a U.S. pledge not to invade Cuba. Khrushchev then wired Kennedy with the same terms, urging that both sides untie the "knot of war." On Saturday an upbeat Ex-Com discussed the note, but that evening a more formal message arrived. Written by hard-liners in the Soviet Foreign Ministry, it demanded the removal of U.S. Jupiter missiles from Turkey, in addition to the no-invasion pledge, as a condition for settlement in Cuba.

This demand was followed by even more bad news. First the Cubans shot down an American U-2 spy plane with a Soviet missile. Then a U-2 straying into Soviet air space was chased out by Russian fighters. Hawks in the Ex-Com rallied for a strike. Rusk feared that the Russians wanted war with the United States; they still could deploy some missile sites in Cuba. In the southeastern United States the largest concentration of U.S. military forces since the Korean War massed, ready for an invasion after the scheduled air strikes. Latin Americans were frantic.

This was the Kennedy administration's shining hour. Instead of panicking, the president decided to answer the first note from Khrushchev and ignore the second belligerent hard-line message. He would not appease the Russians by trading missiles in a deal over Cuba; Rusk endorsed this decision, fearing that to yield would be to invite the Soviets to ask for more. The president had originally judged the offer to trade missiles in Cuba for those in Turkey "a very good proposal," but he had then reconsidered.[25] The Jupiters in Turkey, asserted Rusk and others, were a separate European and NATO issue, not appropriate for negotiations over Cuba. The real issue was the intrusion of Soviet missiles in the Western Hemisphere. The United States would promise not to attack Cuba, but the Russian weapons had to be removed. To show the president's commitment to the deal, his trusted brother delivered the offer to Dobrynin on Saturday, October 27. Awaiting the Russian reply, the U.S. military continued preparations for an air attack on Cuba and for the accompanying invasion on Tuesday, unaware that the Soviet defenders were now armed with short-range missiles with nuclear warheads. American soldiers would have faced annihilation.

True to form, Rusk encouraged participation by the United Nations. That body could oversee the sites, missile removal, and the replacement of the U.S. quarantine. And the United Nations would consider future policy, such as Brazil's idea for a hemisphere-wide nuclear-free zone. Meanwhile, Rusk had prepared a letter for Kennedy to send to Castro, giving the Cuban leader a choice between saving his people and remaining a pawn in the Soviet Union's dangerous game of nuclear brinkmanship.

Secretly, Rusk devised a backup plan in case the Soviets rejected the offer: an exchange, supervised by the United Nations, of Cuban for Jupiter missiles. Rusk was willing to negotiate at all costs, but he also employed calm logic. He drew on an ancient Chinese military notion that an enemy denied an escape route will fight to the end. In the nuclear age that would be global suicide. The United States could neither back down nor force Khrushchev into a corner of desperation.

Rusk's last resort proved unnecessary. On Sunday morning, October 28, the Soviet premier broadcast his reply over Radio Free Europe. The Russians agreed to the quid pro quo: they would crate up their missiles in return for Kennedy's promise not to invade Cuba. Heeding Rusk's advice, Kennedy also agreed to inform Khrushchev that, while there would be no deal on the Jupiter missiles in Turkey, he could rest assured that they would be removed after the Cuban crisis had ended. But the standoff was not over. The Soviets and Americans continued to quibble over the terms, and preparations went ahead for an invasion. Nevertheless, Khrushchev told the Cubans not to shoot at U.S. reconnaissance planes, the Russians began discussions about verification of the removal of the missiles, and U.S. armed forces were eventually instructed to stand down.

The outcome of the crisis hurt those responsible for it. Removal of the missiles proceeded over the next several months, confirmed by U.S. surveillance. Castro felt betrayed and lashed out at Moscow. His appeal in Latin America plummeted. The chastened Khrushchev fell from power within two years, the victim of a struggle for control in which hard-liners in the Politburo belittled his humiliating retreat in the face of American demands. On the U.S. side the Jupiter missiles in Turkey were dismantled in April 1963, replaced by a Polaris missile submarine stationed in the Mediterranean. Kennedy's stock rose as a result of his calm handling of the crisis.

Like the rest of the administration, Rusk was more relieved than exhuberant. He would not gloat, but neither would he ignore the skillful handling of the crisis. Many observers, including Dean Acheson, attributed the peaceful settlement to "plain dumb luck."[26] Rusk disagreed, for if the administration had taken Acheson's advice and gone ahead with an air strike, luck might never have had a chance to materialize in a nuclear war. At times, events had spiraled out of control. The U-2 shootdown was one event that could have led to a nuclear exchange. Ex-Com meetings were often disorderly; people came and went, and new information was presented in a tense atmosphere that made its digestion difficult. Even Rusk admitted that the confrontation in Cuba—"the most dangerous crisis the world has ever seen, because the two nuclear superpowers were at each other's jugular veins and it was not easy to see a way out"—could have turned out much worse if weariness, uncertainty, and tension had led to "fumbling on either side."[27]

Rusk's clearheaded, creative thinking helped ensure that this did not happen. Still, Kennedy upbraided him for letting the Jupiters in Turkey become an issue in the Cuban crisis. In Rusk's defense, however, the Turks had held up removal until Polaris submarines replaced the missiles as a defense system. And Rusk got high marks for his sound advice and careful prescriptions, including the solution—the "Rusk ploy"—to remove the outmoded Jupiters from Turkey if need be. His was a voice of caution in days of withering tension. He had urged Ex-Com members to remain patient and judicious in dealing with the adversary, a lesson he had learned from Pearl Harbor and Korea. Problems had answers, and they need not escalate the crisis further. He applauded Kennedy for wisely taking his time and acting with restraint. Understanding the stakes involved—above all, the danger to humankind—Rusk and Kennedy chose appropriate action to achieve U.S. interests while avoiding a world war.

The Cuban missile crisis provided a reality check for the superpowers. Rusk learned a lesson: future crises had to be prevented "because they're just too damn dangerous." In his view the confrontation might have been avoided if the United States had more clearly expressed the utmost importance of its security concerns regarding Cuba. The clash also raised moral issues that lead him to ask "the ultimate question, What is life all about?"[28] Rusk looked at the crisis as a turning point in superpower relations and a step toward fulfilling his idealist dream of peace. Even though neither side conceded much over the next half-decade, it set arms-control talks in motion.

Détente emerged, but the superpowers vowed to defend their global interests, even if it meant fighting another day. Rusk was bent on a peaceful resolution with the Russians but not at the risk of sacrificing American security. He warned audiences against the foolish notion that the Soviets had veered away from their postwar policy of expansion. Fearing another missile crisis, Rusk hoped for détente, but he also remained vigilant, wary of Russian maneuvers. That was the thinking of a neo-Wilsonian, a classic Cold War liberal.

The Specter of Castro

The missile crisis cast a shadow over Latin American affairs. Kennedy, then Johnson, kept unrelenting pressure on Cuba. Within a few years, all Latin American nations but Mexico had cut ties with Havana. There was still a fear that Castro or his Soviet sponsor would stimulate Communist subversion. In November 1963, Cuba assisted in an unsuccessful attempt to overthrow the democratic Venezuelan government. As Kennedy had proclaimed just a week before his death, "We in this hemisphere must also use every resource at our command to prevent the establishment of another Cuba in this hemisphere."[29] Johnson fully agreed. To combat such efforts, military aid flowed to any nation with anti-Communist credentials, even if it was an oppressive dictatorship. Washington also monitored politics in the region, and Johnson continued subversive acts and training missions to counter guerrilla action. The goal was realized, Rusk exclaimed: by the end of the decade, Castroism was no longer "an exportable commodity from Cuba into other Latin American countries."[30]

President Johnson, a Texan with boyhood ties to Mexican Americans, focused on Latin America. He urged Rusk to devise ways to alleviate poverty in the Western Hemisphere, but promoting order to halt communism became his top priority. Rather than formulate a sweeping reform agenda, the United States assumed a defensive stance to stop Castro. In 1964, for instance, angry that the Panama Canal remained under U.S. control, nationalists in the country rioted when (in violation of a U.S.-Panama agreement) American schoolchildren there refused to fly the Panamanian flag. More than twenty people were killed. When Johnson held that Castro relished the unrest, observers inferred that Panamanian Communists had led the demonstrations. Still, negotiations were begun to give Panama sovereignty over the Canal Zone. Rusk applauded the move as a nod to fairness, yet a treaty would not be signed for over a decade.

Elsewhere Rusk battled Castroism. In Brazil a staunchly anti-Communist regime seized power from nationalist João Goulart in April 1964. Although Brazil's military brought order at the expense of democracy, the United States was relieved. That same year Bolivia's General René Barrientos Ortuño shunned the labor movement and pledged allegiance to U.S. values. And military aid to Colombia, Guatemala, Peru, Nicaragua, and Venezuela brought victories against the left. Rusk oversaw U.S. policies toward these countries, but he also had direct involvement in one instance. His only brush with danger came when a youth in Uruguay attempted to spit on him but nothing came out of his mouth (one reporter enhanced his photograph by dubbing in spit). Such anti-Americanism was equated with Communist subversion, but Rusk refused to press charges against the boy: "That way, he will understand what democracy and liberty mean."[31] Symptomatic of the regimes that the United States found itself encouraging in Latin America, however, the police beat the youth into a coma.

The biggest regional crisis of the Johnson years occurred in April 1965, when civil war broke out in the Dominican Republic. After he was ousted by right-wingers in 1963, Juan Bosch, the country's progressive leader, had vowed to regain power. Because Kennedy had detested the thirty-year dictatorship of Leonidas Trujillo, who was assassinated in 1961, he had sympathized with Bosch's reforms. But after Bosch was elected president, he proved unable to govern. His occasional compliments to Castro also piqued Americans. A savage civil war led to military intervention by the United States. Johnson sought to protect not only American lives but also hemispheric security. He worried that Castro eyed the country for invasion. Fearing that Bosch's return would prompt a counterrevolution by the Dominican military, Rusk looked for alternatives. The objective, he explained, was to prevent "another Cuba" while avoiding another Trujillo tyranny.[32]

Johnson responded by landing over 23,000 marines in the Dominican Republic from late April to early May 1965. Eventually, legalism replaced unilateralism. Quietly supportive of the U.S. intervention, the Organization of American States sent a force to maintain peace until elections brought the anti-Communist moderate, Joaquín Balaguer, into office in 1966. Rusk's goals—"restoration of law and order, prevention of a possible Communist takeover, and protection of American lives"—were fulfilled.[33] He applauded the intervention as the only way to prevent a bloodbath, restore order, and promote democracy. The action had cost lives and money, but it had pulled back the Dominicans from a "precipice into a real catastrophe."[34] This was not an example of nineteenth-century imperialism, he vowed, but a way to avoid chaos. Such damage control served the anti-Communist cause against Castroism, although it did not solve fundamental social problems in Latin America.

Even the most generous of analysts agree that in Latin America, reality never met expectations. In part the fact that the Cold War overran idealism in U.S. policy undercut the push for justice and prosperity. The anti-Communist crusade shoved aside economic and social concerns, with unfortunate consequences for Latin America. Rusk, the internationalist, deplored these setbacks, but he believed that ridding the hemisphere of communism was an essential prerequisite to a successful war on regional poverty. In a perfect world he would have led the social crusade. But the region, he concluded, was not in an acceptable condition as long as aggressive communism existed. Defeating Castro and communism was the necessary first step to fulfilling the Wilsonian mission. Economic and social progress could only occur in the area, Rusk opined, if Communist penetration was first thwarted. That rule held true for the rest of the periphery as well.

Notes

1. Viorst, "Incidentally, Who Is Dean Rusk?" 179.
2. Lindley, *Winds of Freedom*, 126, 128, 132–33.

3. Stephen G. Rabe, "Controlling Revolutions: Latin America, the Alliance for Progress, and Cold War," in *Kennedy's Quest for Victory: American Foreign Policy, 1961–1963*, ed. Thomas G. Paterson (New York: Oxford University Press, 1989), 122.

4. Dean Rusk, news conference, *DSB* 44 (February 27, 1961): 297.

5. Dean Rusk, interview on "Washington Viewpoint," DSB 46 (March 5, 1962): 361.

6. Lindley, *Winds of Freedom*, 131.

7. Rusk, *As I Saw It*, 216–17.

8. Lindley, *Winds of Freedom*, 135.

9. Dean Rusk, interview on Hearst Metrotone / Telenews, *DSB* 46 (January 22, 1962): 126.

10. Rusk, *As I Saw It*, 229.

11. Ernest R. May and Philip D. Zelikow, *The Kennedy Tapes: Inside the White House during the Cuban Missile Crisis* (Cambridge, MA: Belknap Press of Harvard University Press, 1997), 183.

12. Ex-Com meeting, October 16, 1962, President's Office File (hereafter cited as POF), JFKL; May and Zelikow, *Kennedy Tapes*, 255.

13. May and Zelikow, *Kennedy Tapes*, 54.

14. Ibid., 54–56, 87.

15. Ibid., 128–29, 148.

16. Schoenbaum, *Waging Peace*, 310.

17. May and Zelikow, *Kennedy Tapes*, 178.

18. Rusk, *As I Saw It*, 233; May and Zelikow, *Kennedy Tapes*, 198.

19. May and Zelikow, *Kennedy Tapes*, 212, 278, 280.

20. Schoenbaum, *Waging Peace*, 317.

21. Presidential Recordings, 34.1A, October 23, 1962, POF, JFKL.

22. Giglio, *Presidency of John F. Kennedy*, 206.

23. Ibid., 207.

24. May and Zelikow, *Kennedy Tapes*, 417–18.

25. Ibid., 512.

26. Dean Acheson, "Homage to Plain Dumb Luck," in *The Cuban Missile Crisis*, 2d ed., ed. Robert A. Divine (New York: Markus Wiener, 1988), 186.

27. James G. Blight and David A. Welch, *On the Brink: Americans and Soviets Reexamine the Cuban Missile Crisis* (New York: Noonday Press, 1990), 179.

28. Rusk, *As I Saw It*, 245.

29. Lyndon Johnson, *The Vantage Point: Perspectives of the Presidency, 1963–1969* (New York: Holt, Rinehart, and Winston, 1971), 202.

30. DROH III, Lyndon B. Johnson Library, Austin, Texas (hereafter cited as LBJL), 29–32.

31. "What Liberty Means," *Newsweek* (November 29, 1965): 26.

32. Joseph S. Tulchin, "The Promise of Progress: U.S. Relations with Latin America during the Administration of Lyndon B. Johnson," in Cohen and Tucker, *Lyndon Johnson Confronts the World*, 236.

33. H. W. Brands, *The Wages of Globalism: Lyndon Johnson and the Limits of American Power* (New York: Oxford University Press, 1995), 54.

34. DROH III, LBJL, 19.

5

Priorities in the Third World

No secretary of state was as prepared or as committed as Dean Rusk to approach the Third World. His impoverished boyhood, wartime service in Asia, and interest in development as head of the Rockefeller Foundation had given him insights into problems in the periphery. Not surprisingly, he endorsed greater outlays of foreign aid. He lobbied for the Peace Corps, the Alliance for Progress, and the creation of the Agency for International Development to finance construction of schools, housing, farms, and other projects. Rusk, Kennedy, and Johnson met hundreds of Third World leaders during the 1960s. Kennedy, in particular, had embraced these officials, a large number of them from newly independent African nations, irritating European colonial allies in the process. The periphery of Latin America, Africa, the Middle East, and Asia became a top priority.

The coming of age of Europe had reshaped global politics from the fifteenth to the nineteenth centuries. Now, Rusk perceived, independence was the dynamic movement. By 1960 forty nations had come into existence since the Second World War; nearly one-half had broken free of colonialism in 1960 alone. Great empires were splitting apart; a revolution of rising expectations was taking hold. This transformation in geopolitics sparked idealism in Rusk: "Across the world the winds of change are blowing; awakening peoples are demanding to be admitted to the promise of the twentieth century."[1]

But realism was also involved. If the United States let the revolutionary tide blow over, communism would step in. Wherever communism triumphed, Rusk claimed, suffering followed. The 1961–62 famine in China was a case in point, as was poverty in North Vietnam, North

Korea, and Cuba. Economic distress created a metaphorical wall of glass. New nations could peer through to see but not obtain the riches of the developed core beyond, explained Rusk, making them more amenable to the false message of communism, an ideology that obstructed his internationalist mission.

Many developing nations refused to align with either the United States or the Sino-Soviet bloc. Rusk saw such neutralism as a natural movement away from centuries of imperialism. Aid would keep the Third World friendly, boost modernization, and solve the chronic crisis of starvation. The Peace Corps, he believed, would teach them about the successes of democracy. Then they would be more inclined to adhere to the West and to send their resources to Free World economies. According to Rusk, neutralism had been replaced by two forces: "those who want the U.N. kind of world and those who are trying to tear it down."[2] Meanwhile, Third World nations used the Cold War to obtain money and arms.

Rusk balanced security with ideals. The periphery had to be guided toward capitalist democracy while remaining attached to the U.S. camp. A world run by democratic nations was still his dream. America's appeal was not its military might or vast economy but its adherence to the idea that rulers gained power through the consent of the governed. "If we don't quit this world struggle, if we persevere in our efforts, history could come to know the twentieth century as the Age of the Rights of Man," he declared. This neo-Wilsonian creed, Rusk hoped, would lure poverty-stricken countries living behind the "bamboo curtain."[3] Communism, as a result, would be contained as the first step toward instituting liberal internationalism. To be sure, the United States took cues from imperial allies in Africa, dipped delicately into Middle Eastern affairs, and eyed Asia with caution. Still, Rusk argued, it was time for the United States to act with vigor in the periphery.

Africa

No U.S. administration had ever formulated an African policy. The United States had let its NATO allies lead their colonies while it remained a junior partner. Europe aided Africa, the United States focused on Latin America and Asia. Thus, there was no reason "to play Mr. Big in each one of the African countries," Rusk noted. Yet because the United States had long stood for anticolonialism, Africans awaited proof that the leader of the Free World would support independence.[4] With vast quantities of strategic minerals and economic ties to Western Europe, it was essential that Africans be persuaded to identify with the West. Although Kwame Nkrumah of Ghana sought aid from the Soviets, Rusk insisted on carrying out American financing of a $25-million dam on the Volta River. In early 1961 he persuaded Kennedy to back a UN resolution calling for self-determination in Angola, a Portuguese colony. Reaching out, he believed, would turn these nations away from communism.

In one of hundreds of meetings with Third World leaders, Rusk and Kennedy greet Ambassador J. M. Udochi of Nigeria in April 1961. *Courtesy Richard B. Russell Library, University of Georgia*

Typically, Rusk joined idealism with realism. He endorsed independence, self-determination, political stability, and economic gain while remaining sympathetic to European needs. The secretary of state promoted accommodation by all sides, but, above all, the Soviets (who were not very active in Africa) were to be denied footholds on the continent. Preventing Communist penetration without angering allies was tricky, however, as the major African issue of the 1960s—the Congo crisis—revealed. Rusk recognized that the Congo was in disarray. After the Republic of the Congo gained independence from Belgium in the summer of 1960, it fell into civil war. The Belgians exited the country, leaving behind a novice government, and a UN peacekeeping force rushed in to quell violence in the capital of Leopoldville. Meanwhile, the mineral-rich southern province of Katanga, the focus of Belgian financial interests, broke away from the republic, and Moscow, along with its Egyptian allies, backed a rebel faction in the north that sought to take over the entire country.

The central government tenuously held power, imprisoning Patrice Lumumba, a popular pro-Communist leader who had received military aid from the Soviet bloc. Strongman Joseph Mobutu —supported by the CIA—headed the government's army and was bent on stifling Lumumba. He transferred Lumumba from UN custody to the hands of pro-Belgian Katangan Moise Tshombe, who murdered Lumumba in February 1961, thus escalating the conflict. Efforts to control Katanga generated the crisis. Rusk despised the rebels there as white mercenaries in league with European profiteers seeking to exploit diamond, cobalt, and copper mines. He wanted the United Nations to ensure a central government inclusive of all political elements. The alternative, Rusk feared, was "violence and chaos and a ready-made opportunity for Soviet exploitation."[5] He approved when a parliament, elected under UN supervision in July 1961, reintegrated the northern leftist rebels into the government. But Katanga's Tshombe, backed by European investors and U.S. conservatives (who saw Katanga as a symbol of free enterprise in a region full of socialists), encouraged the province's secession.

In September 1961, despite the presence of UN peacekeepers, fighting broke out between the government and Katanga. Tragically, UN Secretary General Dag Hammarskjöld was killed in a plane crash while mediating the dispute. Seeing the futility of military solutions, Rusk nonetheless approved limited armed intervention by the United Nations at the end of the year, as Katangans persisted in their hostilities. Ironically, however, the troublemakers in the Congo were the rightists.

Rusk's approach was rooted in legalism but influenced by the Cold War. Africans wanted to crush the Katangan rebellion, but Rusk feared for the lives and production of the province. French, British, and Belgian investors would surely reject this solution, and

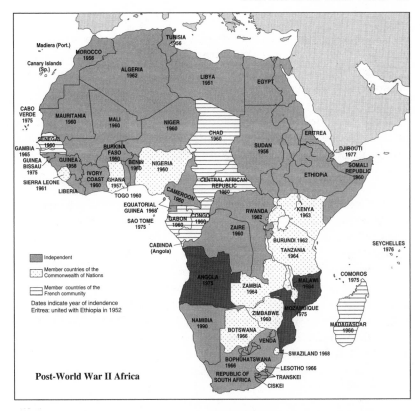

Post-World War II Africa

Rusk did not want the mines to fall into Communist hands. Yet a weak response would tarnish America's image as an upholder of collective security, and it would undermine the reputation of the moderate central government. Communists would exploit the instability, either taking control or helping to break up the nation, and that could lead to more conflict. "Extremists" had to be stopped, announced Rusk, or the Congo situation "would eventually result in a direct military confrontation" between the superpowers.[6]

Eschewing force, Rusk helped negotiate a cease-fire in December 1961 that secured Tshombe's temporary recognition of the central government. Tshombe soon renewed the fighting, but UN forces eventually suppressed him, and Katanga rejoined the central government in early 1963. In 1964, however, Simba leftists in the northeastern Congo drew on Chinese aid to attack the government. Beaten back by government forces in November, they captured and took as hostage over three thousand whites from nineteen nations. Once again the Congo was in crisis. By this time the Katangan Tshombe had become prime minister. To Rusk's disgust, Johnson called Tshombe a loyal anticommunist, and Belgium and the United States consulted on military action. Belgian paratroopers flown in by U.S. C-130 transport planes dramatically rescued the hostages.

The rebellion fizzled out, but the Congo experienced more bouts of violence until 1965, when Mobutu took power in a coup d'état. Europe and the United States, having given up on solving Congolese political problems, reluctantly recognized this strongman. Mobutu, who was pledged to anticommunism, brutalized the Congo until he was forced out in 1997, over three decades later. Rusk had pushed for liberal moderation that would fulfill the goals of African nationalism and block Communist expansion. But in the last analysis he preferred Mobutu to the leftists. However distasteful, Mobutu was pro-Western and could resist Communist insurgencies. A frustrating experience, the Congo saga showed how difficult it was to honor ideals in African policy.

When push came to shove, national security prevailed over Wilsonianism. Portugal was a case in point. Rusk wanted the NATO ally to loosen its control over Angola, but when the Angolans turned to China for aid in 1964, he backtracked. If they continued to press, U.S. officials risked losing from Portugal the lease on military bases in the Azores Islands in the Atlantic. By 1965, charged with hypocrisy, Rusk had stopped pressuring Portugal to decolonize.

Apartheid

The charge of hypocrisy was also issued in regard to the U.S. response to the vicious policy of apartheid in South Africa and the oppression of blacks in Rhodesia. Apartheid, a system of legal separation of blacks and whites, was bolstered by Cold War requirements and defied the civil rights revolution that erupted in the United States in the 1960s. The Reverend Martin Luther King, Jr., and liberals and student activists of all colors, charged ahead of President Kennedy to desegregate public facilities and obtain political and social equality. Rusk supported civil rights and spoke out against discrimination. The first administration witness to champion the 1963 civil rights bill in Congress, he argued that the white race, a minority in the world, "had to come to terms with the various colored races if we're to live in peace with other nations."[7]

Of course, the Cold War was a major consideration. Reforms, Rusk insisted, were mandatory across the board in race relations as the best means to counter communism. In the 1950s he had argued that dealing fairly with minorities was America's "greatest load to bear," for failure to do so played into Soviet propaganda claims that the United States was an imperialist. In the Cold War, a "battle of ideas," this was a major problem in the Third World.[8] The connection of race and ethnicity to the Cold War was obvious in immigration as well.

In 1965, President Johnson initiated the first major overhaul of restrictive immigration quotas in decades. Most notably, the law eliminated both the national-origins quotas that had targeted non-Anglo-Saxon peoples and the racial categorization of immigrants from the Asia-Pacific region. In hearings before the Senate, Rusk testified that immigration curbs by the leader of the Free World set a bad example. "The rest of the world watches us closely to see whether or not we live up to the great principles we have proclaimed and promoted," he admonished. "Our blemishes delight our enemies and dismay our friends."[9] Congress voted to end significant restrictions to immigration.

Rusk's record on civil rights was admirable. Growing up around black people as a child, he had disdained them in Georgia. At Oxford, however, socializing with black students had shown him that Jim Crow was an evil that had to be eradicated. During the 1940s he had integrated the segregated mess of the Defense Department by inviting future Nobel Prize laureate and UN official Ralph Bunche—then a civilian intelligence officer—to have lunch with him at the Pentagon. Rusk also brought African Americans into the ranks of the State Department. Refusing to join clubs where Jews and blacks were prohibited, he had denied his children access to a segregated pool around the corner from their home. For Rusk, integration "came out of elementary liberalism—not the cynical liberalism of modern days."[10] The examples of his racial tolerance abound. The southerner expressed pride when his daughter married a black man in 1967, and he visited the newlyweds at Stanford University (although he offered to resign to save Johnson embarrassment with southern legislators). The event earned him the grudging appreciation of liberals who criticized his Vietnam policies.

Rusk not only integrated State Department functions in segregationist South Africa but also lashed out at the regime. He turned apoplectic in the face of South African racism. In late 1963 the government denied a black U.S. diplomat, Ulrich Haynes, a visa to inspect black enclaves. Rusk went into a fit of rage and demanded an immediate visa, an apology, and Haynes's transport on a South African commercial flight. One official commented that he had never seen the secretary of state so livid and had feared that Rusk would initiate a minor diplomatic war over the issue. Rusk called in U.S. Ambassador G. Mennan Williams and threatened to fight the matter until South Africa relented. Finally, the visa was granted.

At the same time, however, Rusk counseled against exerting too much pressure on South Africa. National security took precedence. Since the Second World War the United States had favored trade over morality regarding Pretoria. As America's top African commercial partner, South Africa held such strategic minerals as gold, diamonds, and manganese and provided missile tracking stations and ports for the U.S. Navy. Even though activist Nelson Mandela and his backers were imprisoned for demonstrating against apartheid, Rusk cautioned that weakening white rule might lead to a race war and "communist infiltration."[11]

Rusk did chide South Africa for provoking international indignity and domestic unrest. Sensitive to America's image, he genuinely desired an end to apartheid. In 1964, Rusk demanded that Pretoria desist in efforts to extend apartheid to South West Africa, and he denounced the unfair trial, conviction, and sentencing of Mandela and his compatriots after their arrest at Rivonia. Constrained by Cold War imperatives, however, he stopped well short of formal condemnation of the government. This restraint led to the charge that, in terms of change, Rusk's criticism of apartheid was more symbolic than meaningful.

Rusk's memoirs are uncharacteristically insensitive to the moral issue of apartheid. He denounced critics for using South African embassies as demonstration sites, arguing that human rights should not be linked to foreign policy. After all, he said, plenty of other countries had "obnoxious practices of one sort or another" that violated human rights. Americans, he warned, should not be the "self-elected gendarmes for the political and social problems of other states."[12] Contrary to the wishes of liberals and black Africans, the United States would not impose economic sanctions or a complete arms embargo on South Africa and would not expel the country from the United Nations. Kennedy began a unilateral arms embargo but then vitiated it by allowing the sale of spare parts. Lyndon Johnson continued this feeble policy.

Such cold-blooded realism allowed Americans to deplore apartheid but cooperate with the racist government. No great crusade was undertaken against official white Rhodesian racism either. Rusk preferred that Britain and Rhodesia settle the problem of political representation for blacks. The United States would nudge the process along by endorsing the UN sanctions but would otherwise avoid involvement. A low profile epitomized Washington's African policy. Expending minimal energy on the continent was the goal.

The Congo and problems with Portugal were not considered crucial, since Africa was a peripheral interest. South Africa was strategically important, but Rusk believed that Africa should not divert the attention of national security advisers from more serious issues. While focused on Europe, Cuba, and Southeast Asia, U.S. administrations hoped that, as long as communism was kept at bay, they could keep Africa off the screen. African dictatorial regimes offered stability and anticommunism. The United States simply held its nose and hoped the oppressors would reform. Meanwhile, Africa stayed a back-burner issue for Rusk, one that needed monitoring and the proper rhetoric but not vigorous intervention. Liberalism did not prevail in Africa. In this region, Rusk's neo-Wilsonianism necessitated a distinctly amoral approach.

The Middle East

More mundane deliberation also dominated U.S. policy in the Middle East. The superpower confrontation was one of three American considerations with respect to the region in the 1960s. The other two were oil and Israel, both linked to the Cold War as well. Since 1945 the United States had worried that the Soviet Union would penetrate the Middle East, attract nationalist Arab states, and imperil the flow of the world's largest source of exportable petroleum. Officials had provided aid to moderate Arab nations, such as Saudi Arabia and Iran, to maintain military and communications facilities.

At the same time, domestic politics, cultural values, and the lingering memories of the Holocaust compelled the United States to support the interests of Israel, a nation of 2.5 million people surrounded by about 90 million hostile Arabs. That stance naturally angered the Arabs, but complex problems defied easy solutions. Choosing between Arabs and Jews was a no-win situation. As Rusk noted, he had gotten "kicked in the shanks" in 1948 by both groups when he worked on the Palestine quandary and "clobbered by both sides" twenty years later when he attempted to negotiate peace.[13] Yet one thing was clear: by mediating between Jews and Arabs in the 1960s, the United States would become more involved in the Middle East than ever before.

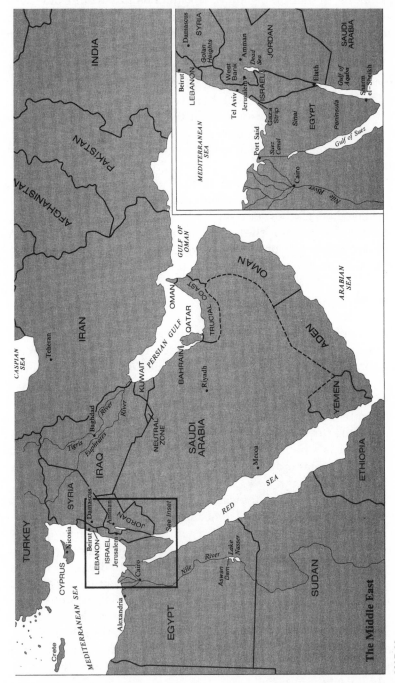

The Middle East

MAP 38

The focus of much of this U.S. involvement was Gamal Abdel Nasser of Egypt, the dynamic Arab nationalist eager to end Western dominance in the region. In the eyes of radical Arabs, he was the hero of the Suez crisis of 1956, during which he had defiantly faced the forces of France, Britain, and Israel. When he had sought aid from the Soviet Union, President Eisenhower perceived him as an enemy. By the Kennedy years, however, Nasser had rejected the Russians to follow an independent course of intervention in any issue that he deemed appropriate.

In 1962, for instance, he sent 70,000 troops to aid rebels in their fight against the royalist Yemeni government, which was backed by conservative, oil-rich, pro-American Saudi Arabia. In this crisis, Rusk considered Egypt, along with Syria and Algeria, to be the leader of the more extreme Arab states. The Saudis were moderates, and Rusk cultivated them and their conservative brethren in Morocco, Tunisia, Libya, Kuwait, and Jordan. But because he did not want to anger the radicals and drive them into the arms of the Soviets—who itched for more involvement in the region—he approved of a UN plan in which both sides would withdraw from Yemen. Still, the imbroglio dragged on interminably.

Nasser had a decisive impact on Arab-Israeli relations. He promised Kennedy that he would keep this rancorous issue in the icebox; indeed, Kennedy was the only postwar president between Truman and Gerald Ford who did not experience a war between the Jewish state and the Arabs. When Kennedy sent an air defense squadron to Saudi Arabia to deter Nasser in the Yemen crisis, however, Israel reacted with alarm. Kennedy had hoped to follow an even-handed approach with Arabs and Jews alike, but by 1963 his optimism had evaporated. Pro-Nasser uprisings in Iraq and Jordan frightened the Israelis, and they demanded protection. Diverging from Eisenhower's policy of keeping a distance between the United States and Israel, Kennedy sent the Israelis Hawk missiles. Indebted to American Jews for his slim election victory in 1960, Kennedy believed that he could do no less. By 1963 an incensed Nasser, feeling pressure from Arab nationalists and Palestinians displaced by the Israelis, turned back to the Soviet Union for aid.

Arms sales indicated a spiral of superpower military support in the region. Johnson readily obliged the Israelis with more military assistance, claiming that Egypt, Iraq, and other Arab nationalists had developed a great weapons advantage. A longtime backer of Israel, Johnson knew that Jews at home—largely liberal in political philosophy—were natural allies of the Democratic party. He proved to be a great friend of Israel. Within two months of Kennedy's death, hundreds of tanks were on their way to the Jewish state. Forty-eight A-4 fighter bombers, as well as ammunition, spare parts, and communications equipment, followed. Rusk rationalized the sales as a way to persuade Israel that it had no need to develop nuclear weapons, but the assistance raised the ante in the Middle East.

Johnson also authorized the sale of weapons to King Hussein of Jordan and King Faisal of Saudi Arabia and cozied up to the Shah of Iran, all conservative Arab allies. But the results were not as expected. Israel enjoyed a boost of self-confidence, the United States became more deeply involved in the region, and U.S. relations with the Arab world suffered. Although Israel and Nasser were at the center of these difficulties, Rusk believed that the Soviets were instigating the problems. When the Egyptian embraced the Russians in 1964, Rusk cringed as Congress tried to cut off food relief to Egypt. Rusk managed to reserve some assistance as a way to shape Nasser's behavior, yet Nasser grew more dangerous.

Palestinian guerrillas attacked Israel from pro-Soviet Syria after Jordan and Lebanon had already permitted similar operations. In 1966, Israel retaliated with a raid on a Jordanian village, and in May 1967 rumors flew around the Arab world that a reprisal against Syria was in the offing. Nasser warned the Israelis that he would defend Syria, ordered a UN peacekeeping force to evacuate the area, and closed the Strait of Tiran, on which Israel was dependent for shipping. The United States had pledged to keep the Strait open, and Israel demanded that the promise be honored.

Rusk talked with the Israelis, the Arabs, and the Soviets in an attempt to prevent war. As in Palestine in 1948, his skills in shuttle diplomacy were put to the test. Congress refused to intervene, and even the Russians, fearing that Egypt had gone too far, counseled calm. Israel, which wanted to attack and had no faith in UN involvement, was Rusk's biggest worry. He nonetheless blamed the Russians for trying to place the onus of aggression on Israel and, by association, on the United States. Hoping to de-escalate the turmoil, Rusk and Secretary of Defense Robert McNamara proposed to reopen the Strait of Tiran either by UN action, a declaration of open seas by shipping nations, or the creation of a multinational fleet to confront Egypt. After Nasser hinted at a blockade, Rusk was concerned that a shooting war was in the offing. His apprehensions were valid.

When Jordan and Egypt signed a military pact, joined by other Arab nations in early June 1967, Israel went on the alert. Despite a commitment to Rusk to withhold action, the Israelis struck as Arab troops moved into Jordan on June 6. Israeli bombers hit Egyptian airfields, and tanks rolled into the Sinai Desert. Within three hours, Egypt's entire air force lay in ruins. Syria and Jordan countered with offensives but were soon dispatched by outnumbered Israel. Six days later the Israelis occupied the Sinai, the Golan Heights, and the West Bank of the Jordan River. They took East Jerusalem, gaining access to the holy Wailing Wall at last. Rusk, whose diplomacy had failed, kept in touch with Moscow to prevent a superpower confrontation. But he was also clear on U.S. support for Israel and the need for the Arab world to recognize the Jewish nation's right to exist.

Rusk never pretended that the United States was a neutral party in the Six-Day War, but he emphasized that, "as a member of the United Nations," it desired peace in the Middle East.[14] That would be a difficult task, for, as he well knew, the Arabs now identified the United States with Israel. He hoped that friendly relations with Tel Aviv would influence Israel's behavior in a positive way; in the immediate term it did not. Israel invaded Syria, and a few days later a truce ended the war. The Jewish state remained a recalcitrant ally. Rusk urged Israeli Foreign Minister Abba Eban not to introduce nuclear weapons into the Middle East, but he refused. Israel also disregarded UN Resolution 242 (which Rusk had worked on), calling for withdrawal from the occupied territory in return for an Arab pledge of peace. Noncompliance discouraged Rusk. He had long supported the rule of law. From this time onward, he grew increasingly disgusted with the resolute Israelis.

Despite Israel's refusal to comply with American wishes, Johnson left this ally alone. Vietnam War protesters were on the march in June 1967. A massive demonstration had just taken place in New York City. Antiwar senators such as J. William Fulbright and Mike Mansfield urged withdrawal from Vietnam but activism against Israel. The irony was not lost on Rusk, who noted that "doves have become hawks, and vice versa."[15] Already faced with grave political difficulties, Johnson did not need to anger Jews at home, especially before the 1968 election. Rusk knew that the United States now confronted a more volatile situation in the Middle East than ever before. By the time he left office, the pro-Israeli stance had resulted in war and in full U.S. involvement in the intractable problems of the region. Rusk realized that the only chance for success was to "make ourselves attorneys for Israel," working with inside contacts to direct policy and temper an unruly ally.[16]

Security considerations reinforced the pro-Israeli tilt of U.S. policy as well. Israel, Iran, and Saudi Arabia were strategic assets. Their influence in regional politics and in the military balance of power, and the Arab nations' supplies of oil, were now essential ingredients in the Cold War. For Rusk, Wilsonianism was a hopeless ideal, considering the violence and complexities of the region. Allies were as difficult as enemies. Yet he took solace in the fact that Middle East containment, as in Africa, was pursued through proxies. That situation would remain in the next Arab-Israeli conflict, the Yom Kippur War of 1973, and until American soldiers aided in UN peacekeeping missions during the 1980s. Having surrogates fight for U.S. interests would not be the case in Asia.

Asia

During the Cold War the superpowers never engaged directly in armed combat. In Asia, however, two hot wars showed the danger of containment. The Korean War, when U.S. troops fought Chinese regulars, had left Mao an archenemy, and the United States had severed relations with the People's Republic of China. Rusk approached Mao with some flexibility, but, like Presidents Kennedy and Johnson, he saw Beijing as a sponsor of revolution in Asia. Once Washington and Moscow began probing for détente in 1963, China became the leader of the world's anti-American forces. Asia was special to the United States, which held bases in the Philippines and Japan (although the Japanese demanded the reversion of Okinawa), as well as trade and resource interests and recent memories of war in the region. Japan now was a cherished ally; so was South Korea, which, although not a member of SEATO, sent two divisions of troops to Vietnam during the Johnson years. Asian allies had to be protected from the menacing Chinese.

Kennedy's fixation on China rivaled his obsession with Cuba. He and Rusk believed that the refusal to recognize Mao, the defense of Quemoy and Matsu (Taiwan's offshore islands) after China shelled them and threatened to take them from Jiang in 1955 and 1958, and the opposition to Beijing's admission to the United Nations were overly rigid positions. Yet changing course would enrage the influential right-wing China lobby in Congress. Beyond domestic politics, Rusk disliked Communist China. He welcomed talks to normalize relations, and, to show good faith, he extended offers to exchange journalists, scholars, and professionals. However, there was little ambiguity in his approach. Before reconciliation could occur, China would have to end what he saw as a belligerent drive for revolution. Well aware of the angry Sino-Soviet debate over ideology, Rusk nonetheless believed that the heart of the bickering between the two nations was merely how to get on with the world revolution—that is, means and technique, not purpose and ends. Fissures within the Communist ranks therefore gave the Americans little comfort. The United States had to meet the Communist challenge, especially the hostility of Beijing.

Mao was aggressive, plain and simple, held Rusk. Refusing to recognize Taiwan, Mao demanded its return to China. In Africa and elsewhere he backed wars of national liberation. China's border war with nonaligned India in 1962, criticism of Russian retreat in the Cuban missile crisis, and development of an atomic weapon in 1964 convinced Rusk that a tough stance was in order. Kennedy even considered teaming up with the Russians to bomb China's bomb. That stance, he reasoned, would hasten the growing division of China and the Soviet Union, strengthening the American hand in Asia.

Rusk was hostile to China because of the great many deaths of Americans in the Korean War, Mao's betrayal of democracy, and the expansionist menace. Mindful of Mao's success as a champion of insurgency, Rusk saw China as a rogue nation. And Beijing was no stooge of the Russians, as he had taunted in 1951. The Soviets were wary of Mao, and Mao disdained Russian weakness in the face of U.S. power (the Cuban missile crisis being a case in point). The People's Republic now carried the disease of communism in Asia by itself.

Adhering to a dual soft and hard line, Rusk hoped to contain Mao. The Communists would not disappear, so Mao must be treated as a legitimate power. Rusk advocated a Two-Chinas policy in the United Nations, to give a seat to the People's Republic while retaining Taiwan's. He welcomed Mao's participation in nuclear disarmament talks; arms control would be vitiated without including the arsenals of all the big powers. When the worst famine in history killed an estimated thirty million Chinese in 1961, food relief was not sent to the People's Republic; Rusk held that it would not change Mao's behavior. Yet neither did he allow Taiwan to take advantage of the situation by attacking the mainland.

In Rusk's overall analysis, nonetheless, China seemed eager for confrontation. Chinese involvement outside of its borders appeared to bear out that view. Indonesia's President Sukarno, whom Eisenhower had tried to overthrow in 1958, leaned toward the Communist camp for assistance. Important in the Cold War, Indonesia possessed valuable raw materials; Kennedy referred to it as "the most significant nation in Southeast Asia."[17] Because of Sukarno's bent toward China, Kennedy lavished attention on him (he even gave him a helicopter as a personal gift). Kennedy also helped negotiate a settlement with Indonesia's former colonial master, the Netherlands, which claimed West Irian on New Guinea. Rusk lost out in his effort to support the Netherlands, a NATO ally, against pro-Chinese Indonesia, which he viewed as a bully illegally seeking to control the territory. The secretary of state was convinced that Sukarno had violated the UN Charter that prohibited aggression. The eventual deal on West Irian called for a vote of self-determination in 1969, after years of Indonesian rule. Rusk felt "queasy" about the ease with which Kennedy shunned principles for pragmatism.[18]

Chinese interest in India also worried Rusk. Democratic and developing India fascinated Kennedy, as did its charismatic leader, Jawaharlal Nehru. But the complexities of the South Asian region overcame his vision that India could serve as a model to other nations that were tempted into neutrality or the Communist camp. China's attack on India in 1962 confirmed the aggressive, revolutionary fervor of the People's Republic and sent Nehru running for military aid, which Kennedy granted on the advice of Chester Bowles, his enthusiastic undersecretary of state. That assistance alienated U.S. ally Pakistan, which then lined up with China. The president thought he could win over both Pakistan and India and resolve their dispute over the territory of Kashmir, but he was wrong. Rusk had no such illusions. He opposed arms sales to Nehru, even though he valued India over Pakistan as an ally. Nehru's invasion of Portuguese Goa in 1961 had infuriated Rusk, who hated colonialism but despised blatant violations of the UN Charter even more. Nehru had benefited from a United Nations dominated by Third World countries, which had ignored his action. India and Pakistan remained at odds. Neither the application of Rusk's principles nor Kennedy's realism succeeded.

In Indonesia, in India, and throughout Asia, China became the focus of Rusk's campaign against communism. Russian expansionism had been checked by the containment doctrine. Now Mao assumed the role of aggressor. The Russians told Rusk as much in explaining the Sino-Soviet ideological split since 1959. China would "resort to overt aggression whenever its expansionist aims are thereby served," Rusk announced in 1963.[19] His diatribes against China grew more strident. Miffed by French recognition of the People's Republic, Rusk explained in 1964 that Beijing not only insisted that Taiwan surrender but also aimed to "extend its tactics of terror and subversion into Latin America and Africa."[20] Mao had become a modern-day Hitler. He had reacted in defiance to the Limited Nuclear Test-Ban Treaty of 1963 by exploding his own nuclear bomb. Rusk viewed China's atomic weapons as having more psychological effect than influence on the strategic balance, and he repeated that the United States had no aggressive designs against Mao. But history was clear; there would be no appeasement for this neo-Wilsonian.

Vietnam would be the classroom to teach this lesson. Rusk understood that Vietnamese revolutionary leader Ho Chi Minh, not Mao, led the revolution in this former French colony of Indochina. By late 1965 it was clear that China had backed away from assertive policies in Asia, as its assault on India and Communist takeover in Indonesia had failed. Even as U.S. bombing edged closer to the Chinese border, the People's Republic did not react. Mao had turned inward in 1966, launching his Cultural Revolution. Yet Rusk worried that once this internal reform program had ended, "a billion Chinese, armed with nuclear weapons," would stand united to carry

STILL TRYING TO SHOOT HIS WAY IN!

Because he viewed Mao Zedong as an aggressor, Rusk was determined to deny China membership in the United Nations. *Courtesy of* The Indianapolis Star-News

out "ideological adventurism abroad." Regardless of its own upheavals, the People's Republic was still considered host to the international Communist movement. Vietnam would serve as a launching pad for Chinese aggression throughout Asia and the world, or so Rusk feared.[21]

In his memoirs, Rusk acknowledged that some of the criticism he received for his "unimaginative Cold War approach to China" was deserved. He later applauded the reestablishment of diplomatic relations with Beijing. But he concluded that, during the 1960s, China "was a militant, aggressive power" that trained troops, arms, and agents in Southeast Asia. Chinese engineers were even reportedly building a road through neutral Laos to facilitate the movement of troops into Thailand. Given this perception of Chinese aggression, Rusk could see no alternative to honoring commitments to save South Vietnam from communism.[22]

Because Chinese aggression in Asia undermined Rusk's Wilsonian dreams for a stable peace, rule of law, order, and the UN system, he took an extreme anti-China stance. In other places in the periphery, he was concerned mainly that stability reign. Rusk did not want affairs in Africa and the Middle East to intrude on his European focus, superpower relations, Asia, and—to a lesser extent—Latin America. Circumstances in Africa and the Middle East were often so intricate and puzzling that he could hope for no more than to quell chaos. Liberal precepts were hard to apply in such conditions, and history gave him little guidance, for the United States had little experience in Africa and the Middle East.

In Asia, however, there was a history of U.S. involvement. There Rusk harbored grave apprehensions. Victory for the Vietnamese Communists would encourage Chinese expansionism, which could weaken the United Nations and eventually bring general nuclear war. As historian Warren Cohen has stated, there was much more to Rusk's view than mere containment. The United States had to prevent China from destroying "the world order to which he was committed."[23] Tiny Vietnam served as the warning light.

At stake in Vietnam was nothing less than the defeat of communism, so that the Cold War could end and the world could finally achieve the Wilsonian vision. Rusk never apologized for his role in Southeast Asia, for he truly believed in the reasons that led the United States to war there. He embarked on an inspired, resolute, and perilous mission to save a small nation from what he saw as outside aggression. In doing so, he also tried to save the world from communism and ultimate destruction. That ideological crusade would ruin a president and tarnish Rusk's reputation, yet it would never weaken his pursuit of liberal internationalism.

Notes

1. Dean Rusk, "American Republics Unite to Halt Spread of Communism in Western Hemisphere," *DSB* 46 (February 19, 1962): 271.

2. "Secretary Rusk Interviewed on NBC's 'Today' Program," *DSB* 48 (February 11, 1963): 204.

3. Dean Rusk, "The Age of the Rights of Man," *DSB* 49 (October 28, 1963): 657.

4. DROH IV, LBJL, 33.

5. Lindley, *The Winds of Freedom*, 222.

6. Schoenbaum, *Waging Peace*, 379.

7. DROH VII, JFKL, 338.

8. Dean Rusk, "Security Problems in Far East Areas," *DSB* 23 (November 15, 1950): 893.

9. Hearings before the Subcommittee on Immigration and Naturalization of the Senate Committee on the Judiciary, February 10, 1965, p. 50, Box 36, IV.D.1.b, Thomas Schoenbaum File, Dean Rusk Collection, UGA.

10. J. Robert Moskin, "Dean Rusk: Cool Man in a Hot World," *Look* 30 (September 6, 1966): 21.

11. Giglio, *Presidency of John F. Kennedy*, 229.

12. Thomas J. Noer, *Black Liberation: The United States and White Rule in Africa, 1948–1968* (Columbia: University of Missouri Press, 1985), 145.

13. Rusk, *As I Saw It*, 378.

14. H. W. Brands, *Into the Labyrinth: The United States and the Middle East, 1945–1993* (New York: McGraw-Hill, 1994), 116.

15. National Security Council (hereafter cited as NSC) meeting on the Middle East crisis, May 24, 1967, Box 36, IV.D.1.b, Thomas Schoenbaum File, Dean Rusk Collection, UGA.

16. Brands, *Wages of Globalism*, 211.

17. Giglio, *Presidency of John F. Kennedy*, 238.

18. Cohen, *Dean Rusk*, 209.

19. Ibid., 171.

20. Ibid., 282.

21. Ibid., 288.

22. Rusk, *As I Saw It*, 289.

23. Cohen, *Dean Rusk*, 289.

III

Applying Principles in Vietnam

6

Collective Security in Indochina

Perception was everything. In Rusk's analysis, China was an aggressor seeking to spread communism throughout Asia. That fear had driven the United States to isolate Mao. It would also lead to a tragic commitment in Vietnam, a former French colony about the size and shape of California. "There'd be peace in Asia if these Asian Communists were to live a normal life alongside of their neighbors there and leave them alone," Rusk argued repeatedly.[1] He was committed to aiding South Vietnam because the United States had treaty obligations to do so that backed up the containment doctrine. It was as simple as that. To the last, Rusk could not comprehend how the Communists could face down immense U.S. military pressure. He was certain why the United States had entered the fray, however. He was neither blindly optimistic about Vietnam nor ignorant of conditions there; he had qualms about intervention. Yet Rusk had no doubts about the sanctity of America's neo-Wilsonian mission of eradicating aggression and creating conditions for a liberal world order to take root.

Decades of Imperialism

Vietnam's history was replete with painful experiences with foreign invaders. The Chinese were a traditional enemy, but the Vietnamese suffered in the modern era under French colonialism. Beginning in the late 1880s, France administered the economy and political life by building an elitist bureaucracy that co-opted a traditional society. Eight percent of the Confucianist populace converted to Catholicism and dominated the civil service. Forced labor, social discrimination, and inadequate educational facilities typified French rule. Justice was often meted out in brutal fashion. Such arrogance and denigration spurred nationalist rebels to lash out at French imperialism.

The nationalists under Ho sought to destroy the regime and then industrialize the economy, reform the educational system, distribute land more evenly, and usher in democracy. During the First World War, this slight, wise, and benign-looking man searched for outside help to oust France from Vietnam. Ho joined the French Communist party in 1920, having been refused an audience with President Wilson at the Paris Peace Conference. Wilson had called for self-determination for all peoples, including those in European colonies, but he did not give Ho much thought. Ho, more a champion of the nationalist than Communist cause in Vietnam, grew disillusioned by the gradualist approach to independence advocated by socialists and democrats alike. He set his sights on revolution, convinced that France would not willingly leave Vietnam. For the next two decades, Ho lived in Russia and China, organizing a Vietnamese Communist party as the vehicle to creating the nation of Vietnam.

The Second World War temporarily expelled the French, but it did not end imperialism. The German defeat of France in 1940 liberated northern Vietnam from European rule, yet by the summer of 1941, Japan occupied the entire colony behind the facade of a French puppet regime. Ho united Communists and nationalists into the Vietminh—the League for the Independence of Vietnam—to fight the Japanese. Stationed in the China-Burma-India theater as chief of war plans for General Stilwell, Colonel Rusk aided the Vietminh guerrillas in their war against Japan, with arms and cigarettes. U.S. officers were impressed by the Vietminh effort. Like Rusk, they cared little about Ho's Communist credentials; they were bent instead on forcing the Japanese from the Asian mainland.

As Japan was pushed out of Southeast Asia, postwar planning began. Ominously, the Europeans demanded the return of their colonies in Asia. President Franklin Roosevelt publicly detested colonialism and sympathized with the nationalists. He suggested that the United Nations oversee the former colonies by creating trusteeships in which the international body would help prepare the way to nationhood. But his own Department of State, valuing relations with Europe above anticolonialism, lobbied for France's reclamation of Indochina. Roosevelt bowed to reality.

The military situation also undercut Roosevelt. In 1943 the British took command of Southeast Asia and allowed French agents and soldiers to return to Indochina the following year. As French parachutists landed in Vietnam, Colonel Rusk asked for a clarification of policy. Roosevelt refused, deferring the issue of independence until the end of the war. By then, he hoped, his idea of a trusteeship would take root. In 1945, Roosevelt acquiesced to naming France the sole trustee in Indochina, provided that Paris prepare the colony for ultimate independence. That concession, and the defeat of Japan, opened the way to French retrenchment.

The field was left to France and Ho's Vietminh. Indochina remained a remote issue for U.S. policymakers, who were preoccupied with Europe and soon the Soviets. President Truman, moreover, was less anticolonialist than Roosevelt. In any case the imperial powers thumbed their noses at U.S. insistence on independence for former colonies. American influence was limited by both the Europeans' position of prominence in Asia and the U.S. need to align them in the containment phalanx as the conflict with Stalin emerged. These constraints frustrated the idealistic Rusk, but he understood the need for compromise.

Aiding the French

The advent of the Cold War compelled the Vietminh to try and force out the French. In August 1945, Ho took advantage of a terrible famine, political instability, and the sudden collapse of Japan to accelerate his revolution. He also connected with U.S. intelligence officers who hinted at support. Vietminh General Vo Nguyen Giap led the insurrection, while the organization's congress asked the Americans—as the champions of democracy—for assistance. Ho urged the United States to block the French return, corral China, and advise on resource and industrial development.

Truman did not reply, but the Vietminh moved forward anyway, capturing the cities. In September 1945, before millions of cheering people in Hanoi, the Vietminh proclaimed the independent Democratic Republic of Vietnam. Ho then read the newly written Vietnamese declaration of independence, complete with references to the U.S. version sure to impress neo-Wilsonians like Rusk. He urged the allies to honor the principles of self-determination and equality enunciated in the UN Charter by recognizing his government.

Geopolitics prevented that course, and as the French gradually reclaimed positions in southern Vietnam, Ho grew frantic for recognition from the United States. Truman was busy with deteriorating

U.S.-Soviet relations. Above all, the State Department warned against weakening French prestige and power by taking an anticolonial stance. Dominated by Europeanists and worried about containing Soviet expansionism, the department placated France. Within a few years this approach would reap rewards in the containment of the Soviet Union in Europe. France became a member of the Marshall Plan in 1948 and of NATO a year later.

Rusk differed sharply from Secretary of State Acheson on matters of colonialism. Although national security made cooperation with France imperative, Rusk disagreed with his own department on Indochina. Acheson, he said, "really didn't give a damn about the brown, yellow, black, and red peoples of the world."[2] Characteristically, however, Rusk adapted, in this case to the Europe-first strategy of containment.

Although functional in Europe, containment was more problematic in Asia. Ho pushed onward, leading a relentless and ultimately successful guerrilla war against France from the end of 1946 until 1954. The United States faced unsavory choices, but the Cold War took precedence. Communism had to be contained. The administration pressed the French to end the war and begin reforms in Vietnam. Yet Truman would not back the Vietminh, regardless of their claims of nationalism, because Ho was a Communist. Aided increasingly by the United States, Paris persevered. Diverting Marshall Plan money to Indochina for the war, the French divided Indochina into three associated states: Laos, Cambodia, and Vietnam, all under the French Union. In 1949, Paris installed the former emperor, Bao Dai, as the titular head of the Republic of Vietnam, but France dominated the nation.

Neither France's military nor political efforts proved effective, and Ho's alarming success, together with the triumph of the Communist revolution in China in 1949, forced the United States to take a closer look at Indochina. In early 1950, China and the Soviet Union recognized the Democratic Republic of Vietnam under Ho's rule, and the stakes rose higher in Southeast Asia. U.S. military and economic aid sustained the French until 1954, financing nearly 80 percent of the war's cost.

Rusk cast aside his remaining anticolonial views during the Korean War. China's willingness to fight the U.S. Army in Korea warned of the "onset of a major Communist onslaught in Asia and perhaps beyond."[3] The weaknesses of independent Southeast Asian nations provoked aggressors. Indochina could "be absorbed into the new colonialism of a Soviet Communist Empire."[4] Chinese aid to Ho in 1951 and 1952 proved that, at the very least, Mao would send his minions into neighboring countries. Indochina was a natural target.

The issue of Indochina had now grown in prominence from a squabble over principles to a strategic marker in the Cold War. Undersecretary of State Rusk was convinced by 1950 that "Southeast Asia [was] in grave danger of Communist domination as a consequence of aggression from Communist China and of internal subversive activities."[5] He hoped to find alternatives to both communism and colonialism—the former, however, being the greater evil. What had happened to his liberalism, his anticolonialism? Rusk retained them, but in his calculations, Wilsonianism was at this time merely a theoretical construct in the context of real aggression. He had become a Cold War liberal in search of security first and global harmony later.

Nation Building

Because Indochina was linked to the Western alliance and because France's effort against Ho was failing, the United States stepped into the breach. In the spring of 1954 the Vietminh's General Giap routed French garrisons at Dien Bien Phu, a stunning defeat that induced France to prepare to withdraw from Indochina. Secretary of State Dulles was worried. To prevent Ho's forces from claiming Indochina, Dulles sought to unite nations of Southeast Asia, the western Pacific, and NATO. An Indochina controlled by Communists, he explained, could disrupt air and naval transport and communications routes between the Pacific and South Asia; threaten the Philippines, Australia, and New Zealand; and forestall access to valuable raw materials such as rubber and tin. Ho was cozying up to the Chinese expansionists. From his post at the Rockefeller Foundation, Rusk agreed with Dulles's assessment.

Unwilling to bail out the French with military support, the Eisenhower administration met with U.S. allies, the Indochinese principals, and the Communist powers to formulate the Geneva Accords in 1954. The agreement ended the war, extracted France from the region, and offered a political solution. Under the Geneva Accords, Vietnam was temporarily split in two. Ho's Democratic Republic of Vietnam, with a population of about sixteen million people, occupied the area north of the 17th parallel. The pro-U.S. Republic of Vietnam, based in Saigon, took the South and its fourteen million inhabitants. The division became permanent, and the

United States—never having signed the Accords—considered itself unbound by the agreement's call for national unification elections (which Ho certainly would have won). Instead, Eisenhower embarked on a program of nation building to create a viable State of Vietnam in the South.

Rusk viewed these decisions as fully defensible. After all, he argued, Ho had joined forces with the Russians and Chinese and wished to dominate neighboring Cambodia and Laos as well. But Rusk overlooked that China and the Soviet Union had joined to compel Ho's acceptance of the division of Vietnam. Beijing proved to be a rather inconsistent friend of the Vietnamese Communists, even competing with Ho for influence in Laos. Ho, believing that unification of Vietnam was possible, signed the Geneva agreement. He was, however, no lackey of the Chinese. Like Dulles, Rusk misconstrued the power alignment. That the United States had to prop up South Vietnam in anticipation of a showdown with the Sino-Soviet bloc was simply an illusion.

From the mid-1950s onward the most significant development was the U.S. commitment to South Vietnam. Truman (and Rusk) had shunned security treaties to defend the Asian mainland, because U.S. forces in the region were minimal and an American presence in Southeast Asia would be divisive. Dulles and Eisenhower disagreed. In 1955 they created SEATO, which united South Korea, Taiwan, Thailand, the Philippines, Laos, Cambodia, and South Vietnam under an American umbrella of collective security against communism.

The treaty was a mistake, lamented Rusk, for it legally obligated the United States to defend South Vietnam, interjecting the Americans into a regional security pact that should have been run by Asians themselves. Collective security was a hallmark of his support of the United Nations, but SEATO expanded the doctrine without due consideration for the extent to which the United States would be committed to fight. Nonetheless, after Dulles explained that the treaty defended South Vietnam from Ho, Congress ratified SEATO by an 82-to-1 margin.

Thereafter, Rusk saw no alternative to honoring the legal promise. Anything short of that commitment would be a bluff that could be called by the Communists, who might then view other security treaties as empty gestures. But like other foreign policy experts, Rusk misunderstood SEATO's terms. The treaty bound member nations to consult one another about aggression only within the parameters of their own political systems. As Eisenhower noted,

U.S. obligations depended on the ability of a South Vietnamese government to govern. Because protégé Ngo Dinh Diem, the leader of South Vietnam, did not perform, Eisenhower had every right to withhold aid. Tragically, neither he, nor Kennedy, nor Johnson did so. All of them interpreted the SEATO document in terms of halting communism in Vietnam. SEATO was a form of "deterrence," claimed Rusk. He took issue with the legal fine points, but the treaty expressed a "kind of thinking" about collective security that he cherished.[6] Despite his initial reservations, Rusk came to venerate the SEATO treaty, and that was a mistake.

With the alliance in place, Eisenhower set out to build the Republic of Vietnam and bolster the rule of Diem, who became prime minister in June 1954. Diem was reliant on support from U.S. politicians and administration planners for his rise to power. After consolidating power with his brother Ngo Dinh Nhu, Diem appeared to provide the elusive third way between colonialism and communism. Diem stirred false hopes. Based on their meetings with him during the two years he spent at a seminary in New Jersey, New York's Francis Cardinal Spellman, Senator John Kennedy, and other Catholics formed the American Friends of Vietnam to promote Diem's cause. Their effort succeeded with remarkable bipartisan ease. Although Diem was a remote, distrustful person bereft of charisma, adaptability, and political skills, he was nonetheless loyal to the anti-Communist crusade. Americans of all political stripes thus kept their fingers crossed, brushing aside his weaknesses in light of his Cold War credentials.

Diem presided over a country divided by political-religious-military sects that exercised control over various areas of South Vietnam. Ironically, the presence of these sects gave nation builders all the more reason to bolster him. There were many Catholics trapped in the Vietminh North, while the one million Catholics in South Vietnam were a distinct minority compared to the Buddhists. Drug dealers, businessmen, and military warlords collected taxes around Saigon. Refusing to include the sects in his government, Diem began a crackdown with CIA assistance in 1955. This action jettisoned any hopes for strengthening what had been his weak point all along: gaining popular support.

Confrontation with the various sects soured some Americans on Diem, but Eisenhower plowed on, for there was no democratic alternative. The support played into Diem's hands. Knowing that the Americans would not leave, he became even more rigid in dealing with internal affairs. Diem defeated the sects and then established the Republic of Vietnam with an army and national police. These forces went after the remaining Vietminh units in the South in a "Denounce the Communists" campaign that killed about one thousand Vietminh operatives and injured over forty-two hundred between 1954 and 1956. This conquest elicited acclaim from U.S. policymakers, who poured economic and military aid into Diem's treasury. It also deepened the U.S. commitment to a leader in Vietnam who would never build a stable political base.

South Vietnam's Ngo Dinh Diem talks with his civil guard during a "Denounce the Communists" campaign in 1955. *Courtesy of the National Archives of the United States, USIS*

The Americans pointed to progress in nation building. From 1956 to 1960, rubber, sugar, and electrical output rose. A new textile industry emerged, while per capita income in South Vietnam increased by 20 percent. Diem built thousands of new schools with an enrollment of 1.5 million children, up from 400,000 in previous years. Village health clinics numbered about 3,500, roads were repaired, and three new highways were built. Land reform schemes even created 123,000 new small landowners. Communists envied these gains, claimed Rusk.

But Diem's political ambitions undermined economic progress. He soon returned control to the exploitive landlord-gentry class in the countryside and installed his Catholic Can Lao party in positions of power, alienating the peasants and non-Catholics who constituted the majority of the nation. They addressed their grievances to the Vietminh. Casting aside hopes for unification through elections, the remaining Communists in the South began a guerrilla war in 1959 and then created the NLF, which organized the revolt. The NLF, later called the Vietcong by the Americans, attracted the hesitant Ho in Hanoi, who also gave up on peaceful reconciliation and soon dispatched North Vietnamese soldiers to fight with the Vietminh cadres against Diem's army.

Like most experts, Rusk misperceived the situation. He believed that Ho had launched a revolution to overthrow Diem. But the rebellion had begun in the South. There the NLF were joined by a number of sects, peasants, and other victims of Diem's ruthless rule. By 1961, 80 percent of South Vietnam's villages had joined the Vietcong, forcing Diem to rely on U.S. aid when he could no longer collect taxes from the countryside. As Rusk took office as secretary of state in January 1961, civil war convulsed South Vietnam. He and his new boss endorsed the containment paradigm in Asia. Kennedy had criticized the French for their colonial blunders, but, presuming the strategic importance of Vietnam, he had earlier called South Vietnam the "finger in the dike" holding back "the red tide of Communism" in Asia.[7] Backing Diem was "a test of American responsibility and determination."[8] Kennedy took these Cold War views to the White House, despite his growing reservations about Diem.

Kennedy and Laos

Goaded by Moscow and Beijing's belligerent talk of wars of national liberation, Kennedy readied for confrontation in the periphery. His priorities included Cuba, the Congo, Laos, and Vietnam, although Cuba drew most of his attention. In Southeast Asia, Laos preoccupied the experts at first. Briefing Kennedy, Eisenhower warned that the situation there merited full regard. Laotian rebels, receiving aid from the Soviets, were gaining the upper hand over neutrals and moderates (who got assistance from the United States). A defeat, Eisenhower warned, would open Southeast Asia to Communist penetration. Eisenhower noted that Laos could ask for military intervention as a member of SEATO, or negotiations could lead to the creation of a coalition government of all parties. The retiring president was clear in his conviction, however, that Laos was a Cold War battleground that the Free World could ill afford to lose. The peaceful people of Laos were being exploited from all sides, and their neighbors such as the Thais feared that the United States would not stem the Communist advance.

With allies in Laos on the run and neutralists leaning toward the Communists, Kennedy decided on a middle course between military action and no action. The "more we looked," explained

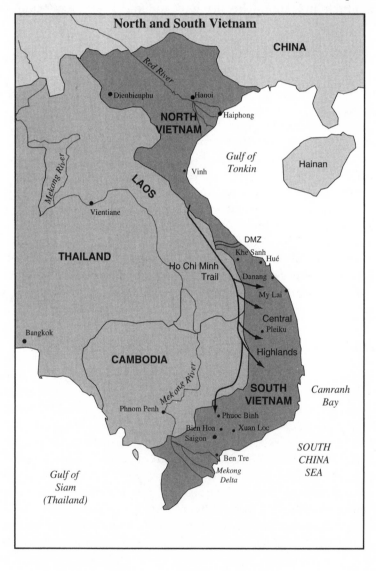

Secretary Rusk, "the more forbidding was the prospect of landing American troops" in this landlocked nation with harsh terrain. Moreover, the Laotian army was weak, the people too passive to fight. The Kennedy administration preferred a political arrangement to build an "island of peace" in the region—a neutral, independent Laos.[9] The Laotians, overseen by the Americans, British, Soviets, and Chinese, gathered in Geneva to talk.

The Geneva meetings of 1961–62 resulted in neutralization. Prime Minister Souvanna Phouma would head a coalition government. As the Soviet, not the American, choice, Souvanna Phouma, in the eyes of Rusk and Kennedy, amounted to a concession on their part. Consequently, Rusk issued a communiqué on March 6, 1962, to Thai Foreign Minister Thanat Khoman, announcing, "The United States regards the preservation of the independence and integrity of Thailand as vital to the national interest of the United States and to world peace."[10] This declaration of collective security served to comfort Thailand, which worried that China and North Vietnam might exploit a weak Laos. Although the Laotian settlement provided the president with a solution to one problem in Southeast Asia, it did not quell criticism from his opponents. Republicans abhorred the deal, and, because of his slim victory in the 1960 presidential election and his apparent lack of force at the Bay of Pigs, Kennedy was vulnerable to their attacks. Still, neutralization seemed the best alternative.

The United States honored Laos's neutrality agreement until the North Vietnamese violated it. Ho used Laotian territory as an infiltration route into South Vietnam and refused to let Souvanna Phouma govern in key areas. "The tragic part of the whole thing," Rusk later declared, was that the Geneva deal was a "fine agreement," but "we got no performance on that agreement from the North Vietnamese—not for a single day."[11] Communist violations of the Accords led Rusk, reluctantly, to endorse covert U.S. activity in Laos. That development bitterly disappointed him, again demonstrating the tension between his idealism and realism. Seemingly, his dream of peace could be achieved only by an unbending application of the tough strategic doctrine of containment. That Rusk would put aside Wilsonian legalism revealed his profound fear of communism in Southeast Asia.

Ironically, the Communist bloc was rife with competitive divisions. Ho vied with Mao for influence over the Pathet Lao Communists. Mao signaled his widening rift with the Russians by walking out of the Twenty-second Congress of the Soviet Communist Party in October 1961. Meanwhile, China had shown little interest in the Vietcong rebellion against Diem. Even as Kennedy decided to act in Vietnam, Ho's benefactors in Beijing and Moscow were cautious. They sent supplies to North Vietnam but preferred to stand by and let the indigenous NLF revolution run its course.

With Laos neutralized, however, Kennedy—refusing to concede any additional territory to communism—prosecuted the Cold War in Vietnam. The Berlin and Congo crises were escalating. In Vienna in June 1961, Khrushchev trumpeted his support for Third World wars of national liberation as he tried to intimidate Kennedy over Berlin. The rhetoric betrayed reality; the Russians were not patrons of Southeast Asian rebels. Yet history, ideology, prestige, honor, and domestic politics drove Kennedy and Rusk.

Noted for his can-do approach to foreign policy, Kennedy took up the challenge. And why not? A superpower boasting a high-tech military, the United States had suppressed rebellions in the Philippines, held off communism in Korea, and protected such clients as Taiwan. Saving South Vietnam seemed an easier task than all of these. When compared with the chaotic political circumstances in Laos, Vietnam—guided by U.S. advisers—seemed more amenable to intervention than to neutralization.

During the Laos talks in Geneva in 1962, Rusk told Soviet Foreign Minister Andrei Gromyko that the United States would not accept the destruction of South Vietnam by outsiders. As Rusk explained, the cease-fire in Laos had been obtained, but Vietnam posed a more dangerous problem. Guerrillas were infiltrating a free country; the number had doubled to 12,800 from 1961–62. This was not a war of national liberation but a "gangster war of terror and intimidation," he announced to the public in March 1962.[12] "If we have to fight for Southeast Asia," Rusk declared, "we'll fight in South Vietnam," a country much more accessible to U.S. military forces than Laos. "Diplomacy had not worked" there, he angrily claimed. And with North Vietnamese troops and rebels "on the march" in the South—"prepared to shoot at all who stood in their way"—the administration was determined to support Diem to the end.[13]

All of the Kennedy men who subsequently claimed that their boss would never have gone to war in Vietnam were wrong, Rusk later argued. They chose to ignore the president's steadfast ambition to contain communism in Vietnam. Rusk's criticism is persuasive; Kennedy made decisions regarding Laos and Vietnam that set the scene for Johnson's disastrous war and Rusk's complicity in it.

Counterinsurgency

According to CIA operative Edward Lansdale, the situation in South Vietnam required emergency treatment. Having helped suppress the Filipino insurgency of the 1950s, he was an expert on such matters. Lansdale reported that Diem would face repeated coup attempts—even from non-Communist forces. The autocrat was unwilling to share power; worse yet, he was unable to root out his foes. The NLF seized most of the countryside in 1961, winning the allegiance of the people. Vietcong successes put Diem, nation building, and U.S. security in jeopardy. Kennedy would have to send more than limited assistance.

By expanding aid, in 1961 Kennedy shifted from defense to offense. He ordered a 50,000-man increase in Diem's army, hiked the number of U.S. personnel to train the soldiers, put 400 Green Berets (U.S. Special Forces commandos drilled especially to fight rebels) in charge of 9,000 border tribesmen to block infiltration routes, and authorized CIA commando raids against Hanoi. South Vietnam's civil guard, based in the provinces, was armed with heavy weapons. American aid to Diem jumped to over $250 million per year.

Diplomatically, Kennedy prodded SEATO to announce that the rebels, helped by outside aggressors, would not be permitted to topple Diem. He also warned Khrushchev at the Vienna Summit to back away from the NLF. Nonetheless, intelligence reports in mid-1961 showed that the Vietcong were gaining. Rusk admitted that the United States was not succeeding in countering the guerrillas; by the end of the year they had killed four thousand of Diem's own officials. The administration continued to look for answers but confronted a deteriorating situation in South Vietnam and resistance from Diem.

Visiting Saigon in May 1961, Vice President Johnson presented Kennedy's plans to Diem, who welcomed the aid but ignored calls to reform his bureaucracy, extend land reform, and broaden the base of his government. He sought assistance minus U.S. control. Stubbornness on Diem's part was understandable, given America's unqualified past support. But Johnson refused to permit such free rein; like most officials, he feared a duplication of the French experience. Yet the United States was stuck; partnership with Diem seemed the only way to contain communism.

If Diem could not be persuaded or forced to reform, other alternatives were necessary. Counterinsurgency was one idea. In this tactic for fighting the guerrillas in rural areas, the Green Berets were an element and strategic hamlets were the key. Strategic hamlets, which had proven successful against Filipino rebels during the mid-1950s, were villages protected behind barbed-wire fences and guarded by the Green Berets, the South Vietnamese army, and the civil guard. The goal was to isolate villages from the NLF, arm the inhabitants for self-defense, and win their loyalty to Diem by providing medical services, schools, and land reform.

One problem, however, was the very unpopular move of forcing peasants out of their ancestral homes and villages, which were often burned down. The other problem was Diem, who put his corrupt brother, Nhu, in charge. Nhu set up makeshift strategic hamlets in remote areas to impress the Americans; then he horded the money allocated for the peasants and used it to control the villagers. Of the eighty-six hundred hamlets that Nhu created beginning in 1962, only 20 percent met U.S. standards. Over 80 percent fell into the hands of the Vietcong within a year. Not surprisingly, disgruntled peasants increasingly fled to the NLF.

By the end of 1961 many counterinsurgency measures were in force. The Defense Department and National Security Council, however, advocated a more concerted and direct way to defend Diem: American troops. Such escalation was a gambit that could lead to war and even superpower conflict. In October 1961, Kennedy sent General Maxwell Taylor, his military adviser, and National Security Council member Walt Rostow to examine the dismal situation in South Vietnam.

After hearing Diem's request for U.S. troops, Taylor and Rostow suggested that Kennedy send helicopter pilots and commit 8,000 combat troops disguised as a flood-control team. More such military "advisers" might be necessary, warned Taylor. Approving the plan, National Security Adviser McGeorge Bundy and the CIA's Edward Lansdale added that the deployment of 5,000 to 25,000 combat troops would be necessary. The Joint Chiefs of Staff and Secretary of Defense McNamara went even further. They called for the introduction of a U.S. task force of 40,000 regulars to fight the NLF and another 165,000 if China and North Vietnam intervened. Taylor and Rostow had advocated a small mission; other officials considered a more dramatic escalation.

Supporters of counterinsurgency expressed their skepticism. Ambassador to India John Kenneth Galbraith and Senator Mansfield argued that Americanizing the war would draw the nation into a losing battle. Only political and social reforms by Diem would succeed. Undersecretary of State Bowles proposed a neutralization scheme similar to the one devised for Laos, but Kennedy would not have it. George Ball, soon to take Bowles's spot, wanted to end the commitment to Diem altogether.

Rusk also questioned the wisdom of sending troops to prop up the ineffective Diem, who ignored advice from U.S. commanders and lacked the ability to coordinate a vigorous effort against the Communists. Furthermore, sending troops might upset the negotiations over Laos then under way, prompt Ho to step up infiltration into the South, and distract attention from the Berlin crisis. Worse yet, China might be provoked into war. "While attaching greatest possible importance to the security of Southeast Asia," Rusk cabled Kennedy, "I would be reluctant to see the United States make major additional commitments of American prestige to a losing horse."[14] Rusk thus opposed Americanization of the war, at least before the president had sufficient time to weigh the consequences.

Still, Rusk confessed that he was no dove, or advocate of withdrawal, on the question of Vietnam. He backed America's ally. The loss of South Vietnam would undercut U.S. credibility, destroying SEATO and confirming to right-wingers at home that Kennedy was weak. Honoring obligations—a fundamental element of Rusk's belief system—was at stake. Honor was "not an empty eighteenth-century concept," he explained, but "a matter of deepest concern to the life and death of our nation. When the president of the United States makes a commitment, it is vitally important that what he says is believed."[15] It was crucial to U.S. credibility in Asia and worldwide, a concept that became an end in itself during the Vietnam War. This position represented neo-Wilsonian logic to Rusk. The United States had to honor collective security treaties in the face of aggression. Vietnam tested resolve but also legal agreements, integrity, and the American word. Because security treaties were really "pillars of peace in a dangerous world," when Kennedy and Johnson decided to stop the forceful takeover of Vietnam, Rusk "felt we had to make good on that pledge."[16] International law required it.

Rusk drew on historical analogies to drive home this point. He referred to Pearl Harbor and the crisis of June 1950 when the South Koreans were nearly pushed off the peninsula by the Communists. "Having lived through dark times before, I was not willing to yield to pessimism in Vietnam just because the outlook was bleak."[17] Faith in collective security would see the United States and South Vietnam through this crisis.

Conscious of his role as the president's top foreign policy adviser, however, Rusk wanted Kennedy's recognition of the gravity of sending ground troops. Although Rusk advocated sending advisers undisguised to show the honorable policy of intervention, he approved the Taylor-Rostow advice. In exchange, Kennedy must insist that Diem take measures to defeat the insurgents. Vietnam was too important to lose. Kennedy accepted the Taylor-Rostow report and prepared to escalate U.S. intervention in South Vietnam and perhaps even make ready for forays into the North. No close adviser or bureaucratic heavyweight seriously considered withdrawing from South Vietnam and letting the Communists overrun the country. Rusk was on board, for in his view global peace and security were at stake.

Thus, the United States, although unhappy with Diem, had become his patron. National security concerns, founded on a fear that communism would destroy the Wilsonian mission, drove the United States deeper into Diem's quagmire. Rusk was no cheerleader for Diem, but in his estimate there was no alternative to supporting South Vietnam. The perceptive Rusk misread conditions, however. He erroneously held that an international Communist conspiracy was behind the rebellion against Diem. He repeatedly claimed that if East Germany went after West Germany or North Korea after South Korea, neither conflict would be called a civil war. So why refer to North Vietnamese aggression against South Vietnam as such? Yet in reality, neither Hanoi nor the Sino-Soviet bloc had been behind the NLF uprising, at least at the start. To be sure, Vietminh cadres in the South had been in touch with the northern leadership, but they had taken the initiative against Diem. South Vietnam had faced a civil war that turned into an international conflict when the United States opted for nation building and containment and when Hanoi, with Russian and Chinese support, had begun to send soldiers and supplies across the 17th parallel.

Furthermore, Rusk—driven by Kennedy—was too rigid. He had experimented in Laos but gave neutralization in Vietnam, which would have extracted Kennedy from Diem's clutches, little consideration. Moreover, sticking to the legal framework of the SEATO arrangements left the United States no room to maneuver, even though the treaty allowed more flexibility than Rusk thought. Finally, Rusk's historical analogies were forced; Vietnam was simply a different case from Munich, Pearl Harbor, and Korea. Rusk was usually correct in his assessments of conflict. He was measured in his response to enemies. But like other Kennedy advisers, he threw the blanket of containment over Southeast Asia. What had begun as a colonial war for independence became a major issue in the Cold War. Vietnam grew out of all proportion to its importance to American security.

The U.S. objective of containment was sound, but the means of pursuing it in Southeast Asia were not. Rusk placed Vietnam in the context of a great battle for universal truths of collective security, self-determination, and legal resolution of conflict. That was a laudable and justified position. But because policymakers were incautious, uninformed, a bit arrogant, and inclined to overstate the Communist threat in Vietnam, they were sucked into a commitment to Diem. And because Diem was a losing proposition, the United States would soon be chastised severely.

Notes

1. DROH III, LBJL, 13.
2. Rusk, *As I Saw It*, 422.
3. Ibid., 424.
4. Dean Rusk, "Underlying Principles of Far Eastern Policy," *DSB* 25 (November 19, 1951): 823.
5. Robert D. Schulzinger, *A Time for War: The United States and Vietnam, 1941–1975* (New York: Oxford University Press, 1997), 42.
6. DROH I, JFKL, 25.
7. Schulzinger, *A Time for War*, 89.
8. Lawrence J. Bassett and Stephen E. Pelz, "The Failed Search for Victory: Vietnam and the Politics of War," in Paterson, *Kennedy's Quest for Victory*, 226.
9. Rusk, *As I Saw It*, 428, 429.
10. Timothy N. Castle, *At War in the Shadow of Vietnam: U.S. Military Aid to the Royal Lao Government, 1955–1975* (New York: Columbia University Press, 1995), 51.
11. DROH I, JFKL, 14.
12. Dean Rusk, "America's Goal—A Community of Free Nations," *DSB* 46 (March 19, 1962): 448.
13. Rusk, *As I Saw It*, 430.
14. Ibid., 432.
15. Ibid., 436.
16. Ibid., 435–36.
17. Ibid., 435.

7

Sink or Swim

From Kennedy to Johnson

Although he had his reservations, on November 22, 1961, President Kennedy decided to fulfill much of the Taylor-Rostow request, and the United States forged deeper into Vietnam. Kennedy did not want to stir up domestic criticism; the influential Senator Richard Russell, chairman of the Armed Services Committee, for example, had spoken out against involvement. Kennedy also did not want to send soldiers to Asia while he focused on Berlin. "And the United Nations provided no help; Communist aggression in this situation was not as clear as it had been in Korea. The United States would go it largely alone in South Vietnam. Still, major advisers—the Joint Chiefs, McNamara, and Rusk—urged Kennedy on. If Diem took the offensive while broadening his political base, the United States should supply more military assistance. The crucial assumption was that Diem would and could honor his side of the bargain if he had support. This faith inexorably Americanized the struggle in Vietnam, in which U.S. soldiers took over the fighting.

Kennedy and Diem

With Rusk's complicity, Kennedy promoted Diem's cause. However, fearing that the move would anger Congress, heighten North Vietnam's infiltration, and incite the Chinese to respond with their own soldiers, the president stopped short of sending regular troops. But the amount of economic aid and the number of military, intelligence, and political advisers rose dramatically. Air reconnaissance, transport, and helicopter support increased. The

Americans told Diem to mobilize to a war footing, expel cronies from the government, and free his generals to act independently.

Diem was uncooperative. Complaining that Saigon was being treated as a protectorate, he refused advice. Because officers had tried to overthrow him in 1960 and had bombed his palace in February 1962, he would not give his generals any leeway. Similar qualms caused his unwillingness to broaden his government to include political sects. He accepted counterinsurgency measures, but, like the strategic hamlets program, they came up short. Diem refused to consider the necessary major reforms. Because Kennedy would not push his purportedly independent ally, their partnership was on Diem's terms, and Diem kept leverage over U.S. designs. Rusk's hope that Diem could be transformed into an efficient and popular leader soon faded.

To be sure, the Americans exuded confidence. Now, the South Vietnamese-U.S. team took to the offensive, supplied by 300 military aircraft and 11,000 U.S. military personnel by the end of 1962. General Paul Harkins (overseeing the military assistance program) believed that strategic hamlets would hold the villages while U.S. advisers and the South Vietnamese army defeated Communist forces through the use of superior air mobility. Indeed, Rusk told journalists that Saigon was "on the initiative," although Americans should keep in mind that the conflict was "a dirty, untidy, disagreeable war."[1] In 1962, in various attempts to deny cover and food to the NLF guerrillas, American pilots dropped napalm (gasoline bombs) and defoliants on Vietcong strongholds and on crops. The destruction by high-tech weapons belied the fact that the South Vietnamese army had made no permanent inroads on Vietcong dominance in the countryside. The incompetence of Diem's forces and the adaptability of the rebels hampered the war effort.

The South Vietnamese army had been instructed in conventional, not guerrilla, warfare. Most officers holed up in their garrisons while poorly trained units went into battle. Unable to speak the language, U.S. advisers could neither mobilize nor command the troops. Air strikes also proved detrimental to the cause. In January 1962, American pilots hit the village of Binh Hoa, killing five civilians, including three children. Rusk recognized the fact that the suffering imposed on an ostensibly friendly populace could hardly garner the people's support for Diem's government. He could only hope that the operations would quickly persuade the rebels to end their war.

Rusk's hope was soon dashed, however. At one time, NLF rebels had fled from helicopters in terror. Now they attacked government forces and then either disappeared or moved their machine guns into trees as cover to reduce their visibility from the air. The rebels also stood their ground. In October 1962 they killed or wounded most of a forty-man platoon of South Vietnamese soldiers near the town of My Tho and shot down five helicopters full of reinforcements. Even U.S. bombing did not cause panic. The Vietcong remained in their foxholes before retreating in an organized fashion.

From a military perspective the situation was not desperate. The Department of Defense claimed that the NLF casualty rate and the rise in strategic hamlets (however untenable) evidenced progress. As McNamara reported after visiting Vietnam in 1962, "Every quantitative measurement we have shows we are winning the war."[2] Unfortunately, he was fooling himself, the president, and Rusk, who read the military assessments every morning. A former tank commander, General Harkins cared mainly about the destruction of the enemy's military capabilities, not social and political reform. With Diem refusing to allow peasants to govern themselves or pay lower rents, they turned to the rebels, and strategic hamlets failed. By mid-1963 only fifteen hundred of the eighty-five hundred guarded villages were free from the Vietcong. Notably, forty-two of South Vietnam's forty-four provinces were paying taxes to the NLF. Diem was not in control.

The massive aid from the United States, however, signaled to Diem that he could go after his critics with impunity. In the fall of 1962 he expelled U.S. journalists who had called him a dictator and had exposed the failures of the strategic hamlets program. Diem proceeded to ban distribution of *Newsweek* magazine. He also managed to alienate the educated ranks and military personnel and terrorize the Buddhist majority. Ambassador Frederick Nolting warned Diem that U.S. public opinion would sour on his regime, but he refused to change his ways. Although Rusk was disgusted by Diem's intolerance, the State Department—preoccupied with the Cuban missile crisis—took no official action.

Such critics as Galbraith, Bowles, and Mansfield warned Kennedy that he was being sucked into Diem's war and could only lose. Kennedy listened, but he had Cuban missiles to worry about. Early in 1963 he sent Roger Hilsman of the State Department and White House aide Michael Forrestal to Vietnam. Although these junior officials found the U.S. effort in disarray, they perceived a glimmer of hope if the administration would toughen up on Diem. The Joint Chiefs chimed in that U.S. advisers might soon come home; victory was possible.

Such wishful thinking made negotiation pointless. In July 1962, as negotiator Averell Harriman brokered the deal in Laos, he offered Ho a similar neutralization arrangement. North Vietnam responded that all U.S. advisers must first exit the South. A cease-fire would then precede the formation of a coalition government including Diem and the Vietcong, and unification elections would follow. When Harriman balked, the NLF eliminated the demand for U.S. withdrawal. But the United States turned aside this plan just as it had done with the 1954 Geneva agreement. Elections, the administration feared, would bring Ho to power over a unified Vietnam. They would also afford the United States a chance to cut its losses and get out, but Kennedy wanted victory and Rusk sought to defend South Vietnam.

Rusk made a futile attempt to coax help from allies. Britain, with its troubles in Malaysia, was in no position to assist. The French urged the United States, as they had years before, to abandon the fight. Europeans, lamented Rusk, cared only about themselves. Yet even SEATO allies recoiled. Pakistan was occupied with India; New Zealand and Australia begged off because of political difficulties. There would be no Wilsonian collective security in Vietnam.

The Fall of Diem

"The spearpoint of aggression has been blunted in Viet-Nam," Kennedy told the nation in January 1963.[3] Positive signs were evident. The ratio of South Vietnamese-to-Vietcong casualties had fallen, more enemy arms had been captured and fewer friendly weapons had been lost, the armed forces had been reorganized, and the strategic hamlets program had been extended. These assessments belied actual circumstances, however. Bad news arrived from the battlefield. In January 1963, at Ap Bac in the Mekong Delta south of Saigon, outnumbered Vietcong troops had defeated Diem's army despite assistance from U.S. helicopters and armored personnel carriers. The NLF had even fought this battle out in the open, abandoning guerrilla warfare. As journalists looked on, three American military advisers were killed, the South Vietnamese suffered heavy casualties, and five helicopters were lost. Reporting the defeat, journalists raised the first questions at home about the confident predictions of victory. Ap Bac was a sign of impending disaster.

Still, the generals continued to pass rosy judgments, and Rusk, who depended on them for information, had to believe them. In February 1963, countering a reporter's claim that the United States had a no-win policy, Rusk retorted that Diem was "turning the corner." In April he maintained that the Communist threat had "been brought under control," although it was "going to be a long and tough and frustrating and mean war." Drawing on history, he concluded that the guerrilla war could be won, just as insurgents in Greece, Turkey, Malaya, Burma, and the Philippines had been defeated by the Free World.[4] Rusk had taken on the role that he would assume for the next six years: point man for fielding criticism of administration policy in Vietnam.

In this role Rusk often sounded like an ideologue rather than the circumspect adviser that he was. This was not civil war; it was "aggression organized, directed, and partly supplied from North Viet-Nam" and China, warned Rusk. Tyranny was on the move, and this neo-Wilsonian lashed out at those who did not perceive Vietnam as "a battle to the end between freedom and coercion."[5] This rhetoric was quite dramatic for the normally composed Rusk, who had cast his lot with the hawks. Even more shocking was that he genuinely believed his analysis, although it is only fair to note that in private he counseled against precipitating a major struggle in Vietnam. He also expressed concern about internal political problems in South Vietnam as he lauded the military situation. The purpose of Rusk's boasts was to cover political failures in South Vietnam and back up Kennedy. The nation, he knew, was in desperate straits. Diem was faltering, and North Vietnamese infiltration of men and weapons, although not at levels seen in 1962, continued.

Diem forced the administration to turn on him. He cracked down on the Buddhists, who disapproved of his Catholic family and who had defied a ban on flying religious banners imposed by his brother, the archbishop of Hue. On May 8, 1963, Diem's army fired on demonstrating Buddhists, killing nine and wounding dozens of bystanders. Buddhists stepped up the protests against their persecution. In a horrifying act of desperation, on June 11 an elderly monk doused himself with gasoline at an intersection in downtown Saigon and burned himself to death. Television film and photographs captured the grisly images for an international audience. An eighteen-year-old girl then tried to cut off her left hand as a sacrifice to the cause. Students took to the streets in Saigon and elsewhere to denounce Diem's dictatorship and oppression. More immolations followed. Shocked Americans, officials and the public alike, urged Diem to appease the Buddhists. When Diem's sister-in-law welcomed an immolation in August 1963 as a "barbecue," Rusk was revolted.The U.S. government could stand no more. Diem promised reconciliation, but he never delivered. Instead, he declared martial law, and his brother's police forces raided Buddhist pagodas in Hue and Saigon, arresting and killing monks.

The U.S. embassy in Saigon went to work. Ambassador Henry Cabot Lodge, a Republican, had been sent in August to replace the pro-Diem Nolting and pressure Diem to reform. Lodge unearthed a plot by South Vietnamese generals to overthrow the government, which Kennedy and Rusk uncomfortably welcomed, but the plan was aborted in late August out of the fear that Diem had uncovered it. Diem and Kennedy were now clearly at odds; Diem suspected U.S. collusion in the plot. Diem's "darker instincts," explained Rusk, had become the dominant element of his leadership.[6]

During several television interviews in the fall, the president denounced Diem as an obstacle in the war and urged him to remove his brother, the security chief. Looking ahead to reelection in 1964, Kennedy worried that U.S. involvement in Vietnam could play into Republican hands. Inaction would heighten press coverage that might judge his policy ineffective. But the GOP would brand him a warmonger if he sent combat troops. Dramatic escalation and defeat were both unacceptable; each would place Vietnam in the political limelight and boost hard-line Republicans. Kennedy began to isolate Diem.

Rusk monitored plans for another coup d'état. Ambassador Lodge was more complicit, however, remaining noncommittal with Diem about a U.S. rescue in the event of an overthrow. This time the generals acted. On November 1, 1963, they killed Diem and his brother Nhu and installed their own leader. Rusk blamed Diem's repressive policies for his downfall. The assassination reverberated in Washington; Vice President Johnson saw the coup as a mistake. Rusk hoped that the new leader, General Duong Van Minh, would elicit support.

Such optimism was more whimsy. Neither Minh's brief tenure nor his numerous successors were improvements. Some were incompetent, others tainted by collaboration with the French. As Buddhist and student protests persisted, the United States continued to recommend reforms in agriculture, health, and education to a revolving door of governments unable to effect change. Americans soon reeled from their own tragedy: on November 22, 1963, three weeks after Diem was killed, President Kennedy was assassinated in Dallas. He bequeathed a Vietnam war to Lyndon Johnson, his successor.

Although friends, staff, and filmmakers have claimed that if he had lived, Kennedy would have pulled out of Vietnam after his reelection, many historians and others, Rusk among them, believed that assessment to be false. "I talked with John Kennedy on hundreds of occasions about Southeast Asia," recalled Rusk, "and not once did he ever suggest or even hint at withdrawal."[7] If Kennedy had made this decision, Rusk would have known about it. And no president would leave Americans in a combat zone for political reasons. The clincher in response to the apologist view is that Kennedy gave ample evidence of his intentions. In September 1963 he spoke of his "very simple policy" on Vietnam. "We want the war to be won, the Communists to be contained, and the Americans to go home," he said. He was "not there to see a war lost."[8] His undelivered speech on the day he died pointed to Southeast Asia as a place where Americans could not weary of the task of fighting for freedom. Contrary to opposing myths, Kennedy would have defended South Vietnam.

The president's commitment had not yielded positive results. By the time of his death he had sent 16,000 advisers and instigated a grueling, dirty war involving the use of napalm and defoliants, helicopter raids, and attrition tactics. One hundred advisers had been killed by the time Johnson took office. Kennedy had come to rely on military solutions to a sociopolitical problem. Worse still, he had so raised the profile of Vietnam that Johnson found withdrawal impossible. Staying the course would not work; running out would call into question U.S. credibility in terms of upholding security treaties the world over. Johnson determined to fulfill Kennedy's mission in Vietnam.

Kennedy, Johnson, and Rusk understood the risks in Vietnam, but they focused on the perceived stakes. Those stakes—lives, prestige, politics, and principles—would rise during the Johnson years, when U.S. soldiers finally went to war in Southeast Asia. Yet confidence in the liberal outlook held. As Rusk asserted, people around the globe trusted the United States: "Most of them want the kind of world we want—not because we want it but because they want it too."[9] His neo-Wilsonian mission still focused on serving that wish.

Lyndon Johnson Takes Over

Top officials were in the air, returning from a meeting in Honolulu where they had heard encouraging reports about Vietnam, when they learned of Kennedy's death. The ranking cabinet member present, Rusk asked the others aboard for their views on global problems. Upon landing in Washington, he advised Johnson to preserve continuity in foreign policy. In his first national speech the new president announced that the United States would "keep its commitments, from South Vietnam to West Berlin."[10] That mission held Rusk at Johnson's side for four years.

Johnson kept abreast of foreign affairs. As vice president, he had traveled abroad, attended National Security Council meetings, and been briefed by a Foreign Service officer assigned as a courtesy by Rusk. The secretary of state credited Johnson, not Kennedy, with a high level of performance in such areas as aid and development. Johnson's effectiveness was due to both his persuasive abilities and his determination to see a decision through to the end. Johnson passionately sought his goals. These "were large and bold. He didn't think in small terms. He thought in the most far-reaching terms," noted Rusk. Fighting poverty, urging forward civil rights, maintaining the commitment in Vietnam—"these were matters that came not just out of his mind but out of his heart and soul."[11] Nobody more fervently defended this liberal agenda than Rusk.

With their shared heritage, Rusk and Johnson developed a close relationship. They were the same generation; Johnson was six months Rusk's senior. Both had been raised in southern poverty, and they competed endlessly and good-naturedly over who had been poorer. Rusk paid frequent visits to the Johnson ranch in Texas, where they once laughed at the sight of the sort of metal bedpan both had used as children. Familiarity bred openness between the usually reserved Rusk and the outgoing Johnson.

Both had also felt the pain of being scorned as outsiders by the Kennedy inner circle. Johnson ridiculed the insiders as aloof intellectuals. Many of those acolytes espoused policies that Kennedy would never have accepted. After his death, however, they touted these positions as key elements of Camelot that the Johnson-Rusk team had sullied. Rusk referred to these people—Arthur Schlesinger, Bobby Kennedy—as "frivolous."[12] Read President Kennedy's inaugural address, he demanded; it put enemies on notice that the United States would defend its interests. That was the real John

Kennedy, the one who had lived through crises since the 1930s, just as Rusk had. Johnson appreciated that demythologized appraisal.

Johnson developed great trust in Rusk. When the secretary of state indicated his desire to resign at the end of 1964, Johnson begged him to remain, as a friend, adviser, and compatriot. Rusk earned the president's highest esteem. According to Johnson, he was a "loyal, honorable, hard-working, imaginative man of conviction," a friend who "stood by me and shared the President's load of responsibility and abuse."[13] Rusk viewed his association with President Kennedy as professionally close, but he was a personal intimate to Johnson. Unlike Kennedy, Johnson did not sidestep Rusk in foreign policy deliberations; instead, he elevated the State Department to a key decision-making position. Johnson preferred a bureaucratic style of leadership. He initiated Tuesday lunches with advisers that propelled Rusk into prominence. Rusk began to formulate and execute policy, helping Johnson with diplomacy. Some even spoke of Rusk as a potential running mate for Johnson in 1964, but the secretary of state let it be known that he would never seek elective office.

Rusk also exhibited his utmost loyalty to the president. He defended Johnson from the press and from enemies, doing damage control when the president committed such gaffes as showing reporters his scar from a gallbladder operation. Rusk's steadfast dedication through thick and thin—during the darkest days of the Vietnam War—shaped his reputation as a sycophant. But, in truth, Rusk sincerely believed in what Johnson stood for. Rusk and Johnson shared a worldview. Both revered liberalism at home and Wilsonian values abroad. They championed civil rights, eager to fulfill American ideals of equality after centuries of wrong. Having risen from poverty, they wanted to provide opportunity for all. And both Cold Warriors had a neo-Wilsonian mission, a vision hinging on a refusal to retreat in the face of aggression or a losing cause. Johnson optimistically held that U.S. power could transform enemies into friends. Rusk had grown skeptical about that mission in Vietnam, but, always the Cold War liberal, he joined the crusade anyway.

Rusk carried Johnson's banner in speeches, news conferences, and testimony to Congress. Liberal internationalism, bolstered by a tough stance, remained fundamental to his approach. The fact that the Communist powers feared that "those fool Americans might even instigate a full-fledged war in Vietnam," he said, "is one of the principal pillars of peace in the world."[14] Regarding Vietnam, the United States would honor its commitments, Rusk declared. Johnson had to stand his ground to show the "totalitarian countries" that we are not "sloppy people with our hands in our pockets," as Hitler had perceived. "When you go into an alliance you have to mean it," Rusk asserted.[15] Credibility was tied to fidelity. The United States would defend not just one nation or selected regions but would try to maintain world peace.

Rusk did not preach an open-ended commitment to Vietnam. He was wary of an endless war and superpower confrontation. He had learned from the mistake made in Korea of presuming that the Chinese would not intervene. He believed they were actively interested in Vietnam, but he would not provoke them and risk touching off a nuclear war. The task must be limited; Ho must be convinced, by American resolve, to end the conflict. Rusk held that the North Vietnamese preferred peace, but getting them to the bargaining table would be impossible until, like the Soviets of the early Cold War years, they realized that the United States would not buckle.

Johnson had a similar perspective. As Senate majority leader he had opposed bailing out the French at Dien Bien Phu in 1954, and as vice president he had frowned on escalation that might bring Chinese troops into the conflict. His predecessors were much to blame for the Vietnam War. Still—taking to heart, as Rusk did, the lessons of Munich and the early Cold War—Johnson pledged to resist aggression. He vowed to support SEATO; he would not desert an ally. "Like his forebearers at the Alamo," writes historian Richard Immerman, "Lyndon Johnson would stand and fight."[16] Rusk applauded such determination.

One of the president's concerns that engaged Rusk indirectly was domestic policy. In 1964, Johnson dedicated himself to creating a "Great Society" of visionary liberal reforms. Johnson sent hundreds of bills to Congress, initiating programs in housing, education, welfare, and culture in a comprehensive war on poverty. Most notably, Congress passed the Civil Rights Act in 1964, ending legal segregation in the United States. Johnson prepared for the 1964 election against archconservative Republican Barry Goldwater, hoping to attract moderate voters by exhibiting this swirl of reformist zeal and by refraining from sending troops to Vietnam. Yet if the conservatives accused him of being soft on communism, he might be forced to prove otherwise by going to war.

That approach would undermine the funds and attention dedicated to his prized Great Society.

Rusk helped by trying to place Vietnam on the back burner. Johnson would delay as much as possible, pushing his domestic reforms in order to win the election and carve out a distinctive niche in history. As spokesman for the administration on foreign policy, Rusk defended his chief from the Republicans by declaring that Johnson would hold the line against the Communists just as presidents had in the past. The country, he said, had fought in such remote places as Korea "to sustain a principle vital to the freedom and security of America—the principle that the Communist world should not be permitted to expand by overrunning one after another of the arrangements built during and since the war to mark the outer limits of Communist expansion by force."[17] Vietnam would be no different.

That tough stance hurt Goldwater. Preferring a vigorous response, Goldwater came off as an extremist who might send American boys to Southeast Asia or even resort to the use of nuclear weapons. Johnson's campaign labeled Goldwater a crackpot. One infamous television spot (yanked off the air after Goldwater protested) pictured a little girl picking the petals off a daisy while a background voice solemnly counted down from ten. When the announcer reached zero, a nuclear explosion appeared reflected in the girl's eyes and a narrator warned that the issues at stake in the election were too volatile to leave to anyone but Johnson.

The president, on the other hand, would be cautious and honor the doctrine of collective security. He would neither give an inch in Vietnam nor risk all-out war. Americans would not replace Asians in the fight in Vietnam. Rusk muddied the waters by avoiding extremes in his public statements. In May 1964, before the American Law Institute, he warned that the United States might expand the war "if the Communists persist in their aggression," but he tempered this statement by implying that his country sought not to destroy North Vietnam but only to end Ho's aggression in the South.[18] This left open the option of escalation, perhaps after the November election.

Beyond the election, however, the president engaged in a tortured search for a middle ground: a way out of Vietnam that would not compromise U.S. interests. McGeorge Bundy of the National Security Council and Secretary of Defense McNamara were Johnson's right arm, pursuing military solutions in Vietnam. Rusk and advisers Abe Fortas and Clark Clifford were his left arm, seeking political and diplomatic answers. Neither hawks nor doves were able to prevent a war, however.

Election-Year Diplomacy

Remembering Truman's indictment on China, Johnson vowed that he would never be accused of losing Southeast Asia. Thus, Rusk would not budge on Vietnam. Because of election concerns, both men rejected the military's request in the spring and summer of 1964 to begin bombing in Vietnam, yet both resolved to keep U.S. advisers in the South. In early 1964 the administration learned that hundreds of North Vietnamese soldiers were headed into South Vietnam along the Ho Chi Minh Trail through Laos and Cambodia. Rusk was angry; Laos was supposed to be neutral. Vietcong attacks multiplied, and a January 1964 coup in Saigon, which brought General Nguyen Khanh to power, sustained political instability. Meanwhile, the strategic hamlets program remained a shambles. The South Vietnamese doubted that their government could stave off the Communists.

Johnson looked for ways to stop the deterioration. A visit to South Vietnam in December 1963 convinced McNamara that all would be lost without prompt, bold action. His pessimism typified the view in the White House, as did the reiteration by top advisers that a Communist takeover would undermine U.S. power in Asia and in the world. The military requested a greater role in the war, including sending more advisers, establishing American patrols along the Laotian and Cambodian borders, and even bombing the North. Rusk particularly resisted the bombing; this enlargement of the war might be inevitable, but it was dangerously provocative.

In the first half of 1964, Rusk participated in a debate over alternatives. By that spring the Communists had begun an offensive in Laos, meeting covert U.S. air strikes that Rusk explained away as reconnaissance flights to prying senators. The military pressured for the bombing of North Vietnam, which the Joint Chiefs deemed the source of the war in the South. After McNamara and Maxwell Taylor, the new ambassador, went to Vietnam in March 1964 and again in May to survey the situation, they advocated strikes against Hanoi to permit Saigon to stand on its own.

Johnson did not want to lose South Vietnam, but neither did he want to risk his election by going to war. Rusk worried that escalation would either bring failure, which would undercut U.S. credibility and the SEATO Pact, or entrench the United States in Vietnam until victory was won at great loss of life. Neutralization, which Rusk viewed as a euphemism for U.S. withdrawal, was unacceptable. Maintaining aid also seemed futile. Rusk had no viable options except one: to expand the war if the Communists persisted in their aggression. He saw no way out short of escalation.

In a characteristic pose, Rusk searched for answers to the deteriorating situation in Vietnam in 1964. *Courtesy Richard B. Russell Library, University of Georgia*

After traveling to South Vietnam in April and May of 1964, he determined not to let Saigon sink. He described South Vietnam as a "gleaming country if only it had peace."[19] The Vietcong, Rusk admitted, had made gains by capturing hamlets, capitalizing on the political coups in Saigon, and launching large-scale attacks. He and Johnson settled on gradual escalation, but not before the presidential election. Rusk did not lie to the public about the situation, but he was careful to avoid undue mention of expansion. By deploying more U.S. troops, Johnson would send a warning to North Vietnam to back off. Americanization was necessary if the government of General Khanh was to survive.

By July, with only one-fifth of South Vietnam under the control of the government, the situation was dire. A series of coups followed a new crackdown on the Buddhists. Rusk hoped that the United States could distance itself from the turmoil. In the likelihood that it could not, he began thinking about preparing the public for war. A congressional resolution was written to alert Americans, as well as Ho and Mao, to the possibility of U.S. intervention. Most advisers believed that Hanoi could not be curbed without bombing. That was also the view of South Vietnamese leaders, who hoped that the Goldwater campaign would pressure Johnson to do so. But Johnson had to avoid a war to placate his liberal base. He needed a pretext to convince Democrats that he did not plan to escalate and, above all, to silence the Republicans. He got it in early August 1964 off the coast of North Vietnam.

U.S. vessels, which were engaged in covert surveillance (referred to as De Soto patrols) in support of the South Vietnamese navy, had routinely sailed within the twelve-mile coastal limit of the Gulf of Tonkin, claimed by North Vietnam as its territory. De Soto patrols pinpointed enemy radars for destruction by South Vietnamese aircraft. The United States recognized a three-mile territorial limit. On the morning of August 2, a patrol led by the destroyer *Maddox* repulsed an attack by North Vietnamese torpedo boats. The next night, South Vietnam conducted a raid, backed by the Americans once again. On the following night, August 4, the C. *Turner Joy* reported that it was under attack and returned fire. The destroyer hit nothing—there were no North Vietnamese vessels in the area—but the president was notified that an enemy assault had occurred.

Johnson and his advisers mistakenly believed the unsubstantiated reports from the Gulf of Tonkin and jumped at the opportunity to exhibit election-year resolve over Vietnam. The president ordered secret air strikes against North Vietnamese naval bases and supply depots and then sent the draft of the previously written congressional resolution, now called the Gulf of Tonkin Resolution, to Capitol Hill. It authorized the president to "take all necessary measures to repel any armed attack against the forces of the United States and to prevent further aggression" in Southeast Asia. These steps included "the use of armed force, to assist any member or protocol state" of SEATO "in defense of its freedom."[20] The Gulf of Tonkin Resolution, in sum, gave Johnson the leeway to do what he wanted in Vietnam without a formal declaration of war.

Republicans had lashed out at Truman for failing to ask for a resolution in Korea. Eisenhower had gotten resolutions to intervene in the Formosa Straits in 1955 and Lebanon in 1958. Congress had given one to Kennedy to guard against Cuban aggression. For all Johnson knew, the U.S. ships had been shooting at whales in the Gulf of Tonkin, but he would not commit Truman's mistake of ignoring Congress. McNamara and Rusk led administration forces in urging congressional passage of the Gulf of Tonkin Resolution.

For Rusk the issue was clear. North Vietnam had violated international law not just by firing on U.S. vessels but by using its coastal waters to infiltrate the South as well. Rusk warned against giving in to Ho's intimidation tactics; the Tonkin incident served as a means to display resolve. "An immediate and direct reaction by us is necessary," he advised the National Security Council. "The unprovoked attack on the high seas is an act of war for all practical purposes. We have been trying to get a signal to Hanoi and Peking. Our response to this attack may be that signal."[21] Indeed, the administration's failure to respond might lead the Communists to believe that the possibilities in Southeast Asia were boundless.

Robert McNamara in foreground listens to Johnson as Rusk shuffles through briefing papers. *Courtesy Richard B. Russell Library, University of Georgia*

Within three days, Congress passed the Gulf of Tonkin Resolution, giving the president authority to defend U.S. and SEATO interests. The vote in the House was unanimous, 416 to 0, while the Senate vote tallied 88 to 2. Only Democrats Ernest Gruening of Alaska and Wayne Morse of Oregon opposed the resolution on the grounds that the United States would be dragged by a duplicitous Johnson into a worthless war that would end in disaster. Rusk believed that the legislators were not hoodwinked; they were not "village idiots," he said, and knew what they were voting for.[22]

Based on the information that Congress had received from the administration, Rusk's assessment seems accurate. Ironically, even Senator Fulbright, who later broke with his friend Johnson over Vietnam, urged prompt passage. Rusk was pleased by the resolution's legal sanction of U.S. involvement in Southeast Asia.

Throughout the fall of 1964 the administration debated reprisal air strikes (demanded by Goldwater as well as the Joint Chiefs) against the North. Johnson did not carry through; his Gulf of Tonkin Resolution made him look tough enough. He focused on stabilizing South Vietnam, where General Khanh had been replaced by a provisional government. The Joint Chiefs itched to augment the military presence to prop up the regime, but only De Soto patrols were allowed. Meanwhile, especially after an attempted coup in mid-September, U.S. advisers in Saigon struggled to keep the government together.

Observers, including the CIA, Ambassador Taylor, and General William Westmoreland, the U.S. commander in South Vietnam, were all pessimistic about ending the turmoil. Eventually, in late October 1964, Khanh was persuaded to resume leadership over the nation's military, but the endless political intrigues dragged on. For his part, Westmoreland abandoned the hope that South Vietnam could succeed without U.S. military intervention. On November 1 an NLF attack on Bien Hoa airfield north of Saigon killed four Americans and destroyed over two dozen aircraft. Westmoreland ran out of patience; he wanted reprisal bombings.

Republican candidate Goldwater was of the same mind. He demanded that the United States immediately bomb the North to end the Vietnam conflict quickly. Johnson, to the applause of the public, recommended moderation. The president had shown his fortitude with the Gulf of Tonkin Resolution. There would be no major war; neither would there be retreat. Bombing would be a last resort; "a war in Asia with 700 million Chinese" would be dangerous.[23] Rusk echoed this sentiment to the press, warning against taking extreme measures. Johnson wanted to win the election first, then deal with his commitments in Southeast Asia.

When it came to the election, Johnson proved his expertise. He routed Goldwater in a huge landslide. Meanwhile, Johnson staked out his position. Americans, he estimated, "knew I would not repudiate the pledges of my predecessors in the Presidency," but they also understood that he would not "wipe out Hanoi or use atom bombs to defoliate the Vietnamese jungles." "I was going to do what had to be done to protect our interests and to keep our promises," he said. "And that is what I did."[24] Given Johnson's determination to stay in Vietnam but avoid taking extreme measures, it is not surprising that his administration leaned toward escalation. Placing a premium on Asian containment, a committee under the National Security Council recommended greater U.S. involvement over inaction or withdrawal. Johnson accepted this advice in early December 1964. The South Vietnamese government would be told to reform, and the United States would begin bombing infiltration routes. The option of hitting the North would be left open, temporarily.

But the "sagging limb" of South Vietnam, as Senate Majority Leader Mansfield called it, came ever closer to breaking.[25] Plotting among the generals heightened as Rusk, among others, appealed for unity. On Christmas Eve in 1964, the Vietcong attacked an officers' billet in Saigon, killing two U.S. advisers and wounding fifty-one Americans and South Vietnamese. Rusk feared that the Communists would cut the country in two. He knew that the United States could not impose solutions on the South Vietnamese, but escalation could not be put off for long. Remembering that delays in the 1930s had led to holocaust, Rusk determined that this mistake could not be made again. As the new year of 1965 dawned, the United States faced a major decision on its military role in South Vietnam.

Despite his worries about provoking the Chinese (who had just exploded their first nuclear device), Rusk had been prepared for a large commitment from the start. Boastful China targeted Thailand, Cambodia, Laos, and Indonesia for wars of national liberation, he claimed. Indeed, Beijing would soon call for "one hundred Vietnams," or wars of national liberation, around the world. Asian dominoes seemed to be teetering. Kennedy had resolved to contain communism in Vietnam. Troubles with Diem and the generals aside, Kennedy and Johnson—supported by Rusk—stayed that course.

Rusk was prominent among those skeptical about Americanizing the war. He feared that the United States simply could not do South Vietnam's business, and, once involved, would be unable to get out and might end up fighting alone. Failure to win in Vietnam, moreover, would irreparably damage U.S. prestige. The entire Cold War consensus at home could collapse. His presidents saw things differently, however, and Rusk went along with their policies. His was a tough position. He hoped to withdraw but understood that it might be necessary to escalate to stop aggression.

The secretary of state sought to find his way through the contradictions. But in the end, regardless of his hedging, two factors governed Rusk's thinking. First, he was not the president of the United States; the final decisions did not rest with him. He could prod Johnson, but the president would demand either loyalty from his aides or their resignation. Some might see that as a lack of backbone, but it was also the bureaucratic reality of life at the top echelon of government. Second, and more important, Rusk had no desire to split with the president. He might have had apprehensions about the means of prosecuting the war in Vietnam, but he was a true believer in the crusade against communism in Asia. Principle overrode pragmatism.

Rusk understood full well that Vietnam was not a threat similar to the Soviet Union during the early Cold War. But Vietnam was a pawn in the bigger strategic battle against China and Russia, a struggle that Rusk determined to win so that he could fulfill his ideals. In defense of Johnson, his own reading of history, and his own principles, Rusk rationalized every move in Vietnam by trumpeting neo-Wilsonian values—even as the United States went on the offensive in what turned out to be the longest war in its history.

Notes

1. Dean Rusk, interview on "Issues and Answers," *DSB* 47 (July 30, 1962): 180.

2. Giglio, *Presidency of John F. Kennedy*, 246.

3. Bassett and Pelz, "The Failed Search for Victory," 243.

4. Cohen, *Dean Rusk*, 186; "Secretary Rusk Holds Press and Radio News Briefing in Los Angeles," *DSB* 48 (February 13, 1963): 364.

5. Cohen, *Dean Rusk*, 186–88; Lindley, *Winds of Freedom*, 195.

6. Rusk, *As I Saw It*, 436.

7. Ibid., 442.

8. Ibid.

9. Dean Rusk, "The Pursuit of Peace," *DSB* 51 (August 17, 1964): 218.

10. Schoenbaum, *Waging Peace*, 409.

11. DROH I, LBJL, 1–7, 12.

12. Ibid., 16.

13. Johnson, *The Vantage Point*, 20.

14. Schoenbaum, *Waging Peace*, 424.

15. Henry F. Graff, *The Tuesday Cabinet: Deliberation and Decision on Peace and War under Lyndon B. Johnson* (Englewood Cliffs, NJ: Prentice-Hall, 1970), 83–84.

16. Richard Immerman, "A Time in the Tide of Men's Affairs: Lyndon Johnson and Vietnam," in Cohen and Tucker, *Lyndon Johnson Confronts the World*, 60.

17. Schoenbaum, *Waging Peace*, 424.

18. Cohen, *Dean Rusk*, 236.

19. "U.S. Reaffirms Commitments to Taiwan and Viet-Nam," *DSB* 50 (May 4, 1964): 695.

20. See the verbatim text in U.S. Congress, Senate Subcommittee on Public Buildings and Grounds, *The Pentagon Papers*, Senator Gravel Edition, 4 vols. (Boston: Beacon Press, 1971), 3:722.

21. Summary notes of 538th NSC meeting, August 4, 1964, Box 35, IV.D.1, Thomas Schoenbaum File, Dean Rusk Collection, UGA.

22. Bob Brewin, "Dean Rusk under Oath," *Village Voice*, April 16, 1985, 16.

23. Schulzinger, *A Time for War*, 153.

24. Johnson, *The Vantage Point*, 68.

25. Schulzinger, *A Time for War*, 168.

8

Limits of a Limited War

The Johnson administration Americanized the war in 1965. The president began a bombing campaign and introduced ground troops. Rusk gave a qualified endorsement to the escalation. Like other policymakers frustrated by Vietnam, he thought withdrawal was no option. The cause was necessary and just: an effort to shore up the security of Southeast Asia within the larger crusade of upholding the rule of law so that peace would ensue. Rusk reluctantly went down the slippery slope of a greater commitment. Privately, he expressed an ambivalence to Americanization, a reluctance to go along with proposals to escalate the war by the more aggressive members of the Johnson administration. Yet calibrated responses to the enemy took on a life of their own. "The war," Rusk said, "will be over as soon as the other side decides to leave its neighbor alone."[1] The other side never reached this decision and Vietnam became Rusk's major preoccupation for the next four years.

Americanization

In January 1965, Secretary of Defense Robert McNamara and National Security Adviser McGeorge Bundy concluded that South Vietnam was doomed without a larger U.S. role. The generals in Saigon played musical chairs over leadership while the war was being lost. Militarily, they refused to move unless supported by the United States. Moreover, Hanoi made the ominous strategic change at the end of 1964 of moving major units into South Vietnam. There had been no regiments at all in the South in 1963, but the following year there were three, numbering forty-five hundred troops. Rusk worried about both the infiltration and a hasty response on America's part.

Rusk obfuscated administration policy in a blur of statements that honored, and limited, U.S. obligations. He warned that withdrawal would have the same effect that appeasement had had in the face of German aggression: world war. Johnson had to remain firm in Vietnam to compel China to abandon its attacks on its neighbors. Rusk assured the Senate Foreign Relations Committee in early 1965, however, that combat troops would not be deployed—that is, as long as Ho Chi Minh did not give Johnson a reason to do so.

Contrary to McNamara and Bundy, who wanted to commit full power to Vietnam, the hedging Rusk insisted that Johnson make present policy work. Escalation would play into the hands of the corrupt South Vietnamese generals and might lead to a wider war. Yet, because Hanoi insisted on U.S. withdrawal, Rusk also rejected negotiations. No matter how desperately Rusk pleaded his case for moderation, the president favored McNamara and Bundy. Present policy, wrote Bundy, was just not working no matter how much Rusk willed it. Consequently, Johnson authorized bombing against North Vietnam on February 28, 1965. Rusk had been less persuasive than the proponents of escalation; military advisers often have the president's ear during a crisis. The United States stepped up the war.

Code-named Operation Rolling Thunder, the bombing of the North arose in response to a February 7 attack on a U.S. Marine base at Pleiku in central Vietnam, which left eight dead and 126 injured. This program of air strikes might buy time until Saigon was stabilized or Ho negotiated, but, as Rusk acknowledged, neither hope was fulfilled. Congress held that bombing aided the U.S. cause, but many Democrats and such commentators as Walter Lippmann warned, as Rusk did, that Johnson might be trapped in a war that was either unwinnable or could ignite into a superpower conflict. Furthermore, they argued, regardless of the destruction, Ho would not give up his dream of independence.

Loyally backing Johnson, Rusk merely delayed Rolling Thunder, banking on a few weeks of ultimately fruitless mediation. He then tried, but often failed, to keep the strikes trained on infiltration routes. Privately, he recalled the Korean War, when complete air superiority had not deterred the enemy. Harassing the supply lines would slow the Vietcong effort, but attacks on the North itself would not be likely to affect the situation in the South. There was also the distinct possibility that China would react by entering the war. Publicly, however, Rusk was tough, demanding an end to North Vietnamese aggression. When North Vietnam refused to relent, Operation Rolling Thunder continued for eight years, inflicting great damage. From 1965 to 1967 the United States dropped over one million tons of bombs on South Vietnam and one-half that amount on the North. Yet Saigon was no more stable, and North Vietnam stubbornly stepped up its infiltration. In 1965 the monthly rate of infiltration reached forty-five hundred soldiers.

Acknowledging these facts, in March 1965, General Westmoreland urged the president "to put our own finger in the dike" and send ground troops. Two battalions of marines had been dispatched to the base at Da Nang on March 6. Rusk approved, reasoning that the marines provided security. To avoid distracting attention from the civil rights bill and other Great Society domestic matters, the deployment occurred quietly. But Westmoreland, pressured by the Joint Chiefs, wanted the 75,000 advisers reinforced with regular soldiers. Bombing was insufficient; a guerrilla war could not be won from the air. The marines alone could not staunch the flow of Vietcong soldiers or build confidence in the South Vietnamese army. A major U.S. commitment was necessary, or Saigon would fall to communism.

Opposed to a combat role for U.S. troops, Rusk countered that Asians would despise non-Asian soldiers. It would be difficult to tell friend from foe. South Vietnam must fight its own war, albeit with U.S. aid. Rusk cautioned, "There is a problem about foreign troops undertaking the kind of pacification effort that is required in South Vietnam."[2] Furthermore, the threat of Chinese entry would be enhanced by sending ground forces, and a nuclear exchange could follow. Americanization of the war was dangerous, concluded Rusk. At this time, he advised doing all that was feasible, including sending marines to reinforce U.S. positions and bombing "to throw back the Hanoi Vietnam aggression," but "without a major war if possible."[3]

At first resistant to Westmoreland, Johnson offered Ho an extensive package of development aid if the Communists would engage in negotiations to end the war. Rusk added that the United States was not looking for unconditional surrender, just a halt in the shooting so that both sides could talk. Ho retorted that the Americans should leave. He would wait out these foreigners, as he had the French, to win his revolution. As the Vietcong began an expected offensive in May 1965, Johnson authorized the U.S. military to assume offensive postures in South Vietnam.

Rusk backed this tactic. It was limited (and thus adhered to the policy of gradualism) but could be effective in handling guerrilla warfare. The bombing and more assertive use of troops testified to U.S. resolve. Contrary to his earlier stance, Rusk now leaned toward Americanization. For one thing, the rest of the administration disagreed with his prior view. For another, until this time, he had perceived problems in Vietnam as internally driven. By mid-1965, with conditions in South Vietnam steadily worsening and North Vietnamese infiltration at a high, the Free World's credibility was at stake. Aggression had to be confronted. It was a position rooted in principles and history. "Surely we have learned over the past three decades that the acceptance of aggression leads only to a sure catastrophe," Rusk pronounced in May 1965.[4] He edged toward the hawks' camp in an effort to defend the Wilsonian ideals of collective security, self-determination, and democracy.

The mission in Vietnam had to be sustained. Westmoreland had asked for 40,000 soldiers in May; a month later he requested an additional 150,000. Rusk relented, hesitant to confront the military experts on the situation. As the Vietcong pummeled the South Vietnamese army, he realized that gradual pressure on Hanoi had not deterred Ho. Perhaps the sudden influx of a large number of troops would bring Ho to his senses. Still, Rusk remained torn between military advisers and their opponents. He balked at Westmoreland's suggestion that the soldiers go on the offensive in search-and-destroy missions. The troops should only secure defensive enclaves, he opined. By late May, however, once the enemy had proved effective, the tactic was jettisoned. Rusk also frowned on a recommendation by William Bundy of the State Department to send a body of troops with the understanding that it would be withdrawn by summer's end if no progress was in sight. Rusk could not allow the abandonment of South Vietnam.

If possible, Americanization of the war must be avoided; if not, the United States had to uphold its pledge to SEATO. The NATO alliance had been tested in Berlin, and the Rio Pact of Western Hemisphere nations had overcome the Cuban missile crisis. SEATO would be honored in Vietnam; the law of the jungle would not be permitted. That "fundamental" commitment, Rusk argued, precluded the Communists from drawing "conclusions that would lead to our ruin and almost certainly to a catastrophic war."[5] Fighting a small war to prevent a large one demonstrated his neo-Wilsonian take on containment in Southeast Asia.

McNamara was in agreement with General Westmoreland. Johnson must send 100,000 troops and ask Congress for legislation to call up 236,000 reservists. Although the plan would not ensure success, wrote the secretary of defense, it "would stave off defeat in the short run and offer a good chance of producing a favorable settlement in the longer run."[6] Johnson understood the risks of escalating the ground war. By this time, academics had organized campus teach-ins to protest Vietnam policy. Rusk ridiculed their naïveté in ignoring Communist aggression. In such matters, he believed, academics lived "in the world of opinion," whereas he, as a decision maker, resided in "the world of decision" where pacifism was an empty gesture.[7] Humane liberalism was fine, but "poets do not make foreign policy or military policy," he noted with contempt. But Johnson, a political animal, worried that the dissent might spill over into Congress and undermine his Great Society. Still, the president listened to his military. The situation in South Vietnam was growing dimmer. Weighing this gravest of issues, he summoned key advisers in late July 1965 to help him decide whether or not to send troops.

Undersecretary of State George Ball, opposing the emerging consensus favoring McNamara's idea, counseled Johnson to cut his losses and get out. For the omnipotent United States to fail against the lowly Vietcong would cause much greater damage to its prestige than withdrawal. Worse yet, egged on by a public showing impatience over a protracted war, Johnson might opt for a dramatic show of strength that could provoke the Chinese and lead either to a Korean-style stalemate or nuclear war. The jungles of Asia were not the place to confront the Communists. The focus should be on the more important European theater. It was time for negotiations, concluded Ball, a staunch Europeanist himself.

Ball voiced concerns that his friend Rusk had held in the past but did not express now. Rusk did not take the analysis lightly, yet he did consider Ball a devil's advocate, not the heretic that historians have portrayed. In fact, Rusk (and McNamara) did not see much substantial difference between their views and Ball's. The undersecretary did not push outright withdrawal; he was just more willing than others to withdraw at this juncture. The problem was that Ball counseled a "political solution" through negotiations but gave no indication of how to implement that solution.[8]

Photographs of these July meetings show an anguished Rusk, head in hands, as he listened to Ball. Yet he ultimately disagreed

At the pivotal July 1965 meetings, George Ball warns Johnson of the dangers of escalation while a morose Rusk looks on. *Courtesy Yoichi R. Okamoto, Lyndon B. Johnson Library*

about withdrawal. The American effort was not like France's; Johnson had no colonial ambitions. The better analogy was Korea, in which the Communist North had overrun its neighbor. Just as in that conflict, the Communists would come to the negotiating table when confronted by the opposition of skilled U.S. troops, superior American technology, and, above all, resolve. "The integrity of the U.S. commitment is the principal pillar of peace throughout the world," Rusk noted.[9]

Rusk sided with McNamara, as did Johnson, under the advisement of a panel of former generals and officials who came to be known as the Wise Men. Rusk opposed invading or bombing the North to avoid Chinese intervention. Instead, troops would be sent as a signal of honor. "If the Communist world finds out [that] we will not pursue our commitments to the end," he said at the last gathering of the critical July meetings, "I don't know where they will stay their hand."[10] Focused on the specter of regional Communist expansion, Rusk voiced an ideology that even Ball shared: a combination of Wilsonian crusading and realist intentions based on historical analysis.

Rusk had no doubt of America's ability to deny Hanoi its prize. North Vietnam had neither the military muscle nor the popular support to attain its objectives. There was, however, a hitch to the

U.S. defensive mission, one that plagued Rusk for years. The administration could not overdo its response. Slow escalation proved loyalty to allies and, by limiting the field of war, deterred China and the Soviet Union from an armed response. But a limited war undermined the goal of stemming Ho's gains. Although it was the best compromise available in light of political and strategic imperatives, fighting with constraints against an unfettered enemy was a losing proposition.

On July 27, 1965, President Johnson announced that he would send 100,000 additional troops to South Vietnam, but he would not call up reserves. Congress approved. Even skeptics believed that Johnson had made the decision in order to avoid a prolonged war. This was not the case. More troops followed; there were 190,000 regulars in Vietnam by 1966 and 535,000 Americans by the end of the next year. Rusk had joined, even led, the group of Johnson advisers who believed that this show of force, even if it failed, was better than no action at all.

A Military Quagmire

Massive firepower, technology, and manpower bore down on Vietnam, but still in a limited way. Johnson adhered to a gradual escalation of troops and bombing. Rusk tried to drum up support from alliance partners, but only regional SEATO members (South Korea, Australia, New Zealand, the Philippines, and Thailand) helped out. The goal was to share the burden of fighting without unduly provoking the homefront or the Sino-Soviet bloc. Rusk understood the difficulties of fighting a limited war. U.S. troops would have to commit to a long war of attrition. The public would have to be patient (a troublesome proposition), so that wider conflict could be avoided. In view of these concerns, Rusk never wished to deceive Americans; the administration, however, cushioned news from the front with vague statements. The handling of bad news was often steeped in artifice. A breach between reality and assertion—the infamous "credibility gap" in which the public began to doubt the administration's honesty—characterized the domestic treatment of the war.

Rusk would not play to the hawkish conservatives who wanted rapid escalation and application of enormous military power. "In a nuclear world," he later explained, "it was too dangerous for an entire people to grow too angry."[11] North Vietnam could have been leveled by bombing and an invasion of U.S. troops. But he worried about the dire consequences to the world if a paranoid China entered the war to honor its security pact with Hanoi. Rusk remembered the Korean War, when General MacArthur had retreated before the onslaught of Chinese troops following the U.S. approach to the Yalu River. Perhaps Mao would not act this time, but Rusk contended that if he did, Johnson would not be able to call off the attack, for he "would have . . . no one to phone in the ensuing nuclear exchange."[12] Restraint guided the effort. Although the subject came up in discussions, nuclear weapons were not seriously considered. And because the State Department helped select bombing targets, Rusk was able to urge the president to avoid civilian casualties. On the ground, unfortunately, this was not always the case, but Rusk rightly claimed that massacres such as the one at My Lai in 1968 were not typical of U.S. conduct.

Meanwhile, Vietcong guerrilla tactics and Ho's willingness to fight a war of attrition hindered Westmoreland militarily. U.S. soldiers poured in, bombers strafed South Vietnam, helicopters quickly attacked. On the ground, search-and-destroy missions killed Vietcong, confirming to McNamara's number crunchers back home—at least for a time—that technology would win the war and minimize the American loss of life. But computer analyses of the "body counts" were wrong about one thing: the increase in troops, bombing, and dead enemy soldiers did not dislodge the NLF. Recognizing this, Rusk judged those figures worthless.

By the end of 1966 the U.S. presence had stabilized South Vietnamese politics, yet combat degenerated into a vicious tally of dead Vietcong and North Vietnamese as an indicator of progress. Rewarded for killing rebels, officers encouraged troops to shoot first and ask questions about the affiliation of targets later, a tactic that caused the deaths of many innocent civilians along with the Vietcong. Random slaughter led to such atrocities as taking enemy "trophies"—ears and noses—or destroying entire villages. The acquisition of territory or the undermining of the NLF command played second to the senseless body counts.

The war of attrition had devastating effects on ordinary people. Chemical warfare came of age; the United States sprayed herbicides (the most infamous being Agent Orange) to defoliate forests and deprive the enemy of sanctuary. Operation Ranch Hand dropped 17.6 million gallons of Agent Orange on 3.6 million acres of Vietnam from 1965 to 1971, prompting soldiers to quip, "Only you can prevent forests." One-half of South Vietnam's timberland was destroyed. Americans ripped through villages, wrecking houses and carting away suspects. Such brutality, in combination with the bombing, created 4 million homeless refugees in South Vietnam, about one-quarter of the population.

The turmoil led to disease and death of civilians and the destruction of a traditional way of life. A black market sprang up amid the shattered economy. Many women were forced into prostitution; thousands bore children who suffered discrimination for being half American. Although U.S. aid to the refugees flowed in, historian Robert Schulzinger sums up the situation: "The misery of ordinary Vietnamese also contributed to a deepening sense that the very people whom the Americans had come to help had seen their lives disrupted or even ruined by the Americans' arrival."[13]

The attrition plan, moreover, did not seem to work. In the fall of 1965 an airmobile division of the U.S. Army engaged a North Vietnamese regiment in the Ia Drang Valley. Down the Ho Chi Minh Trail came the enemy, its forces equipped with rations intended to last two months and uniforms intended to endure five years, lugging weapons ranging from the effective AK-47 assault rifle to mortars and antiaircraft guns. These forces fought for thirty-four days in the Ia Drang, incurring twelve deaths for every U.S. soldier killed. Westmoreland claimed victory, but too soon. North Vietnam's veteran commander, General Giap, took solace in the battles as well. The South Vietnamese army was easy to handle. Moreover, this was the first time that he had confronted the Americans with regular troops, and the result had not been annihilation. He now focused on U.S. forces, believing that the Americans would quit, as the French had, if he inflicted steady losses on them.

General Westmoreland persisted. In the fall of 1966 and again in the winter of 1967, he launched a series of missions to flush out the enemy with superior firepower. Two operations focused on an area northwest of Saigon. Bombers and artillery decimated battlefields; tens of thousands of friendly troops moved in on Vietcong strongholds. Enemy deaths numbered in the thousands, South Vietnamese and U.S. casualties only a few hundred. Villagers were rounded up, interrogated about their loyalties, and either arrested or drafted into South Vietnam's army.

Despite Westmoreland's optimistic assessment, the rebels fought on. There were three massive operations (Attleboro, Cedar Falls, and Junction City), but the vast majority of engagements with the Vietcong were on a small scale that required dangerous foot patrols and permitted little reliance on technology. Most of the NLF squirreled away in an extensive network of tunnels until the offensives ended. Stymied U.S. commanders realized that the enemy was cleverly countering their every move.

The guerrillas, North Vietnamese troops, and peasants loyal to the NLF also showed an amazing resiliency. Forced out of a conventional war by Giap, who adopted his own mobile tactics that tied down U.S. troops, American soldiers began to die in greater numbers. More were killed in search-and-destroy missions by an enemy pledged to resist until the outsiders left and independence was won. In the face of superior firepower and heavy loss of life, the Communists persevered.

Recognizing Giap's strategy, the Johnson administration answered by sending more troops. In late 1965, McNamara reported from South Vietnam that six hundred thousand soldiers were needed to control the Vietcong. By 1967 he had raised his request, warning with chagrin that Johnson must stay the course even at the risk of one thousand American deaths per week. The secretary of defense was by no means sanguine about the possibilities for success with increased troop levels, but he could see no other option short of withdrawal. Rusk, just as worried as McNamara, agreed. Meanwhile, Ho replenished his forces, outmanned his enemies, and maintained the pressure, draining South Vietnamese and U.S. morale in the process. If the United States wanted it that way, this would be a long war.

The political situation was equally discouraging. By 1966, South Vietnam's prime minister, Nguyen Cao Ky, had survived for several months. He lacked popular support, just as his predecessors had. His fellow generals conspired for power. Some even joined a growing movement, spearheaded by Buddhist monks and students, to denounce U.S. influence in their country. McNamara was gloomy, and Rusk saw Saigon's prospects as "grim." The situation was no better in the South Vietnamese military, which was rife with corruption and incompetence. "We haven't begun to see the end of this thing yet," Rusk told reporters in July 1966.[14]

Deterioration was evident on the political front as well. General Giap welcomed the monumental U.S. military operations, each one larger than the one before, because when the high-tech tactics did not defeat the guerrillas, they heightened frustration among Washington policymakers. Ho understood that Johnson could not afford a protracted war—that military morale, public support, and political patience were all limited commodities. By late 1965, Americans had grown increasingly intolerant of a war that seemed to have no end.

U.S. POSITION IN SOUTHEAST ASIA

DETERMINATION

Baldy

"...STEEL!...CONCRETE!...HAMMER!...NAILS!...SCOTCH TAPE!..."

Propping up South Vietnam are (from left) Rusk, McNamara, Johnson, and Henry Cabot Lodge. *Courtesy of Clifford H. Baldowksi*

Dissent

The destruction in Vietnam affected U.S. personnel there. For the 2.25 million men and 11,000 women stationed in the country, the environment was strange, foreign, and hostile. Dampness was a curse in the cold wet months, while the hot dry season was brutal. Search-and-destroy missions were a strain. And soldiers on twelve-month tours, as well as officers who were rotated out of Vietnam every six months, did not develop the bonds of camaraderie of previous wars.

Combat troops in the field, about 20 percent of the force, resented the 80 percent of support personnel who remained in safe, relatively comfortable jobs back at the bases.

Continual sniping from the Vietcong and, for some, the repugnant nature of the body counts destroyed morale. One-fifth of patrols fell victim to booby traps rather than enemy fire. Out of disgust, terror, confusion, or all three, many of those who had volunteered for the cause soon soured on it. Any Asian-looking person could be the enemy, lying in wait. Demoralized and cynical about the war and under intense pressure, some soldiers even killed their officers rather than continue in combat. Rapidly deployed helicopters whisked the wounded to field hospitals, where the majority survived, but they were indelibly traumatized. Nurses, a proud lot themselves, were shocked and depressed by the injuries and deaths. But their disillusionment did not compare with that of the soldiers, for whom Vietnam had become a living hell.

Seething anger also characterized the homefront. Presidents had enjoyed support for prosecuting the Cold War, including the conflict in Vietnam. By the mid-1960s, however, dissent gained a momentum of its own. Vietnam protesters hailed from across the political, economic, and generational spectrums, with varying grievances, but virtually all Americans agreed on one aspect: the conflict had dragged on too long.

Within Johnson's own party, Vietnam opponents were soon joined by dozens who questioned not just the objectives in Southeast Asia but also the very foundations of U.S. foreign policy. It was on these two scores that Rusk's parting of the ways with other liberals became evident. A divergence on basic principles underlay the tragedy of Vietnam. Rusk saw Vietnam as worth the fight in order to back up the containment doctrine. He remained true to neo-Wilsonian Cold War liberalism. Others did not.

Perilous for Johnson and Rusk, at first, was the small band of opponents in Congress. After the 1964 Gulf of Tonkin incident that had led to the resolution legitimizing the war, some—such as Johnson's good friend Senate Foreign Relations Committee Chairman J. William Fulbright—had felt tricked by the administration. Congress would not have passed the resolution, Fulbright angrily claimed, if it had been told the truth or if it had known that over one-half million troops would be sent to Vietnam. Johnson must cease the bombing of the North, insisted such congressional doves, and negotiate with Ho.

Fulbright had broader concerns, similar to those of Ball. In January and February 1966, Fulbright held televised hearings on the war. Vietnam was not worth the resources, he said. It hurt relations with allies and promoted superpower tension. Fulbright, Rusk believed, would have eventually broken with the administration over its intervention in the Dominican Republic, but Vietnam became the senator's bête noire. Academics, military men, and such realists as George Kennan, the father of the containment doctrine, agreed with Fulbright. The senator referred to Johnson's intervention in Vietnam and the operation in the Dominican Republic as the "arrogance of power," in which the United States haughtily believed that its dominance would win victories anywhere in the world. Others, such as Senator Frank Church, said that because he had not voted for the SEATO Pact in 1955, its obligations meant nothing to them.

What were U.S. objectives, and why was the United States fighting in Vietnam? Fulbright asked Rusk, his star witness, during the hearings. The goals were to allow the South Vietnamese to choose their future free from outside coercion, to convince the Communists—through the wielding of U.S. power—that the containment policy lived on, replied the secretary. Vietnam was no different from Berlin and Korea; aggressors would be put on notice that they could not succeed. Surely, NATO allies would be uneasy if the United States abruptly deserted South Vietnam. The logic of containment,

Rusk and Senator J. William Fulbright disagreed on the war in Southeast Asia.
Courtesy Richard B. Russell Library, University of Georgia

borne out by history, was compelling. Rusk might appear rigid to his detractors, but he ably defended his neo-Wilsonian crusade.

In response to Church's views on SEATO, Rusk quipped that although he had not voted for income taxes, he still paid them. Obligations must be honored. But the United States did not rely solely on the SEATO Pact as a rationale for intervention. The statements of three presidents, aid bills approved by Congress, the Gulf of Tonkin Resolution—all built support for the war, Rusk replied. He rebuffed the criticism of his analogies. Rusk would not be branded as a narrow-minded anti-Communist. "I know Hitler was an Austrian and Mao is Chinese. I know the other differences between this situation and the situation in the Thirties. But what is common between the two situations is the phenomenon of aggression."[15] Standing by his reading of history, he asserted that others seemed to have forgotten theirs.

Vietnam was really a civil war, protested the committee's doves, the advocates of withdrawal. Some even likened it to the Korean War. No, replied Rusk, Korea and Vietnam were part of the Cold War. Hanoi, supported by Russia and China, had fomented the Vietnam conflict. China, in particular, was a "blatant advocate of violence" and must be taught "that aggression does not pay. That is the issue involved in Viet-Nam."[16] Rusk did extend an olive branch.

The war would show the Chinese, he continued at length, that the costs of aggression were high. If they exhibited caution, they might be rewarded by an "era of good relations" with the United States.[17]

Because Fulbright was unconvinced that China was a threat, Rusk took a broader tack. He noted the difference between the Communists' brand of liberation "and the kind of revolution which is congenial to our own experience, and fits into the aspirations of ordinary men and women right around the world." South Vietnam was taking part in a revolution of "modernization, economic and social development, [and] education," and feeble North Vietnam was simply jealous. Hanoi had gone to war—as Communists do— to solve domestic deficiencies.[18] Aggression, in this basic liberal formula, emerged from the poverty of communism.

Rusk's reasoning was sensible, but it also showed his intolerance of dissent. He had friends in Congress, including Fulbright, but this was war. Loyalty to the commander in chief was at stake; decisions were for the president, not Congress, to make. The public and press should not undermine their leader. Americans would stomach a limited war if the press halted its quest for the sensational story, stopped distorting the news, and reported the positives, not just the negatives, about Vietnam.

In view of this perception of the press, Rusk provided journalists with as little information as possible. The joke circulated in the press corps that Rusk had pulled a journalist aside and, insisting on confidentiality, had stated that the war would be over if the other side stopped fighting. In actuality, he really believed this to be true. Rusk appeared cool under the klieg lights (although he was known to drink two Scotches before press conferences); his laser-like mind would pinpoint the essence of a problem. But in the eyes of many liberal critics, his mechanical repetition of American doctrines characterized him as unreflective at best.

The result was a public relations crisis. The credibility gap between what was actually going on and what officials were telling the people widened. Rusk shaded the truth regarding war objectives and even progress on the battlefield. The United States was on the defensive, he said in February 1965; yet he knew (and reporters discovered through leaks) that troops would soon go into combat. The United States fought to contain China, but many officials were uncertain about who the enemy was. The conclusion of the conflict was near, he said; it will "end with the freedom of South Vietnam."[19] All the while, military reports told him a different story.

Rusk refused to open up. He did not lie, but he misled. He attacked reporters for their revelations, as if secrecy would win the war. Rusk envied the stonewalling tactics of Cordell Hull, Franklin Roosevelt's secretary of state; he had dodged nosy reporters by assuring them that their inquiries would receive careful consideration. In 1967, Rusk told the cabinet, "There is no evidence of a stalemate in Vietnam." Stalemate was assumed by the press, he said, but in reality the United States had successfully defended South Vietnam from the enemy.[20] Remarkably, as they tried to hold the public at bay, Rusk and Johnson deceived themselves as well.

In actuality, Johnson, who had declared during the 1964 election campaign that he did not seek to widen the war, was responsible for the credibility gap. When Johnson was criticized for failing to honor that pledge, however, Rusk responded by emphasizing the word "seek" in an effort to qualify the statement. Skeptics viewed that defense as tantamount to cunning lawyerese. They expected the truth from the administration's spokesman but never really got it—at least not to their satisfaction. By 1967 a growing number of Americans no longer trusted officials, and Rusk had become a symbol of deceit at the pinnacle of power. Based on his public persona, the view was justified.

Short Cut

HOLLAND, *CHICAGO TRIBUNE*

Many Americans sought victory in Vietnam, not withdrawal. Hawks criticized Rusk for seeking negotiations that would lead to a Korean-type stalemate. Copyrighted by Chicago Tribune Company. All rights reserved with permission

Still, the majority of Americans, like Rusk, saw no other alternative but to fight the war. They endorsed Cold War strategy and loyalty to allies. But with no light at the end of the tunnel, military critics, Republicans, and conservative Democrats decried Johnson's and McNamara's methods of handling the war. Take warmaking out of the hands of civilian technocrats like McNamara, they said, and turn it over to the military. This conservative dissent supported Rusk's principles but not his practice. Others, such as the realists who saw the war as a distraction from the European arena, thought Rusk had gone off course. Millions of youthful Baby Boomers, coming of age during the Vietnam War as the radicalized Sixties Generation, had yet a different complaint.

The Protesters

Popular protests rocked the White House and branded Rusk as a villainous proponent of the war. Demonstrations, coinciding with the decision to escalate in 1965, were held on college campuses. It was not surprising that university students, numbering seven million by 1966, led the charge. Many who had been galvanized by the civil rights movement agreed with Martin Luther King, Jr., that Vietnam drained funds and attention away from the quest for racial equality and the noble war on poverty.

Young people had begun to question the corporate and Cold War values of their parents. They formed such organizations as Students for a Democratic Society, which sought to revolutionize politics, the economy, and society. Led by student radicals of the New Left—who were distinguished from the Old Left by age and by the New Left's break with traditional socialist and Communist organizations—many had campaigned for curricular and social reforms. This generation, which was eligible for the draft, had a personal stake in achieving the goal of unilateral U.S. withdrawal from Vietnam.

Other student protesters claimed the moral high ground. Third World revolutionaries and nationalists merely sought independence from the imperialistic yoke of U.S. foreign policy, they argued. Castro, Mao, and Ho represented those who wished to break free from the oppression caused by capitalist tyranny imposed by U.S. power. Protesters also crusaded against the establishment—the elite ensconced in the government bureaucracy, universities, and corporate boardrooms who profited from the misery of the masses. They adopted the tactics of the civil rights movement by publicly demonstrating against Vietnam.

A most effective forum was the teach-in, the first of which took place at the University of Michigan one day in late March 1965. Three thousand students and faculty discussed the war, and the next morning several hundred demonstrated against escalation. Led by academics whose prominence worried the administration, teach-ins became commonplace across the nation. Many professors had supported Johnson in 1964; now they turned against him. Professors and students became active. On May 21–22, 1965, over 20,000 students on the campus of the traditionally conservative University of California at Berkeley united against the establishment—alleged exploiters, racists, and oppressors. Students also boycotted or demonstrated against the Pentagon, Dow Chemical (the manufacturer of napalm), and U.S. Navy recruiters. In a moral assault on an increasingly irritated but worried Johnson administration, they demanded love, not war. Rusk was one of their main targets.

The radicals constituted a minority of the antiwar movement, but they joined an array of people who opposed U.S. involvement in Vietnam. Liberals doubted that corrupt South Vietnamese leaders would ever garner support. Pacifists, the more radical among them linked to the New Left students, condemned the war. Libertarians demanded an end to the excessive power of the government. Directing its message at elitism, a counterculture mocked U.S. institutions by means of pranks (burning money at the Stock Exchange, plastering recruiting stations with signs that read, "See Canada Now"). Although fundamental disagreement existed between the agendas of these groups, they joined in antiwar rallies that grew to epic proportions and included such influential figures as Martin Luther King, Jr. Demonstrations combined fun, emotional outbursts, serious political sloganeering, and education. Some protests grew violent, however, occasionally even fatal. In late 1965 two men used gasoline to immolate themselves, and a Quaker peace activist died after setting himself on fire in front of the Pentagon, as did a Catholic leftist before the United Nations. They were, perhaps, inspired by the Buddhist monks in Vietnam. Suicide as a form of protest was not the rule.

Though not always successful, liberals, radicals, and pacifists were able to set aside their differences and launch huge rallies in 1967. People attended such events for a variety of reasons—to see a famous leader, to burn their draft cards, or for amusement. Demonstrations grew to attract hundreds of thousands of people. A burgeoning number of conscientious objectors refused the draft, while others either entered colleges and graduate schools (which deferred them from the draft and protected protesters from government retaliation), ignored induction notices, or fled the country. Some antiwar leaders—Herbert Aptheker, Staughton Lynd, Tom Hayden, Rennie Davis, and Jane Fonda—defied State Department bans on travel to Vietnam and visited Hanoi and the NLF in the South. There they found steely determination to fight until the United States withdrew.

Liberals guided the antiwar movement for years, frustrating the New Left, but dissent was not muffled. The Democrats worried about a backlash against their party in the 1966 elections. In California the hawkish Ronald Reagan avoided the Vietnam issue but managed to capitalize on the campus unrest caused by the war to unseat two-term Governor Edmund G. Brown. Republicans gained over forty seats in the House and seven in the Senate that year. In the Senate, two Republicans—Charles Percy of Illinois and Mark Hatfield of Oregon—won on antiwar platforms. Some Democrats talked of challenging Johnson in the 1968 presidential election if the war continued.

It should be noted, however, that a plurality of Americans backed the war and resisted the antiwar movement. Protesters tried to broaden their movement from largely white, middle-class students to the working class, but they failed to change the minds of ordinary people during the 1967 Vietnam Summer campaign, modeled on the 1964 door-to-door civil rights tactics used in Mississippi. After his appearances before Fulbright, Rusk received hundreds of telegrams, which ran 10 to 1 in favor of his testimony. Indeed, five hundred trade unionists called for peace in Vietnam at the AFL-CIO convention in December 1967, but Johnson and Rusk got a rousing ovation from organized labor and the endorsement of union chief George Meany for the war.

Still, the protests profoundly affected the administration. Johnson's approval rating had dropped to 38 percent by the end of 1967, even though most people surveyed backed his rationale of halting the spread of communism. Officials met with dissenters to try to manipulate public opinion, but to no avail. Rusk bore the brunt of the protests. On January 31, 1967, he met with a large group of students coordinated by the National Student Association and antiwar radical Allard Lowenstein. Rusk explained his policy and fielded questions, but he alienated many in the group when asked what would happen if the United States escalated to the point of using nuclear weapons. "Well," Rusk replied, leaning back in his chair, taking a drag from a cigarette, and blowing out the smoke, "somebody's going to get hurt." The stunned group stared gape-mouthed; one participant reported that the students murmured, "My God, the Secretary of State of the United States is crazy. This guy has lost it." Rusk later felt ambushed by Lowenstein, who, he believed, had orchestrated the entire affair to embarrass the administration.[21] The gathering certainly did not help public relations.

The pressure, in fact, got worse. A "Get Rusk" vendetta of anti-Vietnam Democrats in the Senate attacked him to get at Johnson. Speaking to an audience at Cornell University in April 1967, Rusk was startled when several dozen people stood, donned death's-head masks, and faced him. He took questions after the speech, but his wife wept in the car as they left the campus. A few weeks after the March on Washington, activists in New York City pelted him with eggs, stones, and a bag of cow's blood.

In 1967 students at Cornell University protest Rusk's speech on Vietnam. *Courtesy Richard B. Russell Library, University of Georgia*

The October 20–21, 1967, March on Washington began at the Lincoln Memorial and then splintered off to the Pentagon. It attracted over one hundred thousand people, including "beat" poet Allen Ginsberg (who chanted prayers to levitate the Pentagon) and hard-charging New Leftists, some of whom were hospitalized or jailed. Remarkably, Rusk offered his home to his youngest son and two Cornell University classmates who came for the march, but they declined. Such magnanimity aside, the march shook the administration to its core.

Under siege in the White House, Johnson was so alarmed that he urged his attorney general (with Rusk's compliance) to leak rumors that a rabble of Communists connected to North Vietnam and the Soviet Union led the march. In Rusk's view, young people saw war as new: "A lot of the arguments I hear now against the war are the same ones people used once in the thirties, the same sort of things people said to me in arguing against arming or preparing for a war against Germany."[22] References to history held little appeal for the Sixties Generation.

Although the American public at large agreed with Rusk, the administration realized that without progress in Vietnam the president's election in 1968 would be at risk. The March on Washington had been a public relations setback. For the first time since the Bonus March of 1932, the government had called on troops to control petitioning citizens. But protesters simply sat down and sang songs or gave flowers to the soldiers. The antiwar movement had become more than a nuisance; it had awakened people to the stalemate in Vietnam and led them to question authority. In his more reflective moments, which were more frequent than his outbursts against allegedly Communist-led students, Rusk noted that Americans were growing impatient with the war. But, "manning the last outpost at Khesanh on the Potomac," wrote columnist Joseph Kraft in an allusion to the U.S. base in Vietnam, he defended Johnson to the end.[23] Unfortunately, as he would admit later, Rusk never realized the limits of public forbearance.

Americanization of the war had not changed the fortunes of South Vietnam or the United States. That much was clear to antiwar protesters of all stripes. Lack of progress was also abundantly evident to the dispirited Johnson administration. Among these officials, Rusk pledged to persevere. He acknowledged, however, that the possibility of defeat grew greater every day. Like the besieged president, Rusk refused to renege on the promise to stem aggression. As a result, his Wilsonian ideals—even though they were the very reason he doggedly persisted in Vietnam—were difficult to detect. This was a full-blown tragedy; Vietnam was inexorably undermining the reputation of a person who was devoted to liberal internationalism. Rusk was not an evil man, and his basic assumptions about aggressors were valid. His reading of history was accurate, and his fear of communism was legitimate. But his approach to the war, including his refusal to concede anything to the enemy and the specific strategies taken, undercut everything he stood for.

Rusk and Johnson thought they had an escape valve: negotiations. Johnson tapped the secretary of state to conduct peace talks with North Vietnam. Various offers came forth from the administration, interspersed with bombing escalations and then halts. Pressured by Johnson, Rusk directed this effort with increasing intensity. His flexibility in modifying demands for peace would determine his success or failure, but such flexibility would be elusive as he struggled to succeed at both safeguarding American interests and orchestrating Johnson's war.

Notes

1. Kraft, "The Dean Rusk Show," 134.
2. Cohen, *Dean Rusk*, 251.
3. Schoenbaum, *Waging Peace*, 434.
4. Cohen, *Dean Rusk*, 253.
5. Rusk, *As I Saw It*, 448; Cohen, *Dean Rusk*, 258.
6. Schulzinger, *A Time for War*, 175.
7. DROH III, LBJL, 11.
8. Robert S. McNamara, *In Retrospect: The Tragedy and Lessons of Vietnam* (New York: Random House, 1995), 157–58.
9. Cohen, *Dean Rusk*, 258.
10. James A. Bill, *George Ball: Behind the Scenes in U.S. Foreign Policy* (New Haven: Yale University Press, 1997), 14; Cohen, *Dean Rusk*, 258.
11. Rusk, *As I Saw It*, 456.
12. Ibid., 457.
13. Schulzinger, *A Time for War*, 194.
14. Cohen, *Dean Rusk*, 271.
15. Stewart Alsop, "Mr. Dove and Mr. Hawk," *Saturday Evening Post* (June 18, 1966): 18.
16. Dean Rusk, "The Unseen Search for Peace," *DSB* 53 (November 1, 1965): 691.
17. Cohen, *Dean Rusk*, 287.
18. Lloyd C. Gardner, *Pay Any Price: Lyndon Johnson and the Wars for Vietnam* (Chicago: Ivan R. Dee, 1995), 111.
19. Moskin, "Dean Rusk," 16.
20. Robert Dallek, *Flawed Giant: Lyndon Johnson and His Times, 1961–1973* (New York: Oxford University Press, 1998), 473–74.
21. Tom Wells, *The War Within: America's Battle over Vietnam* (Berkeley: University of California Press, 1994), 119.
22. Kraft, "The Dean Rusk Show," 35.
23. Ibid.

9

The Whole World Was Watching

Bombing and diplomacy went hand in hand. After the Johnson administration initiated Operation Rolling Thunder in 1965, Rusk attempted to negotiate peace. As a chief opponent of escalation of the war, he was committed to this course, yet his principled neo-Wilsonian refusal to compromise with aggressors made a settlement unlikely. "You can't end half a war," he remarked.[1] That position slowed progress on the battlefield and at the bargaining table. Despite his reasonable assertion that the United States sought only to honor its commitments and protect its ally, Rusk was rigid in negotiations, and the violence of the air and ground wars persisted. From 1965 onward the administration maintained its basic demand that North Vietnam withdraw. Its only real concession—bombing halts—was not sufficient to persuade the enemy to act. The effects of stalemate devastated not only Johnson but also the very reputation of the United States as upholder of the liberal internationalist values that Rusk tried to defend.

Operation Rolling Thunder

Bombing was first conceived to bolster South Vietnam to give the country time to regroup and revitalize its war effort. The air war did not stabilize the government; ground troops were needed for that. The potential benefit of Operation Rolling Thunder was as a tool in diplomacy. At the time, it was argued that bombing was necessary to limit the infiltration of men and supplies from North Vietnam. The Vietcong and North Vietnam would suffer under a hail of destruction until Ho and the NLF negotiated, or the United States could halt the bombing periodically to encourage the Communists to talk. Either way the air war was a political tactic. McNamara viewed it in these terms; Rusk, too, hoped that bombing pauses would encourage negotiations.

Rusk assessed his own mission as a failure. Whereas McNamara fulfilled Johnson's charge of blocking North Vietnam from seizing the South by force, Rusk was unable to bring peace through negotiations. He mostly blamed the North Vietnamese, who pursued only policies to oust the Americans rather than initiatives for peace. But he also faulted many of his countrymen's naive faith in diplomacy. Although diplomacy had resolved other crises, such as the Korean War, it had no chance against an aggressive enemy bent on victory, he cautioned. Surely, moreover, bombing did not encourage the enemy to take part in a dialogue.

The bombing was ferocious. In 1965 pilots flew 25,000 sorties over the North and dropped 33,000 tons of bombs. In 1966 the effort intensified, as 128,000 tons fell on the North during 79,000 sorties. Much more was aimed at Vietcong targets in the South; the 3,600 sorties over South Vietnam in April 1965 shot up to 4,800 by June. The United States spent $9.60 for every $1 of damage. Downed American planes during the two years numbered 489, while the civilian and military casualties in North Vietnam doubled to 24,000 from 1965 to 1966.

In order to keep Ho worrying about future attacks, McNamara excluded bridges, ports, munitions factories, and utilities as targets. Still, the destruction was immense. In 1967, Americans flew 108,000 sorties; the United States was able to keep 300 aircraft over North Vietnam and Laos for at least thirty minutes each day. But infiltration did not stop; in fact, traffic on the Ho Chi Minh Trail through Laos and Cambodia increased.

Pauses, designed to encourage negotiations, often followed bombing. But North Vietnam never seemed to move in the desired direction. Rusk was frustrated. Reaching back to Kennedy's 1961 meeting with Khrushchev in Vienna, the United States had broached the issue of the arbitration of negotiations by members of the international community. The Soviets and Eastern European nations, Canada, and other countries had tried their hand at mediation, but the answer from Hanoi was always a reiteration of the Vietminh cry for liberation and independence. Rusk never could understand Ho or the essence of Vietnamese nationalism. After all, he reasoned, the United States was not asking for territory or bases. It sought neither to destroy or invade the North nor to alter Ho's regime or its alliance with the Communist world. No economic issues were at stake. Johnson was simply willing to schedule a withdrawal of U.S. forces if Hanoi would do the same with its troops. Yet North Vietnam refused to accept these terms.

From June 1964 to August 1965, Canadian J. Blair Seaborn of the International Control Commission on Indochina (which was created in 1954 to oversee implementation of the Geneva Accords) conducted five trips to Hanoi. America, he said, would withdraw and give aid and diplomatic recognition to the North if Ho ceased to assist the Vietcong. If this offer was rejected, the United States would launch air and naval attacks against North Vietnam. Hanoi, Seaborn reported, had no interest in the offer. UN Secretary General U Thant, in his own attempt to further the talks, got the same reception. Rusk, as he put it, "hoped for a sign that would have made our military efforts unnecessary," but he gave Ho little encouragement—that is, withdrawal from the South aside, he never extended any terms that Hanoi sought.[2]

Rusk placed the onus of responsibility for the war on North Vietnam. He backed bombing and helped choose targets, although he picked military, rather than civilian, locations. For him the air war bolstered the South and exhibited Johnson's will to fight communism, even against worsening odds. Rusk adhered to his fundamental demand that Hanoi must leave the South before the United States would withdraw. It was quite simple for him: "There could have been peace in Southeast Asia if North Vietnam had been willing to live at peace with its neighbors."[3]

Mutual distrust obstructed the peace process. In a speech at Johns Hopkins University in April 1965, Johnson offered negotiations with no preconditions attached. Hanoi called the proposal a fraud. The fact that bombing pauses did not sway Hanoi—a six-day halt in May 1965 achieved nothing—proved to Rusk that Ho was not interested in reciprocal actions by both sides. Although Rusk did not put much stock in the policy of pauses, he had hope for the Christmas bombing halt of 1965–66. A major cessation should occur just once; any more, he reasoned, and the enemy would doubt U.S. resolve. He also advocated the Christmas pause (which lasted for thirty-seven days) because the Soviets had pledged to talk with Hanoi. Polls showed that nearly 60 percent of Americans favored the halt, while even more approved of diplomatic initiatives.

Rusk sent Ambassador Harriman, National Security Adviser McGeorge Bundy, Vice President Hubert Humphrey, and other officials to enlist 145 countries in the effort to bring Hanoi to the conference table. Meanwhile, he gave Hungary a fourteen-point peace plan (by design the same number as Woodrow Wilson's agenda for ending World War I), which included "unconditional discussions" about the future of Vietnam and self-determination for all Vietnamese.[4] The Fourteen Points, the first formal U.S. peace proposals, basically rehashed previous positions. To Hanoi's chagrin, they included no concessions on the status of the NLF in negotiations. Yet the irony could not have been lost on Ho. Nearly half a century before, Wilson had rebuffed him in refusing to apply his Fourteen Points to Indochina. Now the United States was willing to talk about self-determination, but, after years of war, it was too late.

Rusk welcomed Soviet help. He was convinced that Moscow saw peace in Vietnam as a way to stimulate relations with the United States. Russia confirmed Rusk's suspicions that the renegade Chinese had discouraged Hanoi from negotiating. Later, however, Rusk discovered that because Moscow was afraid of driving Ho into Beijing's arms, it had refused to pressure him. Hanoi, Rusk concluded, was "well insulated from world public opinion. They [paid] it very little attention" and cared little for "advice from Moscow."[5]

When Ho did not respond to the Christmas bombing pause, the president and his secretary of state threw up their hands. Military officials had opposed the halt from the start, arguing that Ho would capitalize on it by pouring men and matériel into the South. After five weeks, Hanoi announced that there was nothing to discuss. "Thinking we had gone the last mile," explained the disillusioned Rusk, "I favored resumption" of the bombing.[6] By late January 1966 the peace offensive had little to show. Johnson ordered the resumption of Rolling Thunder.

There would be other halts in years to come, but the idea of coupling bombing with diplomacy faded. Rusk never believed that the air war in the North was worth the effort and risks. Intelligence reports showed that because most of North Vietnam's economy was not industrialized, bombing had little effect on Hanoi's ability to wage war. Infiltration did not slow down; the 7,500 North Vietnamese troops in 1965 grew to 30,000 the following year. Bombing halts seemed to cause results that were the reverse of those intended. "The frequency of our bombing halts and probes for negotiations," lamented Rusk, "might have misled Hanoi to think that we were irresolute and ready for peace at any price."[7] Rusk defended the use of diplomacy; negotiations had resolved such earlier crises as the Berlin blockade and the Korean War. In the North Vietnamese case, however, nobody seemed to be listening.

Hanoi proved resilient. Ho's followers hid supplies or worked at night to evade the bombers. What was destroyed was restored by resourcefulness or Chinese and Soviet military and economic aid, which amounted to $400 million in 1965 and rose thereafter. China sent 320,000 troops to North Vietnam from 1965 to 1969, enough to bolster the defense and civilian efforts and free North Vietnamese men to head south. The 73,000 soldiers the Vietcong had lost by 1966 were replaced in part by fighters from North Vietnam and from the South. The author of Rolling Thunder, Secretary of Defense McNamara, grew so disheartened by its ineffectiveness that he asked for a complete halt to the air war. In November 1967, when Johnson refused, he resigned.

The president had reasons for continuing Rolling Thunder. Bombing would reduce U.S. casualties and possibly stabilize the South, making the air war attractive at home. He also hoped to cripple the North by hitting petroleum depots, which had been targeted by mid-1966. And a new sort of bombing occurred. Pilots dropped propaganda leaflets denigrating Ho and warning of more carnage. This psychological warfare backfired as Ho stirred up patriotic fervor against the cruel U.S. air war. Ultimately, Johnson could conceive of no alternative to the bombing.

Antiwar activists certainly could, however. They agreed with Ho's portrayal of the bombing, and the intensity of the protests soon convinced many Democratic politicians that it was in their best interest to stop the air war. Just as the bombing had not budged the North, Rusk's efforts at negotiation—stepped up from 1966 onward—had gotten nowhere. As Johnson angrily told Rusk in 1966, "I keep trying to get Ho to the negotiating table. I try writing him, calling him,

"IT MAY BE HAZARDOUS TO MY HEALTH."

The undaunted Ho Chi Minh proved to be an unflinching negotiator. *Courtesy of Edmund Valtman*

going through the Russians and Chinese, and all I hear back is 'Fuck you, Lyndon.' "[8]

Negotiating Options

Under pressure at home, Johnson sought a diplomatic way out of Vietnam. A committee chaired by Averell Harriman searched for options if U.S. bombing were halted. Meanwhile, Democrats in Congress questioned the president's earnestness in pursuing negotiations, urging him to look at polls that showed the public's preference for dialogue with North Vietnam. In late 1966, Arthur Goldberg, Johnson's UN representative and a former Kennedy appointee to the Supreme Court, was distraught that the United States had not done enough for peace. He and Rusk had offered a formula, presented through the United Nations, to stop the bombing and withdraw U.S. troops in return for concessions from the North. Hanoi added conditions, including the exclusion of outside influence in the affairs of Vietnam. Goldberg was willing to accept these terms; Rusk refused them as too one-sided.

Polish diplomats offered a more promising plan. Poland's delegate on the UN International Control Commission, Janusz Lewandowski, secretly told Henry Cabot Lodge that he had met with Ho in June 1966. Ho had agreed to talk about the future reunification and neutralization of Vietnam if bombing stopped and the NLF could participate in the negotiations. But Lewandowski was never able to spell out to Rusk what more than pledge to talk the North was willing to do in return. Because Hanoi never issued a word on the Polish plan, moreover, Rusk grew suspicious of the whole endeavor: "We were ready to go to Warsaw and begin talks, but the Poles couldn't produce any North Vietnamese."[9]

When this so-called Marigold Initiative unraveled, Rusk had no remorse. Visiting South Vietnam in the fall of 1966, he lost patience upon surveying Vietcong destruction northwest of Saigon. "The truth is, we simply doubted the authenticity of Marigold," explained Rusk, because, after six months of talking, "we hadn't received any confirmation from the North Vietnamese that they wanted to talk."[10] Bombing reescalated around Hanoi and Haiphong Harbor, and, in an effort to put pressure on Johnson, journalists leaked word of the Marigold discussions to the public.

Rusk knew that the bombings created the impression that the United States was not interested in negotiations, and he told the president so. This was just another "black eye" suffered by the

Americans, who waited on Lewandowski in good faith. Rusk concluded that Lewandowski spoke only for himself, not for Ho. Poland blamed the United States for the breakdown, but in Rusk's view "there was nothing to collapse."[11] The effort at devising a negotiating agenda continued. Acting on his October 1966 call for Hanoi to discuss peace in cooperation with other nations, Rusk drew up a communiqué that pledged a U.S. withdrawal within six months after North Vietnam pulled out of the South. Hanoi failed to respond, and American conservatives censured the plan as a sellout of Saigon.

Rusk pushed on with his program of enlisting international support. In February 1967, after Johnson ordered a bombing pause to honor the annual truce during the Tet holidays, Rusk approved a British- and Russian-devised plan that laid out two stages of negotiations. In Phase A, the United States would stop the bombing on the condition that Hanoi would enter into Phase B: talks. This arrangement would answer the question of what Ho would do if the United States ceased the air war. The Phase A-Phase B agenda excited Rusk because it involved the Soviets and a close ally, Great Britain. Both were briefed on the U.S. position. The British and American negotiator Chester Cooper wrote the Russians that the bombing would halt when the United States was assured that infiltration "will stop." But semantics soon barred the way.

Johnson, Rusk, and National Security Adviser Walt Rostow (McGeorge Bundy had left in February 1966) worked the formula into a letter, which they sent to Ho, stating that the bombing would end once infiltration "has stopped." Johnson demanded this stringent quid pro quo, to Rusk's chagrin. The change of verb tense—from "will" to "has"—dashed the Phase A-Phase B process, which was, Rusk lamented, the closest "we came to setting up talks before 1968."[12] Still, he defended Johnson during the ensuing Anglo-Soviet denunciation of American bad faith. The grammatical mix-up "was just one of those things that sometimes happen."[13] More to the point, Rusk contested the claim of Prime Minister Harold Wilson, who declared that a chance for peace had been missed. Had Hanoi been interested in discussions, the wording would not have mattered, said Rusk. Johnson honored British pleas to delay the resumption of bombing for a few more days, but Hanoi never answered. On February 13, 1967, the air war resumed.

Rusk discussed the prospects for peace on the television series "Face the Nation" a month before the resumption of Rolling Thunder. He expressed optimism only because, as a diplomat, he felt that he had to. In reality he was pessimistic, for the North Vietnamese had not given "one iota of response" to U.S. overtures.[14] The resumption of bombing might persuade Ho to initiate change, but the secretary of state did not hold out much hope. Further endeavors reached the same dead end. Journalists, French intermediaries, and analyst Henry Kissinger could produce no better results. In June 1967, Johnson discussed negotiations with Soviet Premier Aleksei Kosygin in Glassboro, New Jersey, to no avail. In September 1967 he offered the San Antonio Formula: the bombing would stop when North Vietnam engaged in discussions, during which time Hanoi would not increase its infiltration. No word came from Hanoi. The Communists would not negotiate short of an American pledge to withdraw from the country—unilaterally.

Now a symbol of the war after having graced the cover of *Time* magazine in late 1966 as Johnson's foreign policy chief, Rusk pressed on, loyal to the desperate president. Hostile legislators and demonstrators targeted Rusk. Appearances in Congress characterized him as a spartan supporter of a lost cause in Southeast Asia. Neither hawks nor doves liked him; hawks saw Rusk as too compromising, and doves lumped him with the hawks. Because he was Johnson's faithful ally, the hawk imprimatur was hard to shake. Rusk supported the bombing and rejected the charge that the United States was stalling negotiations to save face. He repeated that the air war, along with more effective ground fighting, had brought progress. However, the demonstrators did not believe him. South Vietnam's adoption of a constitutional form of government in February 1967 was a heartening sign, he proclaimed. But the protesters considered such views laughable, and the credibility gap widened.

Regarding peace talks, Rusk always referred to the obstinacy of the "other side" in refusing to come to the table. He stood by those principles—rooted in collective security—that protesters despised. He responded that they should not lose sight of the great question of the day—how to organize a durable peace—or the world might be doomed. "My generation of students was led down the path into the catastrophe of World War II, which could have been prevented," he explained. "We came out of that war thinking that collective security was the key to the prevention of World War III."[15] To the war's opponents such neo-Wilsonian thinking was outmoded and hysterical.

Rusk irritated the protesters by interpreting history to serve his argument. Contrary to their claims, according to Rusk, the Korean War had been more destructive and much uglier than the Vietnam War. Germany's blitz on London during World War II had also been worse. One could not find similar damage in Hanoi, Rusk claimed. Civilian casualties, moreover, had been higher in previous wars. Had not the bombing of Britain stiffened morale against the Nazis? asked antiwar groups. Sure, he replied, but demonstrators must not forget that Germany itself had finally collapsed from the devastation wreaked by bombing.

Rusk's defense of Johnson did not win over the protesters. More joined their ranks. The public must be prepared to hold the line for however long it might take, Rusk explained. But more and more Americans responded that they had had enough. Rusk relied on detailed summaries about America's historic confrontation with aggressors. Students were unimpressed. He even slighted the antiwar demonstrations, maintaining that they were not as huge as they seemed. A few hundred thousand marchers out of a population of two hundred million people was no indication that the country opposed the war, Rusk declared. Protesters were dumbfounded and angry.

Dissenters hated his views on China. In late 1967 he warned of the specter of "a billion Chinese armed with nuclear weapons." This phrase outraged liberals, who accused him of racism akin to the old fears of the "yellow peril." Senator Eugene McCarthy demanded his resignation, and even the Taiwanese admonished him. Rusk was incensed at being branded a racist.[16] In any case he stood his ground. There would be no peace in Vietnam, he pledged, that permitted the intrusion of the People's Republic of China.

Why cite China as the enemy in Vietnam? asked the press, protesters, and many European allies. The NLF, Rusk replied, was a proxy for outside aggressors, having received Chinese small arms, ammunition, food, and sophisticated Soviet weaponry. He was willing to allow the Vietcong to join negotiations, but he would not recognize the body as a government. That struck dissenters as unreasonable. And they grew angrier when the secretary of state woodenly reiterated that if Beijing threw its weight behind peace, then all suffering would halt immediately. The protesters saw not China but a United States guided by Rusk's neo-Wilsonianism as the aggressor in Vietnam.

Behind the scenes, Rusk labored for peace. He counted seventeen peace efforts by U.S. officials and third parties after April 1965, including Johnson's open letter to Ho, the Pope's appeal for talks, a call by Asian nations for a cessation in the warfare, an entreaty by nearly twenty nonaligned countries for negotiations, and numerous bombing halts. Nothing worked—except that many Americans branded Rusk an arbitrary imperialist.

Vietnam consumed Rusk's personal life. Everywhere he went, he met protesters who called him a murderer. To the distress of his wife, Virginia, people picketed his home. He discovered that, without an estimate of when the war would end, not even his Cherokee County cousins supported him. He bit his tongue, deliberately remaining stoic to conceal his emotions, but the criticism hurt. "It's not that I don't have feelings," Rusk told an associate; in fact, although his doctor did not find ulcers, he had frequent stomach pains.[17] Here was Rusk, a Wilsonian, an idealist missionary in the cause of global peace, being accused of warmongering. It chewed him up inside.

Rusk continued to stand by the president. According to the secretary of state, the demonstrators were only encouraging North Vietnam. They were saying, "Now, just hang in there, fellows, and you will get what you want politically even though you cannot win it militarily." He believed that if "self-styled intermediaries" had not probed for a settlement, Hanoi would have faced a united front and sued for peace.[18] As protesters held up "Peace Now!" signs outside the site of one of his appearances in 1967, he told the audience inside that he would like to carry one himself, "but for a genuine peace, not for a phony peace."[19] Rusk admitted that he had underestimated the tenacity of the enemy. He had banked on intense bombing to produce a cease-fire and a favorable response to administration peace plans. The enemy had not answered. At the end of 1967 he looked for a glimmer of hope in Vietnam. There was none to be found.

A Reassessment

A reevaluation of the Vietnam War was long overdue by late 1967 and even more pressing in 1968. General Ky and General Nguyen Van Thieu had both won elections in South Vietnam, but they so disliked each other that political unity was impossible. Rusk had hopes that their October 1967 inauguration would provide a solid basis of support for the government. But persistent internal dissent led to more violence and oppression.

U.S. bombing increased; so did Communist infiltration into the South. By mid-1967 more than 12,000 North Vietnamese trucks wound down the Ho Chi Minh Trail. Over 500,000 peasants went to work in the North repairing bombed facilities. Incredibly, in 1974, after years of Rolling Thunder, North Vietnam could boast the construction of 3,125 miles of fuel pipelines along the infiltration route to supply its army in the South. The Communist government moved the citizenry out of Hanoi, out of harm's way from the bombing; by the end of 1967 the capital's population had shrunk from 1 million to 250,000 people. Over one-half million U.S. troops now fought in Vietnam, and hundreds came home in body bags or on stretchers every week.

Protesters erupted in outrage, marching 100,000 strong to the Pentagon in October 1967 and staging sit-ins at induction centers around the country. "Hey, hey, LBJ, how many kids have you killed today?" they chanted. Johnson turned over evidence of Communist infiltration among the activists to such legislators as House Minority Leader Gerald Ford of Michigan. Fearful of unleashing another anti-Communist Red Scare, Rusk prevented Ford from publicizing the information. But the desolate president became morose as his once faithful advisers, allies, and voters deserted him in droves.

In December 1967, Rusk gave a speech lauding the gains made against Communists in Asia and demanding that South Vietnam be allowed to prosper free from interference and aggression. But critics of the address referred to Vietnam as "Dean Rusk's war," and protesters marched against the administration in greater numbers than ever before. Despite his explanations, Rusk could not cover up the destruction of the war and the administration's failure either to win or to end it. Rusk was trapped in this tragedy, a prisoner of history, principles, and loyalty.

Johnson and his advisers were gloomy—like Rusk, the president was stuck fast. Johnson likened the war to being caught outdoors in a Texas hailstorm: he could neither run nor hide, nor could he make it go away. The president would neither promote negotiations by halting the bombing nor support escalation. That position had led George Ball to resign in 1966. Then, in a big blow to Johnson and Rusk, Robert McNamara, the architect of Vietnam strategy, threw in the towel in November 1967. In March 1968, Johnson replaced him with Clark Clifford, a longtime hawkish presidential adviser who now only tepidly backed the bombing.

With McNamara gone, Rusk stood alone in the upper level of government to defend Johnson. The stress was unbearable. He recoiled at the destruction in Vietnam and winced at domestic criticism. Rusk worried for his family—his wife agonizing with him,

Legislators seek answers to the war from Johnson in 1967. Rusk is at the president's right, Hubert Humphrey is across the table. Facing the camera at left is Senator Richard Russell, the powerful friend of Johnson and Rusk. *Courtesy Richard B. Russell Library, University of Georgia*

two children attending college, another child coming up behind them, and his finances dwindling. The stomachaches sharpened and could be alleviated only by stretching out on his floor at home after long days and late nights. Four packs per day of Lark cigarettes, Scotch, and aspirin helped him stem the pain. But he would not stop working on the war, and he refused to change course in Vietnam.

With the military situation and peace talks stalled, in early November 1967, Johnson summoned the illustrious Wise Men for advice. The group included former Secretary of State Acheson, who told him to hang tough and ignore his critics. McGeorge Bundy, William Bundy, Walt Rostow, Maxwell Taylor, and Rusk agreed. A bombing halt would be futile, they said. In January 1968, in response to harsh criticism of Johnson's Vietnam policy from India, Rusk declared that Washington would not back down from aggressive Hanoi. The United States had shown restraint by not mining the North's harbors or extending the fighting into Cambodia and Laos. But "when a North Vietnamese battalion is marching down the road, we must decide whether to get out of its way or stop it. We have decided to stop it."[20] Although Johnson would talk with North Vietnam, he would also continue bombing because Hanoi was "still weaseling on us."[21]

Putting a positive spin on the war to quell public dissent, Johnson had advisers talk about progress. In November 1967, General Westmoreland informed Congress that in two years the United States would prevail. Although the road to victory would be tough, argued the State Department and the CIA, a year from now things would be better. Hanoi was prepared to hold out, but heavier bombing and stepped-up ground operations would slowly destroy its will to fight. Then a shocking event exploded this myth.

The Tet Offensive

On January 30, 1968, during the Vietnamese New Year, or Tet, Vietcong commandos attacked the U.S. embassy in Saigon. The suicide squad of nineteen blasted through an outside wall, killing several marines before being gunned down. They were part of an enormous offensive coordinated by the NLF and Hanoi to seize the countryside, the provincial capitals, and five major cities in South Vietnam. One observer equated Tet with Hitler's last gasp at the Battle of the Bulge. Similarly, the effort's greatest impact was not on the military situation; rather, the attack sank Johnson's political fortunes.

Over the previous month, General Giap, the North Vietnamese commander, had diverted American attention to the U.S. marine base at Khe Sanh, northwest of Saigon. He shelled the base, which took on symbolic significance for Johnson as his Dien Bien Phu, where the French had made their last desperate stand against Vietminh forces in 1954. Using combat troops and the heaviest bombing of the entire war up to that point, Johnson ordered Khe Sanh defended. Tons of defoliants and bombs fell on the enemy, and the lush area around Khe Sanh was turned into a desert. One hundred thousand tons of explosives from B-52s ignited a five-square-mile area in the biggest air raid in the history of warfare.

With U.S. attention trained on Khe Sanh, Hanoi launched the Tet Offensive in the South. The Vietcong captured and held the ancient city of Hue for three weeks, devastating buildings and people before being pushed out on February 23, 1968. Elsewhere two weeks of bloody battles brought victory for the South Vietnamese and U.S. armies. Failing to hold a single town and having squandered roughly 50,000 soldiers, Giap withdrew his forces to the North. His military strength was cut by about one-third; the

Communists lost about one-fifth of their total forces. Despite the scare, Westmoreland called Tet a disaster for the Vietcong and Hanoi. Militarily, he was right. Defectors to the Communist side were rare, the South Vietnamese army held its own, and no territory had been lost. The enemy had greatly suffered. But the political impact of Tet was devastating.

Rusk understood the psychological ramifications of the Tet Offensive, especially when the sanctuary of the U.S. embassy was penetrated. As the Tet Offensive had begun, however, he had been preoccupied with gaining the release of eighty-three members of the USS *Pueblo*'s crew. On January 23, 1968, Communist North Korea had seized the vessel in international waters in violation of international law. Rusk advised the North Koreans to "cool it," but he prevented a military response to this outrage.[22] At the end of the year, after patient diplomacy on Rusk's part, the sailors were released.

Now a much bigger crisis loomed. Skeptical reporters and the public wanted to know how the administration could claim that the end was in sight in Vietnam when America's own embassy had been invaded. After all, Westmoreland had been forced to take refuge in a command center as the battle raged in Saigon. Perceptions and images proved to be crucial elements of the Tet Offensive. "This could be very bad," said Johnson, realizing that public confidence in his policies might wither. Venerable news anchor Walter Cronkite, who had backed the war, asked during the Tet Offensive, "What the hell is going on here? I thought we were winning the war."[23] The gap between what Johnson and Rusk professed and the reality in the field was widening into a chasm.

The South Vietnamese did not help matters. The chief of the national police shot a captive in the head, point-blank, as an NBC news camera projected the horror to twenty million American viewers. The *Pueblo* incident and Tet Offensive made the United States seem impotent. There was no progress on the battlefield. And what was gained, anyway? A marine explained that the town of Ben Tre had been leveled because "we had to destroy the village to save it." Americans rubbed their eyes in disbelief at such illogic; for most, the war seemed futile. By March 1968, in the midst of an election year, the president's approval rating had plummeted to 36 percent.

Cruelty escalated beyond description in the hamlet of My Lai in March 1968. Although the army covered up the massacre at the time, the barbarity revealed the atrocities committed in the name of anticommunism. Troops under the command of twenty-four-year-old Lieutenant William Calley avenged the losses of the Tet Offensive by killing five hundred unarmed men, women, and children in the village—most of them execution-style.

The usually unflappable Rusk now blamed the press for the domestic reverberations caused by Tet. Filling in journalists on the debacle on February 9, he angrily demanded of a reporter who had expressed doubts about victory, "Whose side are you on? Now, I'm Secretary of State of the United States, and I'm on our side." The remark received national coverage, portraying Rusk as a myopic Cold Warrior, an image that was only exacerbated by his grumbling about people who felt the need "to go probing for the things that one can bitch about."[24] In public he seemed not to mind. "If the United States failed in Southeast Asia and if this led to aggression elsewhere," he stated later, "there might not be any television networks or newspapers."[25] To his annoyance, however, the media seemed to prefer bad news about Vietnam.

Rusk hardened even more. On camera, in his March 11, 1968, testimony before Senator Fulbright's Foreign Relations Committee, and at cabinet meetings, Rusk vigorously defended the war. "If we don't keep our word in Southeast Asia, the inevitable result [will] be isolationism in the country," he said. The Communists were in disarray, but so was the West. Withdrawal "would lead to a major war," he argued, ignoring his own logic that there was little danger of war because of Communist disarray![26]

The confusion can be explained by Rusk's agonizing effort to move Johnson toward a solution in Vietnam while remaining true to the president. In private he endorsed Johnson's decision to reevaluate Vietnam once again. In March 1968 a task force under Clifford, the new secretary of defense, focused on Westmoreland's request for an additional 206,000 troops. The military urged that the war be expanded by conducting major offensives and entering neutral Laos and Cambodia. Westmoreland even hoped to invade North Vietnam and to increase the bombing, hitting Hanoi with the full force of U.S. power. Because Johnson had determined to end all talk of surrender within his administration, Rusk feared that the president would embrace the recommendation.

Only the Joint Chiefs of Staff backed the plan. Clifford and the civilians, including Rusk, were incredulous. This would mean calling up reserves, spending billions of dollars, and drawing personnel from NATO commands in Europe. For its part, NATO might not stand the loss, having recently undergone the shock of Charles de Gaulle's decision to kick the alliance structure off French soil.

Reinforcements would not be any more effective in Vietnam than they had been before. And after Tet the American public would not permit the move. Moreover, the U.S. counterattack had inflicted a major blow on the Vietcong. It was time not for escalation but for new ideas about how to end the war. After the Tet Offensive, Rusk clearly became a force within the administration for deescalation.

Still bent on granting Westmoreland's troop request (as he had done every time in the past), Johnson heard Rusk turn the tide. After discussion of the Clifford task force report on March 4, Rusk emerged from his silence to suggest a bombing halt in those areas of North Vietnam not involved in the war against the South. Clifford and Johnson were stunned. In Rusk's plan the air war could continue against military targets, infiltration routes, staging areas, and in support of U.S. troops. It would be scaled back in other places deemed nonessential to the war. This was consistent with his earlier reservations about bombing the North. Now his idea might restart negotiations. If Hanoi rejected the overture, then the United States would be on record as having made an attempt at peace. With the monsoon season imminent, the air war would be difficult anyway.

After the lack of progress from earlier halts, during which Communist infiltration had continued, Johnson could have sneered at such talk. Coming from the faithful Rusk, however, the idea gave him pause. The secretary of state did not want to give in to Hanoi; he was willing to provide what the military wanted if the Communists did not budge. Yet an attempt at negotiations was worth the effort, at least to show North Vietnam and domestic critics that Johnson preferred peace. The president valued the opinion of his faithful adviser.

The 1968 election was also crucial. An unconditional yet partial bombing halt might placate antiwar enthusiasts. Voters dissatisfied with the war had given Senator Eugene McCarthy a shocking 42 percent of the vote in the New Hampshire Democratic primary and twenty of twenty-six convention delegates against the incumbent—President Johnson—on March 13. McCarthy advocated talks with Hanoi and stated that, if elected, he would consider firing Rusk. Senator Robert Kennedy, who had entered the campaign three days later, also demanded withdrawal. Ever the politician, Johnson was open to Rusk's idea.

As a final step before making his decision, the president reassembled the Wise Men, who had told him in November 1967 to stay the course. Now, four months later, in March 1968, even the hawkish Acheson advised Johnson to seek the best possible peace. Tet had doomed the U.S. effort. Rusk later confessed that he "was not optimistic that our initiative would lead to talks," but in the domestic political climate it seemed like the only viable alternative, and it would, at least, block the sending of more troops.[27] "Everybody is recommending surrender," complained Johnson on March 28, as his aides prepared his nationally televised speech on Vietnam.[28] But Rusk had worked on him. Troops meant more war— a war that Americans did not support and that was hurting the president in the polls.

With the exception of Thailand and South Korea, moreover, allies had not been of great help. Americans had suffered thousands of casualties during the Cold War in the name of collective security, but in the Korean and Vietnam wars the United States had supplied 80 to 90 percent of the foreign forces. "And that's not very collective," Rusk told Johnson. "So if my Cherokee County cousins were to say to me, 'Look, if collective security means 50,000 dead Americans every ten years, and it is not even collective, maybe it's not a very good idea.' "[29] This was powerful persuasion coming from Rusk, who was profoundly disappointed that so few allies had endorsed a most cherished Wilsonian doctrine of unity against aggressors.

Rusk's quiet, persistent entreaties in March 1968 influenced the president. The final decision did not come easily for Johnson; in mid-March he reiterated that the United States would meet its commitments and win the war. Then Robert Kennedy denounced him; the popular Democratic candidate pointed out that despite possessing the strongest military in history, one-half million troops joined by 700,000 South Vietnamese regulars, and total air and sea superiority, the United States could not secure a single city from enemy soldiers numbering a scant 250,000. Sobered by news that 509 Americans had been killed that mid-March week in Vietnam, the president turned again to Rusk.

Aides informed Johnson that hawkish statements were costing him votes. They predicted that he might lose the Wisconsin primary to Kennedy or McCarthy in early April 1968. "I've got to get me a peace proposal," he told Clifford,[30] and he was given Rusk's bombing halt plan. Clifford, with the secretary of state's compliance, urged the president to talk peace. Rusk had made the case. He was not calling for withdrawal, just a reduction in the fighting. It was time to act like a realist and a Wilsonian. Enough was enough. Negotiation was the intelligent course for the United States to take.

Johnson was won over to the partial bombing halt, but he would soon take an even larger step, making one of the biggest political moves of his life.

For his part, Rusk had not made a complete about-face. He had never staunchly upheld military solutions to the war. Americanization and bombing were tactics to convince enemies that aggression did not pay. He had become anathema to the demonstrators, Congress, and reporters for his stalwart defense of Johnson. In reality, though, the war now jeopardized the very principles of liberalism that he had fought for in the first place. The secretary of state realized that the game was up.

Circumstances had changed, and there was an opportunity to extricate the country from war. An election year gave protesters more influence. In January 1968 four hundred antiwar activists had thrown bricks, bottles, and balloons filled with blood and paint at those attending a dinner in San Francisco that Rusk addressed. The Tet Offensive had ridiculed the military's assertions of victory. Perhaps the president could again try his hand at negotiations, succeed in imposing some sort of cease-fire, and then go on to triumph at the polls in November 1968. Then Johnson, with his devoted adviser at his side, could renew his pursuit of justice and equality under the Great Society. Bombing and diplomacy still went hand in hand, but now there would be greater stress on the latter. Rusk, in what proved to be his final year in government service, hoped to obtain the elusive goals in Vietnam so that Johnson could achieve his own at home and abroad.

Notes

1. Kraft, "The Dean Rusk Show," 134.
2. Rusk, *As I Saw It*, 462.
3. Ibid., 461.
4. George C. Herring, *LBJ and Vietnam: A Different Kind of War* (Austin: University of Texas Press, 1994), 100.
5. DROH II, LBJL, 32.
6. Rusk, *As I Saw It*, 466.
7. Ibid., 459–60.
8. James Olson and Randy Roberts, *Where the Domino Fell: America and Vietnam, 1945–1990* (New York: St. Martin's Press, 1996), 171.
9. Rusk, *As I Saw It*, 467.
10. Ibid., 468.
11. Ibid.
12. Ibid., 470.
13. Ibid.

14. "Secretary Rusk Discusses Prospects for 1967 on 'Face the Nation,' " *DSB* 56 (January 23, 1967): 128.

15. Rusk, *As I Saw It*, 503.

16. Schoenbaum, *Waging Peace*, 454.

17. David K. Willis, "A Man Who Has Not Changed," *Christian Science Monitor*, January 17, 1969.

18. DROH II, LBJL, 44.

19. "Secretary Rusk Grows in Stature," *America* 118 (February 10, 1968): 178.

20. Schoenbaum, *Waging Peace*, 467.

21. Dallek, *Flawed Giant*, 483.

22. Kraft, "The Dean Rusk Show," 134.

23. Schulzinger, *A Time for War*, 259, 262.

24. Wells, *The War Within*, 242.

25. Rusk, *As I Saw It*, 477.

26. Gardner, *Pay Any Price*, 444.

27. Rusk, *As I Saw It*, 480.

28. Schulzinger, *A Time for War*, 266.

29. Schoenbaum, *Waging Peace*, 471.

30. Ibid., 473.

10

Fading Out

On March 31, 1968, President Johnson addressed the nation on the Vietnam War. Persuaded by Rusk, he ordered a partial bombing halt over most of North Vietnam. Talks would also begin with the enemy. Johnson then stunned the nation by withdrawing his name from the presidential race. Nobody—except Rusk, who was flying to New Zealand at the time of the speech—had been privy to this decision; the year before, Johnson had discussed with his loyal aide his retirement because of health problems.

With no stake in the election, Johnson was relegated to the political sidelines for the rest of 1968. Nonetheless, he maintained sway over Vietnam policy and the election. The war continued, as did the debate between hawks and doves as the home front grew raucous. Amid the turmoil stood Rusk. He hoped, as Johnson did, that the war would end before he left office. Negotiations proved difficult, however. Still ignoring the fact that the U.S. message essentially demanded that the North Vietnamese surrender their long-held goal of uniting the country, Rusk complained that "we want to talk, but the other side won't pick up the phone." [1]

Decelerated Diplomacy

Johnson's momentous speech changed the domestic political picture and the equation for peace negotiations. The Democrats now had a choice. They could turn to the surging Robert Kennedy, who stole Eugene McCarthy's thunder as the peace candidate and hero of the youth generation. Or they could choose Vice President Hubert

Humphrey, the establishment man and (unjustly) perceived lackey of the brooding Johnson and the Democratic machine. The two men, with McCarthy, would vie until Kennedy's shocking death in June gave the nomination to Humphrey. Still, McCarthy carried the peace banner to the Democratic National Convention in Chicago, where antiwar activists promised to confront the president's men and write a peace plank into the party platform.

Rusk had renewed hope in diplomacy. Johnson's decision not to run, together with the lure of the bombing pause, might invigorate the peace process. It would give Humphrey—Rusk's choice—time to devise a peace plan to counter Kennedy and McCarthy. Indeed, just days after Johnson's speech, Hanoi announced its willingness to talk. Perhaps having suffered enormous casualties in the counteroffensive after Tet, North Vietnam was now ready. But Rumanian sources later revealed that Johnson's withdrawal from the presidential race had been the catalyst. In mid-April, Johnson convened his negotiators, Averell Harriman and Cyrus Vance, and two close advisers, William Bundy and Rusk, to set out the U.S. position. The troubleshooting Harriman had negotiated the Limited Nuclear Test-Ban Treaty and Laos Accords. He was considered a bit too dovish, but Vance, a former member of the Defense Department who had worked on the Dominican and Cyprus crises three years earlier, would balance the delegation.

Rusk noted that the U.S. stance had not changed. Hanoi must agree to a cease-fire, allow South Vietnamese participation in negotiations, withdraw from South Vietnam with the United States, respect the demilitarized zone separating the two Vietnams, return prisoners of war, and honor the neutrality of Laos. Because the president immediately regretted his March 31 address, which limited his military options, he leaned toward Rusk's terms, calling for a resumption—even expansion—of the bombing in the event that Hanoi balked at the demands. In contrast, Secretary of Defense Clifford and the Harriman-Vance team advocated flexibility on all issues and pushed for no time limit on the bombing halt.

After repeated disputes with Hanoi over where to hold the talks, the Harriman-Vance mission left for Paris in May 1968 to end the war and help Humphrey beat Republican candidate Richard Nixon in the upcoming election. Rusk was not sanguine. He wondered whether somebody would even be able to "turn up the warm body of a North Vietnamese" in Paris.[2] Clifford and Harriman grew angry, clashing repeatedly with Rusk, whose negotiating position seemed to harden just when concessions were needed.

Rusk confers with antagonist Clark Clifford. *Courtesy Richard B. Russell Library, University of Georgia*

Johnson, with Rusk's backing, refused to run his diplomacy according to Humphrey's political hopes or to make essential compromises. Indeed, beyond his differences with Clifford over the principles involved in the war was Rusk's charge (and Clifford agreed) that Johnson's secretary of defense placed domestic politics at the fore in the negotiation strategy. In 1948, Rusk had confronted Clifford over the founding of Israel; Clifford, at the time an adviser to Truman, had supported full recognition to help the president in the election that year. Twenty years afterward, Rusk determined not to let electoral politics interfere with foreign policy. As Rusk explained, because Clifford was "much more of a political animal than the rest of us," he was greatly affected by the antiwar sentiment.[3]

As a result, there was little progress in Paris. Hanoi demanded—unfairly, in Rusk's opinion—a total and unconditional pause in the bombing and an end to U.S. aggression against the North. Doubtful that North Vietnam would halt its war, Rusk dismissed these demands, and American policy remained consistent. "Despite the shock of the Tet offensive," he later said, "our policy throughout 1968 remained close to what it had always been. The United States continued to support South Vietnam, preventing North Vietnam from seizing it by force."[4] There was no intent to destroy the North. The Americans merely wished an end to the fighting. Hanoi would have to take its troops home and let the nations of the region work out their own future, concluded this neo-Wilsonian. The stalemated Paris talks gave way to more war. A renewed North Vietnamese offensive in the spring convinced Rusk that this bombing halt, like its predecessors, had failed. On June 4, more out of frustration than in expectation of positive results, he urged Johnson, "Let's hit them and not say anything about it."[5]

Acting on a tip from the Soviets that stopping the bombing would lead to a breakthrough, Clifford urged Johnson to order a two-week halt in all air strikes. Harriman had earlier asked Rusk for a cessation, and now the administration debated again. Rusk counseled caution, taking his middle course. Bombing should not resume, but Vance and Harriman would have to receive specific concessions from North Vietnam before Johnson could agree to Clifford's pause. Accepting Rusk's position, Johnson stalled the Paris negotiations into July. The secretary of state was to blame; his department offered no bargaining options. Visiting Kyoto, Japan, at the time, Rusk faced stone-throwing Japanese protesters who called him "Boss of War Rusk."[6] The pressure remained intense.

A light flickered in July 1968. Either as a result of exhaustion or as a signal, Hanoi slowed its attacks on the South. Clifford, Harriman, and Vance jumped at the opportunity, asking for a bombing halt to rebuild momentum in Paris. The military had other ideas— take advantage of the lull and renew the ground and air wars. Rusk momentarily sided with his negotiators. "I buried my doubts," he explained, because the Communists no longer insisted that Saigon accept the NLF agenda of political reform.[7] Johnson turned away both the military and the diplomats. He did not want to escalate, but, because of past failures, he looked contemptuously on the bombing halt. Rusk did not press the president, reasoning that he had not received one sign that Hanoi "wanted peace in Southeast Asia on any terms other than its own: an unconditional halt to the bombing, the withdrawal of all American forces, and a North Vietnamese takeover of South Vietnam, Laos, and Cambodia."[8]

Rusk would have none of this, and he would not let South Vietnam be excluded from the table, particularly if the Vietcong were included. But Johnson had other motives in nixing the bombing halt. He was livid that his vice president, assured of the Democratic nomination after Robert Kennedy's assassination on June 6, had come out in favor of the suggestion to cease the air war. He would show Humphrey who was boss and thumb his nose at domestic critics at the same time. Johnson conferred with GOP candidate Nixon, who also opposed Clifford's idea of the bombing pause. Soon Johnson's attention was diverted by the startling Soviet invasion of Czechoslovakia on August 21. Rusk, too, turned to the invasion, arguing that the fight for freedom in Vietnam would inspire the Czechs.

Johnson's ambivalence only created more difficulties, as the Democratic convention in Chicago amply showed. As the Democrats prepared to nominate Humphrey, the split between liberals and radicals became apparent to the entire nation. Johnson cast a somber shadow from Texas, refusing Humphrey's entreaty to compromise with the antiwar delegates on the party platform. For the 10,000 protesters milling outside the convention center, this rigidity gave them license to disrupt the proceedings.

Chicago and Paris

The Democrats could not seem to recover after Johnson's withdrawal from the race and Bobby Kennedy's assassination. McCarthy ran a lackluster campaign, and dove George McGovern was unable to remobilize the Kennedy forces. That left Humphrey, a traditional Democrat with exemplary liberal credentials, to take the nomination. Humphrey wanted the war ended and endorsed the Clifford-Vance-Harriman bombing halt. Unfortunately, he could not shrug off Johnson's overbearing presence.

The mix of conventioneers was ripe for an explosion. Old-guard Democrats loyal to Johnson squared off against serious antiwar dissenters. Johnson controlled the nominating process, however, through the smothering direction of his ally and consummate machine politician, Chicago's Mayor Richard Daley. Meanwhile, guided by peace activist David Dellinger, protesters gathered outside. They were joined by counterculturists with their own platforms, including reforms that were far removed from the war, such as the legalization of marijuana and the abolition of money.

Mayor Daley watched, incensed by the spectacle in his parks and streets. Angered by the disruptions and insults to the city, Daley ordered police to break up radical demonstrations. Moving in with tear gas and clubs to clear the parks, the police instigated several nights of riots that were broadcast by television to a shocked nation. As blood flowed in the Chicago streets, the crowds chanted, "The whole world is watching."

Inside, at the convention, the antiwar plank was voted down. Peace delegates, inspired by those engaged in the melee outside, responded to their defeat by singing the civil rights anthem, "We Shall Overcome." Daley barely kept order during the nominating process on August 28. The Democrats chose the forlorn Humphrey, who gazed down in distress from his hotel room window at the carnage in the streets. The political damage was irreparable. Democrats approved of a platform that supported Johnson's Vietnam policy of fighting while negotiating. A majority of Americans supported this stance, but they also equated the disorder in Chicago with the Democrats, who were seen as having brought the nation to the brink of chaos. This so-called silent majority of traditional, family-oriented, middle- and working-class folks did not distinguish between the hippies of the counterculture and the sincere antiwar movement. The protesters were one and the same to most television viewers, many of whom usually voted Democratic.

In the eyes of the silent majority the rebels were only part of the unraveling of the nation. During the late 1960s, the country had endured rising crime rates and urban riots that had burned out cities. The silent majority blamed these problems on a civil rights movement turned militant. They also frowned on cultural change, which they saw as an erosion of morality caused by liberal values rooted in sexual freedom, feminism, and a victim mentality. They also complained that the social spending seemed to bypass the average white American as the government funnelled aid to poor minorities. To top it all off, hard-hat Americans, generally supportive of the war, accused Johnson of mishandling the conflict. By the fall of 1968 nearly 28,000 Americans had died in Vietnam, most of whom were from the poor and working classes. The silent majority was fed up with liberalism at home and abroad. Chicago provided additional evidence that the country was going to hell under the Democrats, and Humphrey fell far behind Nixon in the polls.

The desperate Humphrey saw his election chances sliding away if Vietnam policy did not change. Rusk warned the president that if the bombing stopped "with no conditions, many Democrats would vote for Nixon."[9] Johnson and Humphrey were both well aware of the silent majority's views on the war. Although he was hesitant to confront Johnson, on September 30 the Democratic nominee endorsed the cessation of bombing as a step toward peace. This time, Johnson placated Humphrey. Shrugging off prior failures to get the talks going, Johnson expressed the hope that the North Vietnamese now would come to the table. "Even a blind hog sometimes finds the chestnut," he declared.[10] The announcement worked magic; Humphrey began to gain on Nixon.

Almost on cue the Paris negotiations picked up as well. At the talks North Vietnamese negotiators Le Duc Tho and Xuan Thuy relented in their opposition to formal recognition of South Vietnam and told Vance and Harriman that Hanoi would not take advantage of a bombing pause to raise troop levels in the South. This was the reciprocal action for which Rusk had long searched. Noting that Soviet Foreign Minister Andrei Gromyko had been unusually noncombative at an October 6 lunch, Rusk suspected that the Russians were pressuring Hanoi to agree to terms that would precipitate a total U.S. bombing halt. A week later, Rusk advised the president to proceed, though with utmost caution. As long as the North recognized his government, South Vietnam's President Thieu supported the initiative.

The effort touched off three weeks of complex and hurried deliberations in Paris, Washington, and Saigon. Johnson initially delayed, demanding that the Communists agree to peace talks within twenty-four hours of a bombing halt. Hanoi refused, seeking a two-week period between the cessation of the air war and negotiations. Johnson turned the issue over to Rusk, who counseled slow, deliberate moves to craft a peace plan. At stake was not only peace but also the presidency. Meanwhile, as Nixon heard rumors of a bombing halt that could undermine his candidacy, he frantically appealed to South Vietnam to refuse to participate in the Paris talks before the election.

Furiously working for an accord as the Russians pushed Hanoi, envoy Harriman became irritated at Rusk, whom he viewed as Johnson's yes-man. Exercising typical caution in negotiating with presumed aggressors, however, Rusk merely sought a pledge that South Vietnam would have equal status with North Vietnam at the talks and that the enemy would not use the bombing halt to escalate the war. Harriman obliged Rusk by pressuring Hanoi for a concrete agreement, and on October 27, North Vietnam gave in to all U.S. terms. Peace talks would finally commence a week hence. Johnson remained skeptical, but Rusk assured him that he was fully alert to any maneuvering. The Harriman-Vance mission would proceed after a bombing halt that would go into effect on October 31, Rusk told Johnson, "as long as we recognize this isn't moving us into Paradise."[11] Negotiations were moving awfully close to Election Day, however, which was only about a week away.

In Saigon, Thieu was the single remaining obstacle. Urged on by the Republicans, South Vietnam balked at the plan. Thieu informed Rusk that he could not possibly prepare in time for the talks, which were scheduled to begin on November 2, two days after the bombing halt. He was wary, he asserted, because the Vietcong had rocketed a Catholic church in Saigon on October 31. Thieu wanted more restraints on Hanoi. He may well have thought that he could get a better deal by waiting until Nixon was elected on November 5.

An exasperated Johnson vowed to proceed unilaterally, but both he and Rusk knew that without Thieu's cooperation the negotiations would favor the Communists. Rusk considered putting the bombing halt on hold until he could bring Thieu around. News of another delay infuriated Harriman, but since U.S. Ambassador to South Vietnam Ellsworth Bunker sided with Thieu, Rusk saw no other choice. In the hope that Thieu would change his mind and negotiate, Johnson decided that he would stop the bombing anyway. This was both good and bad news for Humphrey.

The bombing halt began on November 1, but the Paris talks did not: Saigon had not sent its representatives. Desperate to help Humphrey, Harriman (who despised Nixon) cabled that Hanoi had agreed to start negotiations by November 6. After Johnson disclosed this development to the press, Humphrey briefly surged in the polls. Then Thieu declared that he would not participate, and the Democrat's momentum wavered. Nixon defeated Humphrey by a scant one-half million votes. Johnson was accused of throwing the election to Nixon through his lackadaisical action on bombing. Actually, Johnson cared little for either Nixon or Humphrey; both men irritated him. The loss to the Republicans surely disappointed Rusk, but he was more concerned with getting Thieu to the table in Paris. It took a month to accomplish this mission, after Rusk advised the president to "turn on the heat" by telling the recalcitrant leader that the United States would go ahead without South Vietnam.[12]

On December 8, Thieu's delegation showed up in Paris only to have the talks falter over such arcane issues as the shape of the negotiating table. On January 25, 1969, five days after Nixon's inauguration, discussions finally commenced. Rusk had "hoped until the end that an agreement might be possible, but it was not to be" during his tenure.[13] Failure to conclude a peace after so much effort had been exerted, he told reporters, was his greatest disappointment. Did he have even a twinge of doubt that he had been wrong? they asked at one of his last appearances as secretary of state. Rusk replied that all actions in Vietnam were open to reexamination, but, he said, "I think the main lines of policy have been right."[14] On January 20, 1969, he accompanied Johnson to Andrews Air Force Base in Maryland, where the outgoing president bade farewell to Humphrey, Clifford, and his loyal secretary of state; boarded his plane; circled Washington once; and headed west toward Texas.

By the time Rusk was at home, in retirement, it was clear that the intersection of history and personality, of events and ideas, of policies and ideals, had sent him to the sidelines of American diplomacy. This was more than an irony; it was a tragedy as well. At another point in history, presiding over a crisis other than Vietnam, he might have exited bearing the reputation of a great statesman. "Isn't it remarkable that this has happened to me!" Rusk lamented. "I leave office seen as a hawk. And basically I am an idealist and a man of peace."[15] That was certainly true, although it did not appear so to protesters, the American public, and many historians thereafter.

In 1969, removed from the spotlight for the first time in over one-quarter century and seeking sanctuary from the harsh world of public service, he could reflect on the months of anguish that epitomized his last years in office. Poet W. H. Auden's lament about the tragedies of history is an appropriate epitaph for the outcome to Rusk's Vietnam policy:

> The stars are dead. The animals will not look.
> We are left alone with our day, and the time
> > short, and History to the defeated
> May say Alas but cannot help nor pardon.[16]

Peace at Hand

The change in administrations did not end the war; it merely ushered in new tactics. President Nixon brought troops home in 1969 in an effort to Vietnamize the ground war. By 1970 the 543,000 U.S. soldiers had been reduced to 334,000. At the end of 1972 just over 24,000 combat troops remained.

To wrench an agreement from Hanoi, Nixon began clandestine bombing in neutral Cambodia in 1969, and in the spring of 1970 he sent in troops. Despite temporary military gains the effect of the incursion aggravated the situation for Nixon. The war proved as disruptive as before. In Vietnam many soldiers either refused to fight or deserted. A wave of protests, involving 80 percent of college campuses, swept the nation in May 1970. At Kent State University in Ohio, jittery National Guardsmen killed four students.

Two women died when guardsmen stormed a dormitory at Jackson State College in Mississippi. In January 1971, Congress repealed the Gulf of Tonkin Resolution and canceled funds for operations in Cambodia. That same year, Lieutenant Calley was sentenced to life in prison (commuted to parole by Nixon in 1974) for the My Lai massacre that had so horrified the public.

On the diplomatic front, Hanoi and the Vietcong boycotted the Paris talks because of the Cambodia invasion. But by 1972 all sides were back at the table. Domestic pressure on Nixon, who focused on his reelection bid that year, brought him around. So did Communist successes in repelling a South Vietnamese effort to interdict infiltration routes in Laos in 1971 and Hanoi's launching of a new offensive in the spring of 1972. In October 1972, National Security Adviser Henry Kissinger and North Vietnam's Le Duc Tho agreed to a cease-fire, a U.S. withdrawal from Vietnam, the return of prisoners, and—in a major concession by the administration—an allowance for North Vietnamese troops to remain in the South. The accord quelled domestic critics and gave Nixon a huge election victory.

The violence was not over, however. Saigon refused to let North Vietnam maintain its troop presence. Hanoi, meanwhile, held to the October agreement. Wishing to show Prime Minister Thieu as well as hawks at home that the United States would not cut and run, Nixon broke the deadlock in December 1972 by initiating the most destructive bombing of the entire war. B-52s hit transportation and industrial facilities, killing over one thousand Vietnamese civilians in the process. The Americans suffered losses too, as fifteen planes were shot down, ninety-three pilots were shot down and presumed killed, and thirty-one pilots were captured. The Christmas bombings provoked the wrath of critics at home and allies abroad.

The outrage had little effect on Nixon, for the bombing was meant to show Thieu that the United States would stand by him. Still, the president wanted the war to end. On January 23, 1973, the Paris Peace Accords were signed, providing terms essentially identical to those of the October cease-fire. Nixon claimed a "peace with honor." American troops came home, leaving a handful of U.S. officials behind. Two years later, when a South Vietnamese offensive failed and the North launched a broad counterattack, the war ended. On April 29, 1975, North Vietnam and the Vietcong swept through the South. After nearly thirty years of war, both countries were finally united into one—under Communist rule.

After a decade of difficult rebuilding efforts, Communist Vietnam turned toward moderate engagement with the capitalist world, signaling a willingness to reestablish diplomatic relations with the United States. Many Americans, torn by their experiences in the war, tentative about involvement overseas, and resentful of their former enemy, were in no mood to embrace Hanoi. But the breakup of the Soviet empire by 1991 further impelled the push for economic growth along capitalist lines in Vietnam as well as the fading of wartime memories and the abandonment of anti-Communist thinking in the United States. In 1995, President Bill Clinton restored formal diplomatic relations with Vietnam. America's longest war had officially come to an end, three decades after it had begun.

The war had been devastating for all. When Nixon took over, the country had lost 37,000 lives, 62 percent of whom were draftees. The total would rise to 58,000, along with 300,000 wounded, by the time of the cease-fire in 1973. Even the air war took a great human and financial toll—918 aircraft valued at $6 billion were lost, and the downed pilots (many of whom were never accounted for) either perished or were taken prisoner. Returning veterans faced a hostile or indifferent America eager to forget the nightmare. Secretary of State Rusk's son Richard, who opposed his father's stance on Vietnam, suffered a nervous breakdown as one of the war's thousands of casualties.

Vietnam suffered terrible destruction. The United States had dropped over seven million tons of bombs on Vietnam, equal to four hundred atomic bombs. That tonnage was three times the amount released in the Second World War—on Europe, Asia, and Africa combined—and this on a country the size of Texas. The United States had used seven million tons of munitions in World War II and about fifteen million tons from 1964 to 1972 in Vietnam. Millions of acres of forests in South Vietnam were destroyed by napalm and defoliants. Over 1.5 million Vietnamese died in the war. (Two million Cambodians perished in the political aftereffects of the Nixon invasion, as did thousands of Laotians.) Ten million refugees from Southeast Asia remained in camps or fled, including 30,000 Amerasians whose fathers were American. Vietnam faced decades of reconstruction; some areas would never recover from the bombing and herbicides.

The war was also an economic and political calamity. In the United States it fed inflation and unemployment, grinding Johnson's Great Society domestic reforms to a halt. It also destroyed

Democratic unity and the liberal coalition. Nixon's effort to maintain secrecy about his incursion into Cambodia helped precipitate his downfall. The so-called Plumbers, who broke into Democratic National Headquarters at the Watergate Hotel in Washington in June 1972, had been formed to plug leaks to the press concerning the bombing of Cambodia. Their bungled attempt set President Nixon on the road to resignation and disgrace. Vietnam scarred the United States for years. Americans underwent a crisis of confidence, no longer trusting leaders and balking at intervention overseas. They questioned the basic principles and objectives of foreign policy during the Cold War. They doubted whether the nation stood for the Wilsonian ideals of seeking good in the world. Such cynicism fueled an isolationist sentiment that alarmed liberal internationalists, especially retired Secretary of State Rusk.

Vietnam in Retrospect

Well before the peace, Rusk had quietly left the scene. Johnson had offered him an appointment to the Supreme Court, a sure bet because Senator Richard Russell of the Judiciary Committee had cleared him, but Rusk refused. He had never practiced law. He also wanted to get out of Washington. But before he did so, Johnson bestowed on the fifty-nine-year-old Rusk the highest honor for a civilian American, the Presidential Medal of Freedom.

In 1970, returning to his regional roots, Rusk began his tenure as the Sibley Professor of International Law at the University of Georgia in Athens, where he taught until 1984. He jumped vigorously into his pedagogical duties, gave quiet counsel to government officials, and for the first time in years enjoyed family life, including his grandchildren. Rusk sank into public obscurity, but he remained a sage for the foreign policy establishment.

He periodically reappeared in the limelight. In 1976, President Jimmy Carter, a fellow Georgian, looked to Rusk for advice. In 1985 the former secretary of state testified in defense of Westmoreland in the general's libel suit against CBS for the television network's wrongful accusation that he had falsified intelligence data from Vietnam. Rusk also served on numerous national advocacy boards, including the North American Free Trade Agreement's (NAFTA) Future of the Americas Commission.

Never interested in the political games of Washington, DC, he shunned government service. He routinely commented on his tenure as secretary of state and on contemporary policies, but that was all. Younger people, he quipped, should "learn by making their own mistakes, not by following mine."[17] When asked with whom he would like to spend the Hereafter, he expressed his reluctance to nominate someone who might have to live with him in Hell. Rusk knew his reputation was forever tainted by Vietnam.

Prodding from students, reporters, and correspondents led Rusk to comment on foreign policy. He defended his actions by explaining his neo-Wilsonian principles: seek peace through law, uphold democracy, negotiate when possible, and then—if need be—collectively resist aggressors. Stand pat against communism; stay the course in Southeast Asia. "I have not apologized for my role in Vietnam, for the simple reason that I believed in the principles that underlay our commitment to South Vietnam and why we fought that war," he wrote in his memoirs in 1990. "As a private citizen I believe in those principles today."[18]

Vietnam was not Kennedy's war or Johnson's war, he argued. It had always been Ho's war; if Hanoi had kept its troops at home, there would have been no conflict. Thus, Rusk criticized the Paris Peace Accords as "in effect a surrender." The presence of North Vietnamese troops in the South "meant the eventual takeover" of the country by the Communists.[19] Kennedy and Johnson could have had this same deal, but both had insisted that the only way to protect South Vietnam was to force Hanoi to withdraw. Rusk understood why Nixon consummated the deal; the president had no alternative. But Rusk did not trust the Communist aggressors to honor the neutrality of South Vietnam, and history proved him right.

As Rusk saw things, his administrations had actually attained the goal of resisting aggression. The issue was how one defined the term "winning." For Rusk the United States won because the Communists had not been able to overrun an ally. The nation had signaled to its foes that it would stand by its commitments. If only protesters had cooperated with Johnson, negotiations could have led to an independent South Vietnam. Yet in the end, Rusk was wrong. The United States lost the war in Vietnam; communism prevailed, and America's involvement took a great human and political toll on its own citizens.

Rusk never trivialized the casualties of war. Participation in a world war, Korea, and then Vietnam made him view war as "the principal obscenity of the human race; it is horrible in every respect." He genuinely "regretted every casualty on all sides of every war fought in [his] lifetime," and asking American youth to fight was painful for him.[20] He was compassionate. He never forgot the look of contempt from an army nurse he encountered in a hospital in South Vietnam. It depressed him to be accused of allowing his nation to drift into Vietnam without a thought. On the contrary, Rusk pondered every move seriously. He was convinced that his decisions, based on Cold War liberal beliefs, had saved more lives from nuclear catastrophe than had been lost in Vietnam.

That assertion was true, but was it really worth fighting in Vietnam for grand principles and strategic interests? Rusk thought so. He had one objective in Vietnam: to avoid another world war that would bring about the end of civilization. Appeasement had demonstrated that aggression could gain momentum. "That is why we drafted the United Nations Charter and the collective security treaties of the postwar period," he noted. In North Vietnamese actions against South Vietnam, Rusk saw what he interpreted as "the seeds of conflict for future war."[21]

This view did not coincide with the domino theory, which he termed simplistic. Rusk opposed the doctrine of Communist world revolution and its agents of militarism, tyranny, and misery. South Vietnam lived near millions of Chinese and fought against Communists determined to win their revolution. He hoped to give Saigon the strength to survive. It turned out, however, that only American, not South Vietnamese, might was capable of keeping the regime alive.

Rusk readily admitted that mistakes had been made in Vietnam. He erred in gauging the patience of the public and underestimated the staying power of the enemy. Because the administration downplayed the conflict as a police action rather than a major war, Americans were not psychologically prepared for the casualties. Protesters gained the upper hand in a propaganda battle with the government. Rusk faulted officials, himself included, for mismanaging the war by not better accounting for public perceptions and enemy resilience.

Rusk's self-criticism had limits, however. Congressional doves, he believed, were a bit disingenuous about Vietnam. They had not been deceived by the Gulf of Tonkin incident. They knew the stakes and had endorsed intervention. Rusk had no quarrel with those who changed their minds, but he would not accept the claims of deception leveled at Johnson and himself. Johnson had talked to congressional leaders. Rusk had visited hundreds of legislators, accepting every invitation to their clubs and breakfasts, and each Wednesday morning he had held a briefing session in the House attended by between 50 and 250 people. The war had been explained in detail.

Not until late 1966 did significant opposition develop. Up to that time, the administration had enjoyed overwhelming bipartisan support. Wayne Morse, one of the two senators who had opposed the Gulf of Tonkin Resolution, introduced a motion to rescind the document in 1966. Only four senators backed him. In May 1967, Senate doves—including Fulbright, Frank Church, and George McGovern—wrote an open letter to Ho voicing their opposition to unilateral U.S. withdrawal from Vietnam. Indeed, Johnson and Rusk could hardly be blamed for believing that they had congressional support.

Rusk gave little quarter to detractors who believed that officials had exaggerated the Communist threat. From the time he stepped down as secretary of state to the day he died, he put aggression from the North as the central issue in Vietnam. Of course, it was not solely a civil war, at least during Rusk's tenure as secretary of state. In 1978, appearing with George Ball on "Meet the Press," he confessed that his views on Vietnam had not changed. But Rusk also offered a concession. He hoped that historians would be able to say, "Well, Presidents Kennedy and Johnson, and those fellows Rusk and McNamara, *overdid* it, and what they did was not necessary after all."[22] That is, he would happily eat crow if the Cold War ended by means other than the steady application of the containment doctrine that he had long embraced and that the postwar history of confronting aggressors had validated during his neo-Wilsonian mission. If that scenario developed, he would be content, for it would mean the realization of his internationalist vision. Rusk accepted the role of sacrificial lamb on Vietnam as long as his liberal dream materialized. That time had not arrived. Hindsight, moreover, was not very helpful, he asserted. If only one could go back in history and combine the lessons of World War II with the lessons of Vietnam! But that was impossible.

On the other side, Rusk could not abide conservative critics and later Vietnam revisionists who blamed the policy of slow escalation for losing the war. Kennedy, they argued, should have marshaled a huge force. Johnson would have been better off unleashing U.S. power; levying taxes, calling up reserves, maybe using nuclear weapons, and invading North Vietnam. Limited war was the best and only strategy, countered Rusk. Ho would have persisted. China might have intervened, which would have expanded the war. And besides, the United States was in no position to initiate such a massive approach; it was on the strategic defensive, awaiting the moves of North Vietnam. Rusk saw purposeful gradualism as a successful approach that had worked everywhere after World War II. Limited policies had contained communism in Iran, Greece, Berlin, and Korea. Caution had also prevented a nuclear war in these cases, as it had in Vietnam. Aggression could be blunted "without sliding down the slippery slope into general war," even at great human toll.[23] Hanoi may have been encouraged by such restraint, but there was no other option. Launching an all-out drive for mobilization could have been fatal. Whipped into a war frenzy, Americans would have demanded that Johnson use the full extent of the U.S. arsenal. "With nuclear weapons lying around it's better not to have that happen," Rusk sagely concluded.[24]

Miscalculations did not deter him from his principled drive to prevent a Communist takeover, although they did undermine the crusade. Asked by a colleague during the war if he was making a mistake in Vietnam, Rusk shot back, "Well, if I am, it's a beaut."[25] The rationale of stopping aggression, aiding an ally, and exhibiting America's credibility in its commitment to provide global security was sound. The most unforgivable error, he held, was Nixon's withdrawal before a satisfactory security arrangement for South Vietnam was in place. The United States, he maintained, had been a force for good. The Vietnam War put that belief in question for many people, but not for Rusk. Without a U.S. presence all of Southeast Asia might have fallen to communism. Even a war that dragged on in a "slow-bleed" fashion, instead of coming to a finite conclusion, was better than a unilateral retreat, he argued.[26]

Despite the horrors of the war, that view should give historians pause. Rusk did not create Cold War strategic constructs; he only defended them. He misapplied U.S. military power and misjudged its impact, but the anti-Communist crusade was one that had engaged the United States and its allies for two decades, and the mission against perceived aggressors had endured longer than that. To criticize his stand on Vietnam, then, compels a questioning of not only the entire anti-Communist effort since the Second World War but also the liberal internationalist consensus. Why was defending Vietnam any less important than defending the Philippines or Guatemala or, for that matter, the nations of the European core? Whether triumphant or faced with abject defeat, Rusk applied the containment doctrine on a global scale in accordance with accepted American doctrine and practice, and he did so with a certain idealism lacking in most other U.S. leaders. Rusk's generation had embraced collective security as the key to preventing another world war. The price was high, but Cold Warriors could point to significant victories. Communist insurgencies were stemmed, and non-Communist governments were bolstered by American aid. Indonesia, Thailand, the Philippines, and Japan all benefited from U.S. security policies. South Vietnam had too.

If the United States had won the war, Rusk believed, everything would have worked out. He was very likely correct in this opinion. He never recanted, never conceded that the war had been wrong, as McNamara and others did later. In his view, victory would have divided Vietnam as it had the two Koreas, kept Cambodia safe from Communist hands, and insulated Laos and Thailand. There would have been no refugees. The United States would have recovered, as it had following the Korean War. And the public would have continued to treasure the idea of collective security. Just after retiring from the government, Rusk noted, "We have the resources to be able to help countries that are in trouble, and so we help to pay the bill. We did the same thing in the Korean War. I would compare what we've been doing in Southeast Asia to what we did during World War II under Lend Lease."[27] He remained the historian, and the liberal optimist, long after the failure of Vietnam had chased many a liberal from the Cold War camp.

That stance earned Rusk grudging respect from his critics. In reviewing *The Pentagon Papers*, the set of documents that revealed the misbegotten policies of Vietnam, columnist Hugh Sidey saw the error of exaggerating Communist threats in Vietnam and of sending Americans into an unwinnable war. Yet he applauded Rusk for taking responsibility for a policy that he thought was right even if the former secretary of state turned out to be wrong. Rusk had acted honorably, which could not be said of many other officials, for whom self-preservation came first. He did not back down, and he personally survived a war that ruined so many others. Vietnam had tested Rusk's basic principles, which were found lacking when applied in an age of revolution at home and abroad. But he had handled adversity, and he had stood by his Wilsonian beliefs, which—however conventional in the eyes of the protesters—were timeless and worthy.

Still, adherence to neo-Wilsonianism had doomed him. In a most telling postscript, Rusk spoke at a January 1973 memorial service for Johnson. Rusk's remarks applied just as equally to himself as to a president who had pushed liberalism to new heights. "Today's writers are inclined to discuss Lyndon Johnson almost solely in terms of Viet-Nam, and such questions as whether he did too much or too little in that tragic struggle. The historian will take a broader view," predicted Rusk, considering "the many other initiatives aimed at building the peace."[28]

Indeed, looking back on his service as secretary of state, Rusk saw much that had been beneficial to the world. Perhaps most important of all, he had changed history by easing superpower conflict. At the end of 1968, he explained, "I think in this last eight years it has become apparent that it is too late in history for opposition blocs to pursue a policy of total hostility, that an effort must be made to find points of agreement, if possible, which are in the mutual interest of both sides."[29] Despite the shadow of Vietnam, Rusk had truly advanced the Wilsonian objective.

In Cold War victory, allies were emboldened by U.S. power. In defeat, as in Vietnam, they could take solace in the fact that America had sacrificed 58,000 lives, tens of thousands of wounded, and a tremendous amount of resources to defend the Free World. The United States had honored its alliance obligations, impressed the Communists with a will to resist, and thus, perhaps, avoided a general war. For that reason, Rusk believed that "the American commitment to South Vietnam was the right decision." He went to his grave never having changed his mind on that score.[30] Liberalism had taken its blows, but Rusk's thinking was not lost on astute observers. After the Tet Offensive, news anchorman Walter Cronkite issued a calm but devastating statement about the hopelessness of the war. He urged a negotiated way out "not as victors but as an honorable people who lived up to their pledge to defend democracy, and did the best they could."[31] These words captured the tragedy, but also the contribution, of such well-meaning men as Dean Rusk.

Notes

1. Kraft, "The Dean Rusk Show," 134.
2. DROH II, LBJL, 15.
3. Wells, *The War Within*, 246.
4. Rusk, *As I Saw It*, 486.
5. Immerman, "A Time in the Tide of Men's Affairs," 85.
6. "Boss of War Rusk," *New York Times*, July 5, 1968, 1.
7. Rusk, *As I Saw It*, 486.
8. Ibid., 487.
9. Clark Clifford, *Counsel to the President: A Memoir* (New York: Random House, 1991), 572.

10. Olson and Roberts, *Where the Domino Fell*, 193.

11. Schoenbaum, *Waging Peace*, 487.

12. Immerman, "A Time in the Tide of Men's Affairs," 95.

13. Rusk, *As I Saw It*, 489.

14. Secretary Rusk, interviewed on "Face the Nation," *DSB* 59 (December 1, 1968): 650 (hereafter cited as "Face the Nation" interview).

15. John B. Henry II and William Espinosa, "The Tragedy of Dean Rusk," *Foreign Policy* 8 (Fall 1972): 189.

16. *The Oxford Dictionary of Quotations*, 3d ed. (Oxford: Oxford University Press, 1979), 20.

17. F. Willey and E. Shannon Willey, "Comeback of Dean Rusk," *Newsweek* (November 22, 1976): 60.

18. Rusk, *As I Saw It*, 492.

19. Ibid., 491.

20. Ibid., 494.

21. DROH II, LBJL, 23.

22. "Meet the Press" interview, April 30, 1978, Box 2:27, V:A, Dean Rusk Collection, UGA.

23. Rusk, *As I Saw It*, 499.

24. DROH I, LBJL, 42.

25. Quoted in Viorst, "Incidentally, Who Is Dean Rusk?" 181.

26. DROH I, LBJL, 44.

27. DROH III, LBJL, 20.

28. Dean Rusk, remarks at memorial service for Lyndon Johnson, January 24, 1973, Folder 10, Box 23, Series IV:A, Dean Rusk Collection, UGA.

29. "Face the Nation" interview, 647.

30. Rusk, *As I Saw It*, 502.

31. Frank E. Vandiver, *Shadows of Vietnam: Lyndon Johnson's Wars* (College Station: Texas A&M University Press, 1997), 287.

Conclusion
The Liberal Missionary

Dean Rusk "has the compassion of a preacher and the courage of a Georgia cracker," Lyndon Johnson once said. "When you're going in with the marines, he's the kind you want at your side."[1] That statement was a wholly fitting tribute to a loyal aide, a solid and good liberal who was willing, at great sacrifice, to defend the world against aggression. Looking back, Rusk grasped why he had faltered in Vietnam. Many Americans questioned the precepts of Cold War liberalism, the belief that their country must commit resources to containing communism and must uphold collective security, self-determination, and free-market prosperity. Rusk represented this neo-Wilsonianism both at its zenith and as it came under fire.

Rusk was liberalism's most effective advocate at the highest ranks. George Ball counseled caution on Vietnam. He was, however, a corporate lawyer ensconced in finance capitalism and, like Dean Acheson and other establishment liberals, an elitist attached to the European core. Rusk was more humble. He believed that policy was made at the grass roots by the people, that such populism was the true expression of democracy and the only way to stay attuned to the needs of the weak and poor. J. William Fulbright was a great critic of the Vietnam War, yet his opposition to racial equality betrayed his liberal credentials. Rusk was no racist; he campaigned enthusiastically for social justice. The list of contrasts goes on. Presidents Kennedy and Johnson were politicians who often compromised their ideals; Chester Bowles and Adlai Stevenson were Wilsonians, but, like other liberals, they existed only on the fringes. Kennedy listened to his brother Robert, who, late in his life, championed the left-liberal cause, but Johnson did not seek the younger Kennedy's counsel.

Rusk's post-retirement endeavors, which focused on aiding the less fortunate, were testimony to his innate liberalism. Through the creation of scholarships and his active leadership of the Black

Student Alliance at the University of Georgia, Rusk showed his liberal stripes. To honor his contributions, Atlanta named an elementary school for him; and Canton, Georgia, established the Dean Rusk Middle School. Rusk stood for something. He was neither a politician acting out of expediency nor a bureaucrat on the make. Far from being a muddle-headed idealist, Rusk was a liberal ideologue who unswervingly championed moral absolutes. That placed him squarely in the American internationalist tradition. The mission was to defend freedom the world over, and Rusk had contempt for those who would take a different course. "Don't ask me to call a man a liberal who wants to turn over to a totalitarian regime more than fourteen million South Vietnamese," he said, for that "kind of liberalism is jaded and cynical."[2] He was no cynic, pacifist, or ostrich. "Liberal means something about freedom."[3]

Democrats and Republicans were united by anticommunism, but Rusk had a more profound drive. He sought peace and liberty. Many held this vision, yet few tried to carry it out. As the exemplar of the Wilsonian ideal, the United States was obligated to spread democracy. Rusk adhered to universal values of peace, justice, and happiness under international law. He had learned these principles in his youth, and he put them into practice during his long, centrally placed career. What distinguished Rusk from others was his activism, which rivaled Woodrow Wilson's. Dynamic liberal internationalism typified his mission.

During one-half century of U.S. preeminence, Rusk made no apologies for his principles. Undertaking a cause embedded in Wilsonian internationalism, World War II universalism, and Cold War globalism, he dedicated his career to resisting aggression. Defense of democracies, of the weak, and of the Free World was his article of faith. Wilson, charged radicals and realists alike, had believed that he could end all war; he was proved wrong. Because Rusk still believed in Wilson's mission, he set out to adapt Wilsonianism to Cold War pragmatism. If he had been unable to frame the issues in terms of internationalist values or show a drive to prosecute the Cold War, he would not have climbed to the pinnacle of power. And surely, without the loyalty he showed to Kennedy and Johnson and the practical advice he provided, Rusk would never have become the longest-serving secretary of state of the postwar years. Rusk understood the constraints they faced, overseas and at home. His job was to help them steward Americans and allies toward the vision of a just, global system.

Conviction in the sanctity of constitutionalism compelled Rusk to heed the wishes of the presidents. They were the elected representatives of the people. Considering his closeness to Johnson, Rusk might have swayed him on Vietnam. In fact, he tried to do so gently, working within the consensus of the administration. Although he succeeded in persuading Johnson to order the bombing halt in 1968, Rusk had already lost key battles. Rather than resign, he continued to serve the government to keep his hand in determinations that would lead, he hoped, to the war's end. Presidents Kennedy and Johnson, elected by the American people, made the decisions; these were not Rusk's to make.

Still, Rusk believed in the cause that critics jabbed at him for so doggedly espousing in Vietnam. They saw Rusk as giving too little consideration to the will of people around the world and too much to the Cold War. Some were downright uncharitable, such as dove Senator Frank Church, who told a reporter, "We might have done better with Mickey Mouse than with Dean Rusk."[4] Rusk was clearly single-minded in reflecting on history. He viewed aggression, perpetrated by the Sino-Soviet bloc, as the greatest threat to world peace. Collective security, which he would orchestrate among allies, would save the Free World. Rusk was a sentry, guarding Wilsonian values from what he referred to as the "snapping hounds of Hell."[5]

One criticism of Rusk and other postwar U.S. foreign policy architects was that Cold War globalism perverted Wilsonianism. These liberal detractors contend that he sought to contain communism without distinguishing between circumstances or the importance of different areas to U.S. security. In Rusk's pursuit of his vision, they charge, he did not know when to stop. The United States, in conflict with the UN Charter, often acted unilaterally. Moreover, NATO, which engaged just one set of nations in collective security, was divisive. Rusk, they conclude, was really a conservative realist.

This view ignores Rusk's historic angst that liberal internationalism was stymied by war and superpower tensions. Ironically, even Wilson acted unilaterally and clandestinely—in Mexico and Russia, for instance. Furthermore, however imperfect the analogy of Stalin and Mao to Hitler, the Russians and Chinese proved to be genuine threats to peace. The United Nations or collective security pacts could restrain them. Neo-Wilsonianism more accurately explains Rusk's approach—internationalism adapted to the Cold War, idealism tempered by realism. That is, Rusk modified liberalism with considerations of national security. This cracked the Wilsonian mold but conformed to internationalist doctrine. Rusk was devoted to international law and the UN Charter. He long refused to compromise with the Communists, arguing with such realists as George Kennan that the Soviets would simply nibble the United States to death with probes, infiltration, and subversion. Rusk was, as one historian has put it, an "idealist in a realist world."[6]

Realists call Rusk a naive patriot. He held to anachronistic assumptions about the Cold War, they argue, and he applied them to Vietnam. He did not change with the times and steer Johnson off the wrong course. He exaggerated strategic threats and failed to match ends with the appropriate means. Withdraw or apply all-out force—those were the options, declare the realists. Abandon the anticommunism of the past; forsake fixed ideas. Regarding Vietnam, the realists are particularly critical. They argue that some areas were more important than others. Vietnam was not critical to U.S. security; a Chinese or Soviet threat was mere illusion. Beijing was preoccupied by its Cultural Revolution; its support for wars of national liberation amounted to glib rhetoric. The Russians, meanwhile, were at best ambivalent about the region, fearing trouble with rival China if they became overly involved. And South Vietnam itself never approached viability, regardless of tremendous U.S. effort. The Vietnam War was propagated by unwise statesmanship, realists claim. Worse, the Wilsonian crusade on behalf of principles was both fruitless and dangerous.

Was not Rusk somewhat a realist, however? He frowned on the Bay of Pigs operation in Cuba, balked at Americanization of the war in Vietnam, urged mediation in the Congo to forestall direct U.S. involvement, and continued support for South Africa despite his contempt for apartheid. He offered partnership to Europe but backed away when the Grand Design was rejected, gave development as well as military aid to Latin America, and, not insignificantly, directed much attention to Asia. In the Middle East he helped Israel, bowing to political reality, yet he cultivated relationships with moderate Arab states. The Berlin deal and Rusk's machinations following the predicament, as well as his recommendations during the Cuban missile crisis, were a brilliant display of realist tactics. Rusk believed that armed force undergirded the olive branch of peace. He stood for law and a peaceful world order only as the means to provide America's own answers to calls for Communist revolution. As he pursued superpower disarmament, Rusk never claimed that the Cold War was over, only that it must be controlled. He harbored no illusions about an easy peace. Neo-Wilsonianism absorbed enough realism indeed.

He misjudged the situation in Vietnam, as did so many other experts. Yet the contention that U.S. policy and Rusk's way of thinking were sterile artifacts of the past missed the point. Rusk fought for principles that were timeless. There was no need to adjust to supposed "new ideas," he correctly noted, for democracy was the world's most explosive concept, as it had been for centuries. And "unlike the Communists," he said in 1966, "we really believe in social revolution and not merely in power cloaked as revolution. We believe in constructive change and encourage it."[7] Rusk expressed basic American values.

Clearly, Rusk recoiled at Communist China; Mao seemingly disdained his principles and fomented revolution in Asia. The war to defend South Vietnam therefore became a test for liberalism, a way of showing China that Wilsonian principles were sound. Indeed, in 1994, Rusk urged President Bill Clinton to push for civil rights in China, whose leaders had crushed a democracy movement five years earlier. Although Clinton appreciated Rusk's view, he preferred not to focus on human rights. Realists saw no reason to sacrifice economic growth for high-minded ideals.

The liberal Rusk saw every reason to fight for principles—even in Vietnam. It was there that Rusk became most prominent, or infamous, depending on one's perspective. Because Vietnam represented the practical pitfalls in his belief system, it has, unfortunately, detracted from his achievements, scrupulous tenets, and otherwise estimable reputation. It would be unfair to Lyndon Johnson to excuse Rusk from culpability in Vietnam on the grounds that he was merely carrying out orders from his boss, however. Rusk endorsed Johnson's policies. The secretary of state could have just as forcefully advocated any other approach as he staunchly defended Johnson's in Congress. Yet he also compelled the president to ponder failure. Retaining leverage with Johnson, Rusk tried to wean him away from the war.

Rusk admitted his errors. He had wandered into a quagmire. However honorable, collective security proved ineffectual in this war of national liberation. North Vietnam was resilient. He misperceived the nature of the enemy and the conflict. Communism might spread from Vietnam to the rest of Asia and beyond, but the real fight involved a civil war. Undeniably, Rusk helped lead the United States to a terrible war. And the enemy had changed this time. There were no ultimatums, showdowns, monumental battles; guerrilla tactics were the method of warfare. Ho and the NLF fought not for territory but for ideals, for liberation from a colonial past. They were not aggressors but nationalists campaigning for freedom from imperialism, people stirred by a brutal history of injustice. Rusk emphasized the parallels between Hitler and Ho. These thieves might have different names, he noted, but "what they have in common, namely robbery, is what sends them both to prison."[8] But the Munich analogy was a stretch; the Vietnamese presented a more complex and subtle set of challenges than did a traditional big power such as Nazi Germany. Near the end of his life, Rusk acknowledged that basing policy on historical analogies was fraught with danger. There were always variations.

History weighed heavily on Rusk, but protesters viewed him as a dinosaur of foreign policy. A new generation, unschooled in the lesson of Munich, the sacrifice of world war, and the need for U.S. leadership around the globe confronted the supposedly stodgy establishment led by Rusk. It was not that revolutionary currents had swept him by but only that young people found Cold War liberalism lacking. Rusk did not err by striving toward Wilsonian ends; the crusade simply did not apply in Vietnam. The goal of resisting aggression was laudable and enduring. However, disaster befell those who remained wedded to the Wilsonian mission in Vietnam. To guard his career and preserve his place in history, Rusk might have retreated to the safer confines of cyncial conservative realism, or he might have joined the idealistic left and applied the brakes.

Rusk did not, and—like Johnson, tens of thousands of Americans, and hundreds of thousands of Vietnamese—he paid a price. He has gone down in history as a forgotten secretary of state, a nonentity to all except those who remember him as a toady to the tragic Johnson. Worse than the damage to his reputation, Rusk's great fear was realized. He observed with trepidation that Americans so hated the war that, disillusioned with internationalism, they embraced dreaded isolationism instead. Ironically, Rusk helped create the new mood. This was not isolationism of the 1930s sort; instead, Americans favored withdrawal from Vietnam, slashes in foreign aid, and a release from NATO obligations. The Vietnam War and, within a few years, the worst economic slump since the Great Depression soured them on foreign affairs. They preferred to focus on the domestic scene.

The United States would, of course, remain in the world, but public weariness endured. Presidents tried to kick the Vietnam syndrome of disillusion. With the end of the Cold War—despite the age of economic globalization, which both excited and alienated people—the predisposition to turn inward reemerged. Rusk's Wilsonian mission encountered a challenge rivaling fascism and communism: building an equitable global order amid chaotic market capitalism and increasing disunity among people the world over, including Americans.

For an internationalist this sentiment was distressing, and Rusk hoped it would be a passing phase. Differing from realists in one respect, he cherished the UN Charter. After Vietnam, and even before, others held the charter in contempt. People "do not read the UN Charter with the reverence with which we drafted it, with a prayer on our lips, knowing that this time we simply cannot fail," he lamented.[9] And he was right. He wanted the United States to continue "to organize a peace in the world" rather than "pretend that the rest of the world is not there," and thereby "undo a great deal that has been done in this post-war world" for good.[10] Americans could not be inattentive toward the world. That indifference would be even worse than misadventures abroad.

For Rusk the lessons of history (appeasement), the evil of the times (Sino-Soviet communism), and the belief system that underlay U.S. foreign policy (collective security and democracy) were beacons. They were also the bedrock of neo-Wilsonianism, a doctrine that compelled a crusade against aggressors. It was an idea and policy that was very much in the American mold. Collective security was not American, however, until—having learned from the bitter experience of war—Wilson, Roosevelt, and Rusk made it so. Wilson had offered his Fourteen Points. Roosevelt had rushed aid to the democracies, fought a two-front war against powerful military machines, and formulated a blueprint for peace. Rusk had confronted the tyranny of communism by joining together like-minded nations. Leadership during the Cold War hinged on the promotion of collective security, a doctrine that became more American than the splendid isolationism pursued since the founding of the country.

To call Rusk a hawk on Vietnam or to accuse him of narrow-minded anticommunism, then, belies the complexity of his views. To argue that this wise statesman was an unreconstructed hardliner is simplistic. He was not a single-minded anti-Communist.

Instead, Rusk defended a middle position, between the extremes of isolationism and militarism. He sought neither to appease aggressors nor ignite a third world war. That tortured but reasonable approach confused his critics, to whom Rusk appeared both humane and rigid. Yet he staked out the essense of liberalism.

Rusk was, simply, a Cold War liberal. Patience would wear out the Communists. Containment drew on Wilsonian doctrines of collective security and democracy. He faithfully pursued the universal values that had served U.S. foreign policy for most of the twentieth century. That he was caught in the three great struggles of the midtwentieth century—World War II, Korea, and Vietnam— was a twist of fate for this man of peace. Still, on his eightieth birthday in 1989, he expressed his satisfaction that he had had a large part in preventing a nuclear holocaust that would have destroyed the world. At the end of the day, Rusk proved the soundness of neo-Wilsonianism. National security policies deterred aggressors who, after the Second World War, were armed with weapons of mass destruction. He also cautioned that his own nation's military-industrial complex kept the country on a war footing and was capable of provoking conflict in a dangerous world. By the 1990s the collapse of the Soviet empire and, he hoped, the reduction of large U.S. defense budgets validated his tough liberal stand.

Rusk was a standard-bearer for the American mission abroad. Law, fairness, justice, freedom from want and fear—these were values claimed by Wilson and taken to heart by Rusk. War and conflict—which had so shaped the history of the twentieth century— drove him to defend his beliefs at all costs. In Vietnam the crusade continued for too long. Yet his career and life—whose context were much, much larger—should not be judged on that issue alone, for elsewhere he brought to bear aid, wisdom, even courage. Rusk stood up to the Red-baiters of the Truman era. He stewarded the Rockefeller Foundation toward developing the poorest reaches of the world. He counseled moderation in Cuba, restraint in Laos, aid for Latin America, integration in Africa, diplomacy in the Middle East, reciprocity in Western Europe, negotiation with the Soviets, even caution in Vietnam.

Rusk's generation had brought the United States through the Great Depression, world war, and totalitarian challenges. The entire perspective of history in the midtwentieth century and the full range of U.S. obligations around the globe—going well beyond Southeast Asia—provide the proper framework for understanding him. Against that background must be held the truism that life is an original experience. Historical conditioning, cognition, and even personality compel decisions that one might not make in retrospect. A judgment based on these factors must find Rusk's service admirable. He was not always right, as no decision maker can be. But at the highest level of public life, when integrity was often not the rule, he earned a reputation for honesty and foresight. Under his leadership the United States did much good. With Rusk's career of principles defended on behalf of mankind, he should be salvaged from the dustbin of history and accorded his place as one of the most important figures in American foreign policy.

Rusk died on December 20, 1994, one-quarter century after he had left Washington with the belief that the overriding issue for human beings around the planet was the avoidance of nuclear war. He passed away most likely thinking that this problem no longer ranked as a crisis issue. The Cold War was over; his side had won. Other difficulties were magnified—the environment, race relations, terrorism, the gap between rich and poor. These matters required work. Faith in liberal internationalism—in "the common law of mankind"—convinced him that they would be solved, for only ideology separated nations. In 1970, Rusk had predicted that Communists would answer their problems by moving toward individual responsibility, while capitalists would embrace greater social responsibility. The two camps would merge, closing the ideological gap.[11]

Rusk was right. He confessed in 1991 that the fall of communism had been beyond his wildest dreams. Neo-Wilsonianism had paid off after all. The mission of liberalism continued, but Rusk had done his part. With the fundamental characteristic of the liberal, he remained ever the optimist. He truly believed that the United States and United Nations would succeed wherever they turned their attention.

Near the end of his life, as a venerable Cold Warrior whose time had passed, he declared to a group of college students his confidence in their prospects. Unlike many other senior citizens, Rusk trusted American democracy and the ability of these young people to shape their destiny. Expressing his regret that he would not be able to accompany them on the nation's next adventures, he noted that the " 'family of man' is taking form."[12]

A man who had lived through a turbulent history, created much of it, and defended his principles, Rusk believed that the future would be bright for, above all, he understood change to be inevitable. If met with resolve and creativity, it could be harnessed to fulfill the aspirations of mankind. "It is not for us to fear the great winds of change that are blowing today," he eloquently remarked in 1962. "They are the winds we have long known and sailed with, the winds which have carried man on his unending journey, the winds of freedom."[13] Borne out by a sense of history, this liberal's creed provided the impetus and framework for a lifetime of commitment.

Notes

1. George C. Herring, *America's Longest War: The United States and Vietnam, 1950–1975*, 3d ed. (New York: McGraw-Hill, 1996), 218.

2. Graff, *The Tuesday Cabinet*, 84.

3. Moskin, "Dean Rusk," 16.

4. Leroy Ashby and Rod Gramer, *Fighting the Odds: The Life of Senator Frank Church* (Pullman: Washington State University Press, 1994), 361.

5. Dean Rusk, "Reflections on War and Peace, Collective Security, and the Snapping Hounds of Hell," *Law Review* (1975), Box 4:23, Series V:A, Dean Rusk Collection, UGA.

6. David Steigerwald, *Wilsonian Idealism in America* (Ithaca: Cornell University Press, 1994), 167.

7. Dean Rusk, "The U.S. Commitment in Viet-Nam: Fundamental Issues," *DSB* 54 (March 7, 1966): 352.

8. Yuen Foong Khong, *Analogies at War: Korea, Munich, Dien Bien Phu, and the Vietnam Decisions of 1965* (Princeton: Princeton University Press, 1992), 183.

9. Rusk, *As I Saw It*, 504.

10. DROH IV, LBJL, 40–41.

11. Ibid., 45–46.

12. Rusk, *As I Saw It*, 634.

13. Dean Rusk, "Five Goals of U.S. Foreign Policy," *DSB* 47 (October 15, 1962): 557.

Bibliographical Essay

The two basic sources for this book were Thomas Schoenbaum, *Dean Rusk: Waging Peace and War* (New York: Simon and Schuster, 1988), and Warren I. Cohen, *Dean Rusk* (Totowa, NJ: Cooper Square Publishers, 1980), both of which sketch Rusk's internationalism. Schoenbaum is the more gentle of the two; Cohen presents a favorable view, particularly in regard to Rusk's liberalism, but offers a more pointed critique of his Vietnam policy. Cohen broke ground by defining Rusk and his policies and by processing numerous Freedom of Information Act requests to declassify documents for the use of researchers. Schoenbaum drew on those files and on numerous others (as well as on oral histories) that he has compiled in a sizable collection on Rusk and the 1960s at the Richard B. Russell Library at the University of Georgia in Athens (UGA). His copies of documents of meetings, memoranda, and the like from Boston's John F. Kennedy Library (JFKL), Austin's Lyndon B. Johnson Library (LBJL), and the National Archives are a convenient resource for those studying the era.

With an even more favorable view toward Rusk, my book broadly follows the arguments of both Schoenbaum and Cohen. I stress more than do the two authors the role that history and experience played in the development of the secretary of state's way of thinking. And, too young to remember the Vietnam War or Rusk's service, I provide a certain objective distance in contrast with the others. Published a full decade after Schoenbaum's book and almost two decades after Cohen's, my study has benefited from the most recent information gleaned from declassified sources on Vietnam as well as a range of other topics. One final distinction is that, where my predecessors told Rusk's story in chronological fashion, I have used an approach that combines chronology, themes, and topics.

The Dean Rusk Collection at UGA includes the Schoenbaum Files and the Parks Rusk Files, which are valuable sources of information about Rusk's early life. Richard Rusk, son of the secretary of state, has also deposited material in the collection. The holdings are divided into six categories, which cover Rusk's childhood, Rockefeller Foundation years, State Department tenure, publications, speeches, and correspondence, all of which pertain to his life in general as well as his administrative agenda.

Oral histories were also a key source. The Dean Rusk Collection at UGA, JFKL, and LBJL hold extensive interviews by Rusk and with those who participated in the events that shaped his life. Of special importance to this book were the Dean Rusk Oral History interviews at the Kennedy and Johnson libraries. The UGA oral histories, many by Schoenbaum and Rich Rusk, were integrated into their books. The latter work—Dean Rusk, with Richard Rusk, *As I Saw It*, ed. Daniel S. Papp (New York: W. W. Norton, 1990)—is the closest that the former secretary of state came to a memoir. It is part autobiography and part his son's attempt to come to terms with his father, whose views on Vietnam he opposed. The oral record is supplemented by Bob Brewin, "Dean Rusk under Oath," *Village Voice*, April 16, 1985, 16. Other interviews that were useful, especially in voicing liberal positions (and criticism of Rusk), are at JFKL: Charles Baldwin, Charles Bohlen, Chester Bowles, Abram Chayes, Harlan Cleveland, William O. Douglas, Frederick G. Dutton, Robert Lovett, and Benjamin Read.

A selective collection of Rusk's speeches from the early Kennedy years is Ernest K. Lindley, ed., *The Winds of Freedom: Selections from the Speeches and Statements of Secretary of State Dean Rusk, January 1961–August 1962* (Boston: Beacon Press, 1963). Rusk's appearances before congressional committees and his speeches in the U.S. Department of State *Bulletin* round out the extensive oral record. Schoenbaum's bibliography lists all of Rusk's public communications as well as articles about him. Researchers can also gain an appreciation for his rock-solid views by watching the twelve-hour 1985 interview by Edwin Newman, produced by the Southern Center in Atlanta.

Contemporary articles that provide useful information about personal background, character, and values are Joseph Kraft, "The Dean Rusk Show," *New York Times Magazine*, March 24, 1968, 34–140; J. Robert Moskin, "Dean Rusk: Cool Man in a Hot World," *Look* 30 (September 6, 1966): 16–21; Edward Stillman, "Dean Rusk: In the American Grain," *Commentary* 45 (May 1968): 31–37; and Milton Viorst, "Incidentally, Who Is Dean Rusk?" *Esquire* (April 1968): 98. A probing look at his views and record is found in John B. Henry II and William Espinosa, "The Tragedy of Dean Rusk," *Foreign Policy* 8 (Fall 1972): 166–89.

On Wilsonianism see John Braeman, ed., *Wilson* (Englewood Cliffs, NJ: Prentice-Hall, 1972); Lloyd E. Ambrosius, *Wilsonian State-craft: Theory and Practice of Liberal Internationalism during World War I* (Wilmington, DE: Scholarly Resources, 1991); and, especially, Arthur S. Link, *Woodrow Wilson: Revolution, War, and Peace* (Arlington Heights, IL: Harlan Davidson, 1979). For a dissection of both internationalism and how Wilson's agenda differed from Cold War globalism see Thomas J. Knock, *To End All Wars: Woodrow Wilson and the Quest for a New World Order* (New York: Oxford University Press, 1992). David Steigerwald, *Wilsonian Idealism in America* (Ithaca: Cornell University Press, 1994), countering Knock's view with an analysis of the trials and transformations of Wilsonianism, rationalizes Rusk's approach. A good overview of American ideology in practice is Alonzo L. Hamby, *Liberalism and Its Challengers: From F.D.R. to Bush*, 2d ed. (New York: Oxford University Press, 1992).

Regarding the historical analogies of Munich and Korea to which Rusk referred (and the flaws in such analogies), see Yuen Foong Khong, *Analogies at War: Korea, Munich, Dien Bien Phu, and the Vietnam Decisions of 1965* (Princeton: Princeton University Press, 1992), and Ernest R. May, *"Lessons" of the Past: The Use and Misuse of History in American Foreign Policy* (New York: Oxford University Press, 1973). For a defense of analogies see Amos Permutter, *Making the World Safe for Democracy: A Century of Wilsonianism and Its Totalitarian Challengers* (Chapel Hill: University of North Carolina Press, 1997).

Both as an overview and superb visual resource, the twenty-four-part video series by CNN (Turner Original Productions, Inc., 1998), "The Cold War," is useful for explaining events and movements of the 1960s as well as the other decades of superpower conflict. The Cold War and the 1960s are now well-traveled ground for historians. James N. Giglio, *The Presidency of John F. Kennedy* (Lawrence: University of Kansas Press, 1991), gives a balanced look at Kennedy's foreign policy. Indispensable for their panoramic treatment of the Kennedy years, despite their hagiographic treatment of the president and less friendly consideration of Rusk, are Arthur M. Schlesinger, Jr., *A Thousand Days: John F. Kennedy in the White House* (Boston: Houghton Mifflin, 1965), and Theodore C. Sorensen, *Kennedy* (New York: Harper and Row, 1965). Thomas G. Paterson, ed., *Kennedy's Quest for Victory: American Foreign Policy,*

1961–1963 (New York: Oxford University Press, 1989), is also essential. Interesting cultural observations are made in Robert D. Dean, "Masculinity as Ideology: John F. Kennedy and the Domestic Politics of Foreign Policy," *Diplomatic History* 22 (Winter 1998): 60. And a readable study that counts Soviet-U.S. relations as the central concern is Michael Beschloss, *The Crisis Years: Kennedy and Khrushchev, 1960–1963* (New York: HarperCollins, 1991).

The wide-ranging articles in Diane B. Kunz, ed., *The Diplomacy of the Crucial Decade: American Foreign Relations during the 1960s* (New York: Columbia University Press, 1994), and in Warren Cohen and Nancy Tucker, eds., *Lyndon Johnson Confronts the World: American Foreign Policy, 1963–1968* (New York: Cambridge University Press, 1994), employ new sources in a sweeping look at issues of the decade. The Cohen and Tucker book is, to date, the most complete work on the Johnson years. Robert Divine, ed., *The Johnson Years: Volume One: Foreign Policy, the Great Society, and the White House* (Lawrence: University of Kansas Press, 1987), contains chapters on Vietnam and Latin America. H. W. Brands, *The Wages of Globalism: Lyndon Johnson and the Limits of American Power* (New York: Oxford University Press, 1995), is a survey that places Johnson's policies within the context of the containment doctrine.

The comprehensive Robert Dallek, *Flawed Giant: Lyndon Johnson and His Times, 1961–1973* (New York: Oxford University Press, 1998), includes an exploration of the contradictions of Johnson's Vietnam policy: determination to win along with recognition that the war would undermine the administration. Crucial to any study of the Johnson years, though they should be read with caution, are Johnson's memoirs, *The Vantage Point: Perspectives of the Presidency, 1963–1969* (New York: Holt, Rinehart, and Winston, 1971).

Two Frank Costigliola essays, "The Pursuit of Atlantic Community: Nuclear Arms, Dollars, and Berlin," in Paterson, *Kennedy's Quest for Victory*, and "Lyndon B. Johnson, Germany, and 'the End of the Cold War,' " in Cohen and Tucker, *Lyndon Johnson Confronts the World*, hold that America's European policy was an exercise in U.S. hegemony. A more positive assessment, sensitive to the transformations in U.S.-European (especially West German) relations over the decade, is contained in Thomas Alan Schwartz, "Victories and Defeats in the Long Twilight Struggle: The United States and Western Europe in the 1960s," in Kunz, *Diplomacy of the Crucial Decade*. Vladislav M. Zubok, "Unwrapping the Enigma: What Was Behind the Soviet Challenge in the 1960s?" in the Kunz collection, provides fascinating insights into Khrushchev's thinking and policies. For trade and economic relations with the Common Market and Japan, see Thomas W. Zeiler, *American Trade and Power in the 1960s* (New York: Columbia University Press, 1992).

On Latin America, William O. Walker III, "Mixing the Sweet with the Sour: Kennedy, Johnson, and Latin America," in Kunz, *Diplomacy of the Crucial Decade,* is most useful for its investigation of the motivations behind and effects of U.S. foreign aid to the region. It concludes that aid was a subset of anti-Communist national security policy, as does Stephen G. Rabe, "Controlling Revolutions: Latin America, the Alliance for Progress, and Cold War," in Paterson, *Kennedy's Quest for Victory.* For a hemisphere-wide critique of Kennedy's obsession with anticommunism, see Stephen G. Rabe, *The Most Dangerous Area in the World: John F. Kennedy Confronts the Communist Revolution in Latin America* (Chapel Hill: University of North Carolina Press, 1999). Jerome Levinson and Juan de Onis, *The Alliance That Lost Its Way: A Critical Report on the Alliance for Progress* (Chicago: Quadrangle Books, 1970), indicts the administration for the alliance's failure. Walter LaFeber, "Latin American Policy," in Devine, *The Johnson Years,* shares the consensus opinion that the alliance failed. The most balanced (but critical) analysis of the United States in Latin America is Joseph S. Tulchin, "The Promise of Progress: U.S. Relations with Latin America during the Administration of Lyndon B. Johnson," in Cohen and Tucker, *Lyndon Johnson Confronts the World.* For a discussion of the Dominican intervention see Piero Gleijeses, *The Dominican Crisis: The 1965 Constitutionalist Revolt and American Intervention* (Baltimore: Johns Hopkins University Press, 1978).

Thomas G. Paterson, *Contesting Castro: The United States and the Triumph of the Cuban Revolution* (New York: Oxford University Press, 1994), thoroughly studies the rise of Fidel Castro and the deterioration of Cuban-U.S. relations until the Bay of Pigs. Paterson then takes his rather damning story through the Kennedy years in "Fixation with Cuba: The Bay of Pigs, Missile Crisis, and Covert War against Fidel Castro," in Paterson, *Kennedy's Quest for Victory.* Richard E. Welch, Jr., *Response to Revolution: The United States and the Cuban Revolution, 1959–1961* (Chapel Hill: University of North Carolina Press, 1985), although less comprehensive, shows the pervasiveness of anti-Communist sentiment toward Castro. On the Bay of Pigs, Trumbull Higgins, *The Perfect Failure: Kennedy, Eisenhower, and the CIA at the Bay of Pigs* (New York: W. W. Norton, 1987), explores flawed CIA planning. Peter Wyden, *Bay of Pigs: The Untold Story* (New York: Simon and Schuster, 1979), with its detailed look at the cast of characters and their maneuverings, tells the dramatic story. For a participant's view see Richard M. Bissell, Jr., *Reflections of a Cold Warrior: From Yalta to the Bay of Pigs* (New Haven: Yale University Press, 1996).

Robert A. Divine, ed., *The Cuban Missile Crisis*, 2d ed. (New York: Markus Wiener Publishing, 1988), lays out the perceptions and debates regarding superpower motivations and the propriety of President Kennedy's actions. Valuable in assessing the crisis and providing scholarly and participant views is James G. Blight and David A. Welch, *On the Brink: Americans and Soviets Reexamine the Cuban Missile Crisis* (New York: Noonday Press, 1990). Philip Nash, *The Other Missiles of October: Eisenhower, Kennedy, and the Jupiters, 1957–1963* (Chapel Hill: University of North Carolina Press, 1997), fills a gap in the diplomatic history. A useful approach using biographies of the major participants is followed in Mark J. White, *The Cuban Missile Crisis* (Basingstoke, England: Macmillan and Company, 1996). Aleksandr Fursenko and Timothy Naftali, *"One Hell of a Gamble": Khrushchev, Castro, and Kennedy, 1958–1964* (New York: W. W. Norton, 1997), provides a look at Soviet files. The indispensable transcripts of Ex-Com and other meetings are included in Ernest R. May and Philip D. Zelikow, *The Kennedy Tapes: Inside the White House during the Cuban Missile Crisis* (Cambridge, MA: Belknap Press of Harvard University Press, 1997).

On South Africa, Thomas J. Noer, *Black Liberation: The United States and White Rule in Africa, 1948–1968* (Columbia: University of Missouri Press, 1985), looks at the U.S. middle-of-the-road handling of apartheid. Richard D. Mahoney, *JFK: Ordeal in Africa* (New York: Oxford University Press, 1983), focuses on key arenas during the Kennedy years. For an overview of civil rights and of relations with several African nations see Gerald E. Thomas, "The Black Revolt: The United States and Africa in the 1960s," in Kunz, *Diplomacy of the Crucial Decade*. For the thesis that U.S. officials hoped to ignore Africa see Terrence Lyons, "Keeping Africa off the Agenda," in Cohen and Tucker, *Lyndon Johnson Confronts the World*.

H. W. Brands, *Into the Labyrinth: The United States and the Middle East, 1945–1993* (New York: McGraw-Hill, 1994), is a concise but comprehensive survey of themes in U.S. policy toward the Middle East. For the perspectives of the whole range of participants in the region see Charles D. Smith, *Palestine and the Arab-Israeli Conflict*, 2d ed. (New York: St. Martin's Press, 1992). Highly critical of Kennedy and Johnson, particularly concerning the ways in which policy backfired, are Douglas Little's essays, "From Even-Handed to Empty-Handed: Seeking Order in the Middle East," in Paterson, *Kennedy's Quest for Victory*, and "A Fool's Errand: America and the Middle East, 1961–1969," in Kunz, *Diplomacy of the Crucial Decade*. Offsetting Little's view is the milder Warren Cohen, "Lyndon Baines Johnson vs. Gamal Abdul Nasser," in Cohen and Tucker, *Lyndon Johnson Confronts the World*, which does not perceive the president's shift toward Israel as a mistake.

Vietnam and China cast shadows over U.S. policy in Asia. For a superb study of U.S.-China relations in the Cold War, though it has comparatively little coverage of Johnson, see Gordon H. Chang, *Friends and Enemies: The United States, China, and the Soviet Union, 1948–1972* (Stanford: Stanford University Press, 1990). See also the more critical Rosemary Foot, *The Practice of Power: U.S. Relations with China since 1949* (Oxford: Clarendon Press, 1995). On the rigidity of President Kennedy's approach see James Fetzer, "Clinging to Containment: China Policy," in Paterson, *Kennedy's Quest for Victory*. On Johnson see Nancy Bernkopf Tucker, "Threats, Opportunities, and Frustrations in East Asia," in Cohen and Tucker, *Lyndon Johnson Confronts the World*. Arthur Waldron, "From Nonexistent to Almost Normal: U.S.-China Relations in the 1960s," in Kunz, *Diplomacy of the Crucial Decade*, addresses the problems of Chinese flexibility and U.S. initiatives with a kinder view of the American position. Michael Schaller, "Altered States: The United States and Japan during the 1960s," in Kunz, *Diplomacy of the Crucial Decade*, records the influence of Vietnam on the budding global power of Japan. Follow, too, the embitterment generated by U.S. policy in South Asia in Robert McMahon's chapters in Paterson, *Kennedy's Quest for Victory*, and in Cohen and Tucker, *Lyndon Johnson Confronts the World*.

My study drew heavily on Robert D. Schulzinger, *A Time for War: The United States and Vietnam, 1941–1975* (New York: Oxford University Press, 1997), for the narrative and analysis of the Vietnam War. Its detail and use of new documents sheds light on all aspects of the war, especially administration decisions. The book joins the classic George C. Herring, *America's Longest War: The United States and Vietnam, 1950–1975*, 3d ed. (New York: McGraw-Hill, 1996), as well as Marilyn B. Young, *The Vietnam Wars* (New York: HarperCollins, 1991), which provides a look at both the Vietnamese and U.S. sides as standards on the war. A lively and perceptive account is James Olson and Randy Roberts, *Where the Domino*

Fell: America and Vietnam, 1945–1990 (New York: St. Martin's Press, 1996).

Still useful is George McTurnin Kahin and John W. Lewis, *The United States in Vietnam* (New York: Dial Press, 1967). George McTurnin Kahin, *Intervention: How America Became Involved in Vietnam* (New York: Alfred A. Knopf, 1986), provides one of the best analyses. On the enemy see William J. Duiker, *Sacred War: Nationalism and Revolution in a Divided Vietnam* (New York: McGraw-Hill, 1995). A complete listing of sources for the Vietnam War can be found at the Website compiled by Edwin Moise: http://hubcap.clemson.edu/~eemoise/bibliography.html/. On the debate over whether Vietnam policy was right or wrong and why the United States lost, see Todd Gitlinger, ed., *The Johnson Years: A Vietnam Roundtable* (Austin: LBJL and LBJ School of Public Affairs, 1993). See also the thorough David L. Anderson, *Shadow on the White House: Presidents and the Vietnam War, 1945–1975* (Lawrence: University of Kansas Press, 1993), which includes contributions from a wide range of top scholars.

The critics are many. Lloyd C. Gardner, *Pay Any Price: Lyndon Johnson and the Wars for Vietnam* (Chicago: Ivan R. Dee, 1995), indicts policymakers for their Cold War assumptions. In a more constrained way so does Michael H. Hunt, *Lyndon Johnson's War: America's Cold War Crusade in Vietnam, 1945–1968* (New York: Hill and Wang, 1996). Equally reproachful, Lawrence J. Bassett and Stephen E. Pelz, "The Failed Search for Victory: Vietnam and the Politics of War," in Paterson, *Kennedy's Quest for Victory,* claims that because President Kennedy was driven by politics, he exaggerated the Communist threat. The classic analysis of the bureaucratic failures is David Halberstam, *The Best and the Brightest* (New York: Random House, 1972). Three critics of U.S. policy (George McGovern, who blames the war on ignorance; Edward Luttwak, who attributes failure to bad military strategy; and Thomas McCormick, who points to the U.S. quest for economic hegemony) and one proponent (William Westmoreland) voice their opinions in a collection of lectures: Patrick J. Hearden, ed., *Vietnam: Four American Perspectives* (West Lafayette, IN: Purdue University Press, 1990). For a Marxist view see Noam Chomsky, *Rethinking Camelot: JFK, the Vietnam War, and U.S. Political Culture* (Boston: South End Press, 1993).

A more favorable biographical slant is given in Frank E. Vandiver, *Shadows of Vietnam: Lyndon Johnson's Wars* (College Station: Texas A&M University Press, 1997). George C. Herring, *LBJ and Viet-*

nam: A Different Kind of War (Austin: University of Texas Press, 1994), faults the president's decision-making style in a limited war, but not necessarily the motives behind the war. Johnson's poor leadership is the theme in Larry Berman, *Lyndon Johnson's War* (New York: W. W. Norton, 1989).

For insights into administration thinking see Robert S. McNamara, *In Retrospect: The Tragedy and Lessons of Vietnam* (New York: Random House, 1995). Anne E. Blair, *Lodge in Vietnam: A Patriot Abroad* (New Haven: Yale University Press, 1995), provides information on Diem and the U.S. ambassador's efforts against him. For the celebrated dissent of George Ball see David L. DiLeo and George Ball, *Vietnam and the Rethinking of Containment* (Chapel Hill: University of North Carolina Press, 1991); George W. Ball, *The Past Has Another Pattern: Memoirs* (New York: W. W. Norton, 1982); and James A. Bill, *George Ball: Behind the Scenes in U.S. Foreign Policy* (New Haven: Yale University Press, 1997). On the clashes with Rusk's principles and policies in Vietnam see Clark Clifford, *Counsel to the President: A Memoir* (New York: Random House, 1991).

Among the contemporary critiques of Vietnam is Randall Bennett Woods, *Fulbright: A Biography* (New York: Oxford University Press, 1995), a realist reproof issued through the influential head of the Senate Foreign Relations Committee. A harsh indictment of Rusk is found in Leroy Ashby and Rod Gramer, *Fighting the Odds: The Life of Senator Frank Church* (Pullman: Washington State University Press, 1994). See also Gregory A. Olson, *Mansfield and Vietnam: A Study in Rhetorical Adaptation* (East Lansing: Michigan State University Press, 1995). Excellent coverage of the antiwar movement is given by Terry H. Anderson, *The Movement and the Sixties* (New York: Oxford University Press, 1995); Charles DeBenedetti, with Charles Chatfield, *An American Ordeal: The Antiwar Movement of the Vietnam Era* (Syracuse, NY: Syracuse University Press, 1990); and Tom Wells, *The War Within: America's Battle over Vietnam* (Berkeley: University of California Press, 1994).

A number of important works treat selected issues. Timothy N. Castle, *At War in the Shadow of Vietnam: U.S. Military Aid to the Royal Lao Government, 1955–1975* (New York: Columbia University Press, 1995), addresses the United States and Laos. Larry Berman, *Planning a Tragedy: The Americanization of the War in Vietnam* (New York: W. W. Norton, 1982), chronicles the key summer 1965 meetings that led to escalation. Edwin Moise, *Tonkin Gulf and the Escalation of the Vietnam War* (Chapel Hill: University of North Carolina Press, 1997), is an excellent analysis of this critical offensive. For the key turning point in Johnson's war, see Don Oberdorfer, *Tet!* (Garden City, NY: Doubleday, 1971). Finally, David Farber, *Chicago, 1968* (Chicago: University of Chicago Press, 1988), provides the background for the pivotal Democratic National Convention.

Index

ABM (antiballistic missile) defense system, 61

Acheson, Dean: as realist, 14, 15, 17–21, 207; rescued by Rusk, 24–25; in Korean War, 26; knows Rusk is Cold Warrior, 32; gives advice during second Berlin crisis, 46; during Cuban missile crisis, 74; as member of Wise Men, 178, 183

Adenauer, Konrad, 49

AFL-CIO, 162

Africa, 86–93, 101–2, 214

Agent Orange, 152

Alliance for Progress, 66–68, 85

Amerasians, 197

American Friends of Vietnam, 113

Angola, 87, 90

ANZUS pact, 28

Apartheid, 90–93, 210

Ap Bac, 128, 129

Appeasement, 9, 10

Aptheker, Herbert, 161

Arab world. *See* Middle East; Palestine

Asian communism, 13, 25, 27–29, 98–102, 141

Atlantic partnership. *See* Grand Design

Balaguer, Joaquin, 83. *See also* Dominican crisis

Balance-of-payments deficit, 52–53, 57. *See also* Common Market; Japan; Trade

Ball, George W.: and Cyprus crisis, 57; orchestrates European policies, 58; and Cuban missile crisis, 76; and Vietnam, 121, 149–50, 156, 201; resigns, 177

Barrientos Ortuño, René, 82

Baruch, Bernard, 59

Batista, Fulgencio, 68

Bay of Pigs invasion, 43, 46, 68–70, 117, 210

Belgium, 88–90

Ben Tre, 180

Berlin: crisis of 1948, 23, 171; second crisis over, 32, 45–49, 54, 61, 62, 118, 156, 210; access agreement (1971), 60; as point of Russian retaliation, 69, 74, 76

Berlin Wall, 48

Bien Hoa, 140

Binh Hoa, 126

Bismarck, Otto von, 7, 49

Bombing. *See* Vietnam War

Bosch, Juan, 82–83. *See also* Dominican crisis

Bowles, Chester, 32, 33, 68, 100, 121, 127, 207

Bretton Woods monetary system, 57

Bridge-building campaign: in Eastern Europe, 60, 62

Brierly, John, 8

Brown, Edmund G., 162

Bruce, David, 33

Buddhists, 127, 129–30, 137, 161

Bunche, Ralph, 91

Bundy, McGeorge: and Cuba, 69, 74, 77, 120; and Vietnam, 135, 145, 146, 169; resigns, 173; as member of Wise Men, 178

Bundy, William, 148, 178, 188

Bunker, Ellsworth, 194

Calley, William, 181, 196

Cambodia, 110, 112, 141, 168, 181, 190, 195–96